A HISTORY OF
CHRISTIANITY

A HISTORY OF CHRISTIANITY

OWEN CHADWICK

CONTENTS

Author's Acknowledgement

To illustrate the text I have had indispensable help from
Julia Brown and Richard Atkinson.

Picture researcher: Julia Brown
House editor: Richard Atkinson
Design by Bradbury & Williams
Designer: Bob Burroughs
Maps by ML Design

Title page: The Annunciation, an enamelled terracotta relief by
Andrea Della Robbia or one of his pupils for the hospital of Pistoia in Tuscany.
He liked to surround St Mary with a garland of flowers and fruit.

ISBN 0 312 13807 5

First published in Great Britain by George Weidenfeld & Nicolson Ltd.

First U.S. Edition
10 9 8 7 6 5 4 3 2 1

INTRODUCTION

All religion is the yearning of humanity for what lasts. Therefore history, which is of time, and changes each moment, looks as though it cannot be religion's first interest. In Christianity or Judaism or Islam the first interest is God, not what Christians or Jews or Muslims said or did about God in the past.

Christians began with almost no interest in history. They were not interested in the past because they fancied that with the coming of the Messiah all history would stop. But even before they realized that the world was not going to stop, they had interests which can be called historical:

1) How and why did their Messiah die? The stories of the passion of Christ in the four gospels are the earliest attempts by Christians to tell truth about the immediate past.

2) In telling what he had done, they saw that he was to be understood in the light of the long history and expectations of the Jews. The Old Testament (as they later called it) was at once important to them; and in it the record of the Jews from Abraham onwards. They needed to know who Moses was, and Elijah, and David, and King Solomon, and Isaiah.

3) Luke had travelled with Paul on his missionary journeys. He tried to tell how this faith, which started with a few people in Jerusalem, reached out until it was professed within Rome, the capital of all the Empire. He did not know much about the early church in Jerusalem. But he knew quite a lot about Paul's journeys. His *Acts of the Apostles* can be called the first effort at a Christian piece of history.

When the world did not end, and the memory of the apostles was further and further away, Christians began to make lists of bishops in the big towns. Peter the apostle was bishop of Rome and was succeeded by X and X was succeeded by Y and Y was succeeded by Z and so on, until our bishop who is in church on Sunday. It was their first form of dating church history; not with the intention of making dates, but of proving truth – we are the heirs of the apostles and this is how we know we are their heirs. It was not really a work of history, but it showed how the idea of the past, and knowing about the past, began to matter.

By the third century a few Christians began to ask whether they ought to be recording their past. To say much was not possible while they were still illegal. The first historian of the Church is recognized to be Eusebius, the Bishop of Caesarea in Palestine. He endured the last of the great persecutions, but had begun to collect materials for his history even before that danger. He started with a chronicle of world history, with the idea that now the world had reached its climax. Then he turned to writing the history of the Church, with the claim that he did what no one had ever done before. There were good libraries in Jerusalem and Caesarea and he used the documents which he found there; we should know far less about the first three hundred years of Christianity if he had not copied the sources in these libraries. When he came to his own time and the last persecution, he was much less helpful. But how indispensable he was felt to be was shown when later historians, for two hundred years and more afterwards, made their histories into continuations of what Eusebius wrote.

But now there began to be Lives of saints. Most of these Lives were sermons, and useless as history. The ideals that were represented seemed much more important to the authors than what actually happened. It did not help history when the most important thing to record of a person seemed to be, for example, to say how an epileptic had been cured at a tomb. But in the high Middle Ages some of these Lives of saints were written by people who had known them. John of Salisbury was in Canterbury near Thomas Becket when he was murdered, and then wrote about what happened. This was of real historical interest. Thomas of Celano knew St Francis of Assisi and after he died was ordered to write his life.

But in both East and West different collections of lives of saints swept away some of the stories which might have been valuable. In his *Golden Legend*, James of Voragine, a Genoese of the thirteenth century, collected the Latin stories of the lives of saints with the object of devotion; the book became enormously popular all over the West, conditioning the ideas about saints until the Reformation. Much earlier, in the tenth century, Simeon Metaphrastes, a civil servant in Constantinople, did the same for the Greek lives in what he called the *Menologion*; and did it so well that, to the regret of later historians, some lives of saints ceased to be copied and vanished. Like the *Golden Legend*, this *Menologion* had an enormous circulation; we still have at least 603 manuscripts of it.

Some went on with the lists of bishops. By far the most important was 'The Book of the Popes', *Liber Pontificalis*,

Noli me tangere, 'touch me not', the words from Jesus to
Mary Magdalene when she met him in the garden outside
the empty tomb; probably by Martin Schongauer (died 1491).

which was written about 530 and tells the reader something about each of the bishops of Rome; on the early ones the author knew nothing and made it up, on the later ones scraps of real information were brought in. Then other authors added matter about later popes; the later the additions, the more true history. In this present book we shall find a picture of Platina in the Vatican library. Platina's work was the climax of the *Liber Pontificalis*, and almost – but not quite – worthy of the epithet scholarly.

When the Germans became Christians, their authors wanted to say how it had happened. And, surprisingly, this motive caused the two best histories of one part of church history that had yet been written; Gregory of Tours wrote the history of the Franks, and the Venerable Bede wrote the history of the English nation.

Until the Renaissance much the commonest form of history was in annals – a monastery, or a cathedral (like Rheims), or a see (like Hamburg) wished to record its past year by year. These entries were contemporary and so have offered indispensable help to future historians. And monks extended these annals into wider histories; Ordericus Vitalis was an English Benedictine monk who lived in Normandy and started annals of his own monastery, and then included in his work a history of the Norman conquest of England; the result is very useful. The scope of annals by a monk could take in the history of kings as well as of bishops; as in two exceptional English Benedictine examples, by William of Malmesbury and Matthew Paris of St Albans, without whose aid we should hardly be able to write the history of England.

So when Renaissance scholarship came, and printing could make texts easier to find, the foundations of the modern study of Christian history could be laid; but they were only a new form of an endeavour which had existed over the centuries, from Eusebius of Caesarea, if not before. Authentic history was possible now.

The person who started the great change in the writing of history was a Lutheran pastor, Matthias Flacius, a Croat working in Germany, and a person of rare truculence. While annals have their value (we must keep one thing after another; we cannot understand history unless we know in what order things happened), the space of a year is not long enough to understand things. We must do it century by century. In the *Magdeburg Centuries* which Flacius planned but did not write, and which were published at Basle in Switzerland (1559–74), there was suddenly room, a hundred years of room, to treat history by themes within a century, social life, religious ideals,

the analysis of what happened instead of the mere recording of what happened. The modern way of writing history had begun. The *Magdeburg Centuries* were used as a fundamental book for two and a half centuries, far longer than most books of history.

In modern times came far better knowledge of Buddhism and Hinduism and Islam, and the world witnessed barbarous calamities which forced a new value by Christians for the Jewish faith, and the study of 'primitive' cultures in Africa and the Americas meant they could no longer be written off as *primitive*, and the nations developed a moral and religious idea of 'human rights', which had a strong Christian content but rested upon axioms which were not only Christian. All this meant a recognition that other faiths mattered, not only in themselves, but in the way in which the Christian faith was known and practised.

In this way the history of Christianity took on a new importance. The light on the Damascus Road, as on the front of this book, was beyond history and time, it came from eternity. But the humanity which it came upon was changing all the time and yet rooted in its past.

To attempt an overview of the whole, by a single hand, is bound to contain an element of the personal, and the interest of a particular mind. The question which this author asked himself was how the presentation of the gospel affected ordinary men and women, a majority of whom were illiterate; and in affecting them, whether the axioms about the world which they already took for granted could affect the nature of their faith.

Owen Chadwick
Cambridge
June 1995

CHAPTER ONE

JEW AND GREEK

THE JEWISH INHERITANCE

Christianity was one form of the faith of the Jews, and not only in its first years. Jesus was a Jew. When Hitler and his Nazis began their mad campaign against the Jews, they were faced with a block. Most of the German people called themselves Christians and in doing so declared themselves followers of a Jew. A few of the wilder Nazis said that St Paul was not a real Christian because he was a Jew and he made the faith of Jesus more Jewish; but no one can claim that St Paul was not a Jew, because he himself says so with pride. Christian faith began as a way of following the Jewish faith.

The Christians of the first years read the Bible; but the New Testament as we know it did not yet exist. For them, as for the Jews, the Bible was what we now call the Old Testament. They interpreted these texts in the light of the faith of Jesus, but they were the same texts that the Jews read. More than one Christian leader of those days tried to stop the reading of the Bible of the Jews. They said that it was not a Christian book. Some said that the God of the Old Testament was a God of justice and the God of the New Testament was a God of love; that the God of the Old Testament taught an eye for an eye and a tooth for a tooth, and the God of the New Testament taught forgiveness; and that these two were not the same God. Such critics did not get their way, for the young

The young David, by Andrea del Castagno (died c. 1457); Goliath's head below.

Christians wished to keep the Bible of the Jews as their own. They wished this even when they had their New Testament, in which the words and deeds of Jesus were collected with letters of apostolic men.

They took their prayers from the same Old Testament. Their hymns were from the hymn book of the Jews, which was the psalter of King David; for David's name was attached to 73 of the 150 psalms, and the Hebrews were persuaded that he had inspired the collection. The psalms were sung in the temple at Jerusalem, and in the synagogues which Jesus visited. They were poems full of the grace of God, that touched the heart and wept for sin and gave thanks from the depths of the soul. The psalms gave voice to some acts of praise and faith which were at the centre of the Christian way of prayer:

The Lord is my shepherd; therefore can I lack nothing.

Praise the Lord O my soul: and all that is within me praise his holy name.

They also echoed all the ferocity of the cries of battle as the Jews fought for their land in Palestine:

Blessed shall he be that taketh thy children and throweth them against the stones.

When the Christians used such words they had to take them in the sense of a war with the enemies of the soul, rather than a fight against another tribe. But they used these songs of death all the same, and gave them meanings of their own.

Soon they were not all Jews by race, and most of them abandoned the Jewish practice

The Creation, in one of the
first German translations of the
Bible (here, the first words of
Genesis), printed at Nuremberg
in 1483 by Anton Koberger;
a landmark of printing. Note
the unicorn.

Pentecost, the birthday of the Church; by Giotto (died 1337). Tongues of flame (= fiery inspiration to spread the gospel) on the heads of the apostles.

of circumcision. But in a way they remained Jews in their faith, and used the book of the Jews with its prayers and songs. When in early days they quoted from the Old Testament they most often quoted the Psalms and the book of the prophet Isaiah, whom they understood to have foretold Christ. Their God was the God of the Jews; the God who made the earth and brought them through the Red Sea as they fled from Egypt, who lived high in a cloud upon Mount Sinai, who showed them the way to live and what is right and wrong, who was their guide and guardian, who pledged that they were his own people.

All Jews waited in their faith for the coming of one who would save his people; a Messiah, God's own revelation, who would turn this world of pain into the realm of God. How he would do it they did not know; by force it might be; but it would come as an act of God. Their idea of God was deep. He is God, the sole God; no other god is real. He is the 'holy' God; that is, set apart, high above the earth and pure from its dust. He rules what men and women do, and judges them when they do ill. He hates wars and killers, thieves and tyrants, men who lie with women and women who lie with men when they should not. Yet he is a God of pity who, some day, will come to help them out of the hells into which they have turned their towns and their homes. The Jews learned all this from the words of the prophets of the Old Testament; Isaiah, Jeremiah and the others. The God of the prophets of 600 BC was also the God of the Christians.

They took over Jewish feasts like the Passover and Pentecost, and gave them a new base in the work of Jesus. How deep was the Jewish strand in Christian faith may be seen by the words of the Christian creed when it was first drafted. It was the Jews who could first say from the heart, 'I believe in one God, the Father Almighty.'

The Jews had a law which they believed God had given them from the top of Mount Sinai. Part of the Law was to do right. It was in the Law that they should not kill nor steal, that they should help their friends, the sick and the old and those in need. A part of the Law was rules about food, and about rites and ways of prayer. These rules were not about being good, but were a means of marking out the race of God which he had chosen to help the world. Some of these rules set the Jews apart from the non-Jews among whom they might live. They circumcised their boy children; they would not eat pork; they kept Saturday as their day of prayer; and they could not sit down as guests to eat in the house of a non-Jew.

When Jesus was born Palestine was still the home of the Jews. Jerusalem was their sacred shrine and would be so for all time. Jews who did not live in Palestine would try to go to the holy city from time to time, and if they could not they sent money to the temple there. But while Jerusalem, Mount Zion, was their shrine, it was not now the centre of Jewish life. Under the guard of Roman rule the Jews moved into other towns all over the eastern Mediterranean. There were many Jews in the great commercial city of Alexandria, groups of them in all the towns of Syria and Asia Minor, some in Greece, more in Rome. Some of their thinkers now spoke and wrote in Greek, the common language of the East, rather than in the Hebrew or Aramaic tongues which were spoken in Palestine and Syria.

This move of Jews into the lands of the Greeks, and their use of the Greek language, were the first cause of the spread of the Christian faith. All the books of the New Testament had authors who were Jews by race. But all of them were written in Greek; some in bad Greek, some in the people's Greek of the East which is called *Koine*, 'the common tongue', and two at least in good Greek. Not one of the books was written in Hebrew. It has been suggested that St Matthew, who was at first a tax collector in Palestine and then one of the apostles of Jesus, wrote his gospel in Hebrew and that another turned it into the Greek text we now have.

An early fifth-century Greek Bible with uncial letters; the Codex Alexandrinus, one of the three most important Christian documents. Written in Egypt, it may have come from there to Mount Athos, then to Constantinople, and was given by the Patriarch Cyril Lucaris to King James I of England; now in the British Library. Note the difficulty of reading a lesson aloud when there are no spaces between words. This page starts at St Luke's gospel 5, verse 10, the draught of fishes. In the fifth line IC is JS, abbreviation for Jesus.

The ground for this idea is that of the four gospels about the life of Jesus, Matthew's is the most Jewish in its insight into the Christian way. But it is now almost certain that this idea of a lost Hebrew text is not true, and that all the books of the New Testament were written in Greek. Whoever wrote St Matthew's gospel, he was not the tax collector who rose from his table to be an apostle.

The Jews made it hard for themselves, in that Greek-speaking and Roman-ruled society, by resolutely refusing to do what other people did. The usages of their faith marked them as different. They would have no other gods but God. Roman emperors might be mad enough to claim that they were gods and insist that their subjects should make offerings to show their obedience. These might be only a drop of incense, but they were an acknowledgement that there were gods who were not God. Few took this trivial rite to heart; it was like rising to one's feet for the national anthem. The Jews could not do it; it was banned by their Law. Thus it seemed to others that they were not loyal subjects of Rome; and this was right, for they longed for a Messiah to save them from the hard rule and taxes of Rome. One of the emperors, Caligula, set up his own image in the temple at Jerusalem. No act could do more to ensure that Jews saw the rule of Rome as a tyranny.

It might be thought that as the faith of Christians parted from the faith of the Jews, the Christians would not so much mind a statue of Caligula in the temple. On the contrary, they thought it an abomination. Since the earliest Christians were Jews, the insult shook their own obedience to Rome. St Paul wrote to his followers in Salonika of a proud enemy who sits in God's temple and claims to be a god himself; such was Paul's horror of this act that he thought that it might be a sign of the end of time.

The Jews who made new homes in the wide Greek world found that their faith attracted Greeks.

In these towns where religions and cults were everywhere, yet moral standards were as low as those of the later twentieth century, the sanity of the Jewish faith began to pull at Greek minds; the one God, the care for the sick and the poor, the stern law to do good and shun evil, the strict rules of sexual conduct, the God who cares, and cares not only in this life. In many of the towns of Asia Minor and Greece the Jews began to convert Greeks. They did not ask the Greeks to be circumcised or to be meticulous in keeping their rites. These Greeks were not full members of the Jewish congregation. They sat at the back during prayers, and heard the Bible and the psalms, and made the faith their own without quite becoming Jews. They were called 'God-fearers'. It was as if the faith of the Jews shed many of its rites and laws so that it was free to convert all the Greek world to its truths and its ways of prayer.

This was what the Christians did. They were Jews who turned Judaism from a faith for the few into a faith for all. Most of the earliest Christians who were not Jews were 'God-fearers'. The Christians took the faith of the Old Testament and, over three or four hundred years, used it to convert the peoples of the Roman Empire.

During the same three or four centuries there were Christians who were also Jews in every sense, by race and by rites, and who kept the Law. St Paul, who did more than any other to open the faith of the Jews to non-Jews, and let them have the faith without most of the rites, kept his past as a Jew: 'Are they Hebrews? So am I. Are they Israelites? So am I. Are they the seed of Abraham? So am I. Are they ministers of Christ? (I speak as a fool) I am more.'

Not all the Christian Jews were like Paul. Circumcision was such a key to the rites of the Jews that as late as 1993 some undertakers in the state of Israel still circumcised Russian immigrants before burial. A few early Christians who were not Jews by race let themselves be circumcised. The act was done for the sake of peace in the Church; they did not want a clash between Christians who were Jews and Christians who were not. Paul did not like it, for he knew that the heart of faith was in love and not in rites. But even Paul, despite his qualms, let it be done to his companion Timothy, a Greek, so that he could work easily as a Christian among Jews. In some Christian churches circumcision is found to this day, as in Ethiopia. Some other modern African peoples, who had the rite of circumcision in their old cults before they were Christian, retained it when they became Christians, and made as sore a problem for recent European missionaries as the early Jewish Christians made for St Paul.

The Jewish-Christians were the start of the Church. The twelve original apostles were Jews, as were those called later: Paul, Mark and Barnabas. Jerusalem was the centre of the young Church. Their chief was 'James the Lord's brother', who may have been the brother of Jesus; reason enough for his position. But for a time Peter was in Jerusalem and in the memory of the apostles they saw him as their leader.

Groups like this first one in Jerusalem, of Christians who were Jews by race and kept the Law, and were circumcised and ate no pork and kept the Sabbath day, are found for three hundred years and more; most of them in Palestine or Syria. They became isolated. Their fellow Jews saw them as traitors. Non-Jewish Christians, who soon outnumbered them, could not see it as the act of a true Christian to keep the Jewish Law; they looked without sympathy at those who kept it, and felt no pride that these were the heirs of the first Church, and did not think that they might be the way by which one day more Jews might find their faith.

The first Christians did not think that they were a sect of the Jews, or that their task was to end the faith of the Jews. They thought that they were the true ideal of that faith, that the Messiah of the Jews had come.

In their hope for a Messiah, some of the Jews looked for a man of force to make them free. Jesus died in pain with a single blow struck for him, an act which earned his rebuke. He had not made them a free people,

The infant Jesus' presentation in the Temple, here shown by Juan de Borgoña (died about 1535, Spain), was a sign of the early Christian sense of continuity between their faith and that of the Jews.

but seemed to have lost. But this Christ, who failed in pain, fitted a hope in the minds of some of the best Jews. The old prophets had linked the Messiah with a strand of pain:

> O go not from me, for trouble is hard at hand: and there is none to help me.
>
> (Psalm 22:11)

> He is despised and rejected of men; a man of sorrows and acquainted with grief . . . surely he hath borne our griefs and carried our sorrows; yet we did esteem him stricken, smitten of God, and afflicted.
>
> (2 Isaiah 53:3)

The Christian way of prayer, then, was at base the old way of the Jews: to read from the Bible, to hear a teacher tell us how its words fit our cases or the needs of the world, to sing the Psalms with joy, to be sorry for what is wrong, to thank God, to pray for those in pain.

NSAM MEAM IN REGNO MEO

But into this way came a Messiah who died on a cross; and a few hours before he died, at his Last Supper in an upper room in Jerusalem, he asked his disciples to keep alive their memory of his death by eating bread and drinking wine as they did at that supper. So into the heart of the way of prayer came a new rite – of a sort which some Jews had known before, but now given a unique meaning for this group of Jewish Christians by the link with the death on the hill of Calvary outside Jerusalem. Much later, Latin speakers were to call this a *sacrament*; an act that is of the body but has meaning for the soul and power to affect the soul.

This new rite stamped the Christians as different from the Jews in their way of prayer. Because the disciples had found the empty tomb of Jesus on a Sunday, they had this rite on that day rather than Saturday, the Jewish Sabbath. Jewish Christians kept both Saturday and Sunday holy; the Ethiopian Church follows the custom to this day. But the growing majority of non-Jewish Christians dropped the keeping of the Sabbath, though they might still mark it as a day of fasting. When they kept the rite on Sunday, which for most was a working day, they sometimes celebrated it in the evening, probably because Jesus himself had done it at that time. Sometimes, they celebrated it early in the morning before work because that was when workers could attend.

They loved texts from the Old Testament. To this day in shrines and sanctuaries we read on the walls words from the Old Testament, which are understood in a Christian sense. Abraham and Moses, Gideon and Samuel, David and Jeremiah were still Christian heroes though they lived long before Jesus. In the burial chambers which line the catacombs of Rome there are pictures of Daniel in the lions' den, the three children in the burning fiery furnace, Abraham sacrificing Isaac, and Jonah being saved by the whale. At times in their prayers they used the words of the Jews, though not all of them understood what was meant. They marked the end of a prayer by saying *Amen* – 'truly' or 'so be it', an assent to

Domenico Ghirlandaio's *Last Supper*, painted about 1490; St John on Jesus' breast; Judas Iscariot without a halo; above, a peacock, symbol of eternity. The Latin text is Luke 22, verse 29, Jesus' promise that they will eat and drink at his table in the Kingdom.

The portrait of St John the Evangelist in the Grimbald Gospels, written about 1020. Note St John's symbol, the eagle. Probably written at Winchester because at the end is a letter from the Archbishop of Rheims to King Alfred commending Grimbald, a Benedictine monk, to be the abbot of Newminster, Winchester.

the content of the prayer. They sounded their praise with the word *Alleluia*, 'God be praised'.

One strand in the faith of the Jews was strong in their early years. The Jews thought the Messiah brought with him the end of time, when God would judge the earth. The Christians knew that the Messiah had come, so they waited for the end. They asked themselves whether it was sensible to marry when time was so short. They took little trouble to set up an order for their Church though the Church was in need of it; for an order would be a plan for the age to come and there was no reason for such a plan.

The Gospel of St John

Before the end of the first century an early disciple, John, wrote a gospel full of insight, feeling and beauty. This John may have been one of the twelve apostles of Jesus, the son of Zebedee. But John the son of Zebedee was a fisherman on the Sea of Galilee before he followed Jesus, while the John who made this book had a trained mind and wrote good Greek. For eighteen centuries the churches thought that this author was John the fisherman, and in our century good scholars have still thought so. But it is hard to accept that a fisherman whose first tongue was Aramaic, and whose skills were those of his trade, could use the Greek tongue with such contemplative power.

This John of the gospel did not think that the world would end soon. He wished to tell his people that their Lord lives now and will continue to live.

St Paul at first thought that the end was imminent. But as he moved among the Greek towns he found this not to be a truth he could commend to the Greek people who sought for God. He saw that the world was not about to end or, even if it were, that it was not the key truth about Christ and his words.

The Revelation of St John

A book by another John almost upset this view that the world was not likely to end quickly.

The other St John writing the book
of the Revelation on the isle of Patmos;
an icon (late fifteenth century) from the
St Sergei monastery of the Holy Trinity
not far from Moscow, the greatest of
Russian shrines, founded by St Sergei in
1340, and famous for its school of icons.

He wrote it on the Aegean island of Patmos, then a Roman penal colony. John hated Rome as the tyrant, the killer of saints. How could this tyranny end? Only by an act of God which destroyed the tyrant; the destruction of the world itself and the judgement of all in it. His book, called the *Apocalypse* or Revelation, expressed his hope of a world that ends now, at any hour.

The churches asked themselves if this John was a true apostle who knew the truth, and whether his book was fit to be read in church. Some meetings rejected it; others accepted it because they thought this John was also John the son of Zebedee who had known Jesus, and every word of an apostle was precious. It took a long time before they could agree. But in the end – though only in the fourth century AD – John of Patmos was finally accepted. His book won its place in the New Testament because its author's name was John, because it came from the age of the apostles, and because mixed with the message of hatred was an awe of the majesty of God in the words of a true poet; the consolation of eternal life given to those who were killed by the tyrant's sword: 'Blessed are the dead who die in the Lord.'

Through the ages some readers accepted this vision as a literal truth. John saw an angel who came from heaven with a key and a chain, and chained the evil one for a thousand years. Ever since, there have been sects whose members expected this to happen at any moment. Two hundred years after the book was written, a bishop was so sure that the end of the world was at hand that he walked out with his people into the desert to meet the Lord, and they would have died if the police had not sent food and water to save them. One of the best Christian thinkers of that day, Hippolytus, felt obliged to write a book to prove that Old Testament texts foretelling the last judgement did not mean that we must act as though the end were coming this day or the next.

At several later times a crisis in Europe revived the fear of the end of the world. As the year 1000 approached, some were afraid that the last trump would sound.

In modern times some have argued that when Jesus talked of the last things and the reign of God, he meant the cross and what came after it, the fulfilment of the faith of the Jews in the Messiah; and that we should read all those books in the light of the Gospel of the other St John, who did not think that the world was in its last days. Yet to this day, several churches have continued to teach the doctrine as a basis of their moral code – the Seventh Day Adventists, the Plymouth Brethren and the Jehovah's Witnesses – while in Christian Africa itinerant preachers at times strike dread into large congregations with a message of imminent doom.

THE RELIGIONS OF THE NON-JEWS

The apostles and the people they chose at first worked in the towns among the God-fearers linked to groups of Jews. Soon they turned to the pagans and those who adhered to the numerous cults in the hubbub of faiths. Here the Christians met ideas quite different from those of the Jews. They found a 'natural religion' in the world which took one shape after another. Some of these ideas were wild, some absurd, some insipid, some ecstatic, some secretive, some for males only. Some were superficially attractive, such as the Manichaean doctrine, which solved the riddle of pain by saying that there are two gods, one good and the other evil.

Still, they met in these faiths men and women who sought the truth about God, and who prayed. Was there a link here that they could use? In Athens a group of Greeks heard St Paul preach and, finding his doctrine strange, asked him to come and speak to them. Paul had seen an altar with the inscription 'To the unknown god', and used this as an introduction in his address to an audience of educated and sceptical persons. Most of them remained sceptical, though polite. But he converted a few; we shall hear of one of them, Dionysius the Areopagite, later.

If educated Greeks became Christians, they were likely to bring with them ideas that were

not drawn from those of the Jews. They might have learnt from the Stoics of a universal spirit in the world, and of the need to bow before the fate that comes to us. They would not find it hard to transfer such ideas into their new faith, with its sense of God everywhere upon earth, guiding men and women. They might also find that some of the rites of their former religions still had value for their faith, and might wish to use those old rites in their new membership of a Christian congregation. In this way some ideas and rites which did not come from the Jews, and which were not mentioned in the letters of the apostles, started to be used by Christians, who put their own stamp upon them.

The rite of communion or the Lord's supper drew Greeks from other faiths. If they had worshipped the Persian god Mithras, for example (a religion for males only), they were used to the rite of a sacred meal. Mithraism and other 'natural religions' were concerned with life: the force of life, the fertility that bears life, the miracle of birth. Their symbols were to do with food, death, blood, birth and motherhood, the warmth that keeps alive. To eat is to live; to eat together is to place life in each others' hands. The sacred meal was a rite common to many of these people who, in their own ways, were looking for a god they could have faith in. The Christians often called it their 'eucharist', from the Greek *eucharistia,*

The Madonna of the Meadow, **by Giovanni Bellini, painted at Venice about 1485; notice that this generation of artists preferred not to put in haloes.**

'thanksgiving'. At first it formed part of an ordinary meal which they called the *agape*, '(the feast of) love'.

This supper gave rise to vile stories. Because they might be hunted by the police, or because it was the only time when they could all meet, they often came together at night, secretly. They talked much of love, and at their supper they spoke of eating the body and the blood of the Lord. It was put about that the rites were secret because they were full of sex, or even cannibalism. These rumours, however, did not last. The Christian sacred meal was no obstacle to Greek seekers after truth, already familiar with other sacred meals.

In the religion of the Egyptian goddess Isis the chief symbol was that of motherhood. She was often portrayed as a mother with a baby on her knee or suckling at her breast; the loveliest of all symbols of life. At first those who came to be Christians from the cult of Isis, or of Cybele, the goddess of Asia Minor known as the Great Mother, may have missed a certain warmth in their new faith. The Christians seem to have been slow to realize how the birth and childhood of Jesus and the lap of the Virgin Mary were symbols of the best in humanity. This could not easily happen until they had works of art in a church.

The sun
The chief gift to the Christian cult that did not come from the Jews was the symbol of light. Here was a source of life, the sun which gives warmth, and sheds its rays upon the earth so that humanity does not grope and stumble; a symbol in another sense of the light of truth in a dark night where we can be sure of nothing. The cult of the sun was practised by many of the Romans, who would stand at dawn to face the rising sun and feel the first rays of warmth on their face as they prayed. They would celebrate the winter solstice, when the sun had passed its lowest point and once more began to climb in the sky, and the days started to lengthen.

This non-Jewish cult fitted the need of Christian prayer; already the Jewish prophet Malachi had written that 'the Sun of right-eousness [shall] arise with healing in his wings'. Christians began to say their prayers towards the east. They did not face Jerusalem, in the way that the Muslims were later to pray with their face towards Mecca. If they were north of Jerusalem they still prayed facing the east, for it was not the holy city that was the symbol, but light. They began to bury their dead so that their faces might look towards the east. When at last they built churches, wherever the site allowed, they would *orient* them – align them with the east – so that the congregation faced the east window and looked to the rising sun. The first known Christian hymn which is not a psalm of David is the third-century Greek *Phos hilaron* (in John Keble's translation 'Hail, gladdening light'), a lyric of praise to the Son of God as he reflects the rays of his Father's glory.

Sunday
Sunday, *dies solis* in Latin, was the day of the sun god. A Christian who thought about this could not like the customary name. A few early Christian writers in Latin called the day *dies dominica*, the Lord's day. This usage passed into Romance languages (Italian *domenica*, French *dimanche*) while Germanic languages, spoken by people who were not converted till much later, retain the old name.

Christmas
The high point of the Christian cult of the sun as a symbol of light was the making of Christmas Day. No one knew exactly when Jesus was born in Bethlehem; St Luke's Gospel tells us it was 'when Cyrenius was governor of Syria', and St Matthew that it was before the death of Herod, which was 4 BC. Christian scholars made guesses, at first that it was in spring or in autumn. But they were overtaken by the growing cult of the sun. Here was the Light of the World, and we must remember his birth at the time that the sun is reborn at the winter solstice.

They had a pastoral reason for choosing this

The coming of the three wise
men, painted by Roger van der
Weyden about 1450; the three
now of different ages but
not yet of different races.

date. The Roman people kept the winter solstice with a feast of drunkenness and riot. The Christians thought that they could bring a better meaning into that feast. They tried to persuade their flocks not to drink or eat too much, and to keep the feast more austerely – but without success. They also tried to persuade them to give money to the poor who could not take part in the feast, and here they were more successful.

For a time different parts of the Church kept the feast on different days. Some kept it on 25 December, others on 6 January, the date of an old Egyptian festival. The earlier date was nearer to the solstice and prevailed – though not finally until the fifth century. The celebration on 6 January was not lost, but was turned into the festival of *Epiphany*, 'manifestation' – some Greeks called it *Theophany*, 'God appearing'. In Spain, Syria and Cyprus and some other countries the feast of Epiphany, in the East commemorating the baptism of Jesus and the marriage at Cana, and in the West celebrating the reverence of the three wise men, was for a time more important than the feast of Christmas.

So Christmas in our age is a harmony of three elements: the junketings of the Roman crowd trying to relieve the gloom of winter; the Roman cult of the sun and of its light; and, at the heart, the memory of a birth in a manger in the Palestinian town of Bethlehem. To that harmony, much later, the North added elements from folklore, such as the

The three wise men, on a sixth-century mosaic from Ravenna (Sant' Apollinare Nuovo). The upper part was restored later, the names (Caspar etc) are not earlier than this. Notice 'SCS' (= sanctus, saint) used as a prefix like our 'St'. Greeks and Latins linked the Phrygian cap with Easterners, especially if they were religious persons. Roman freed slaves wore them and so the Jacobins of the French Revolution adopted them as their symbol.

Germanic Christmas tree. But Father Christmas was the fourth-century bishop St Nicholas (*Sinterklaas* in Dutch, hence Santa Claus), renowned for his kindness to children, and whose feast day was 6 December.

The wise men

A part of the cult of Christmas, and associated with the dates of both 25 December and 6 January, was the story of the three wise men. St Matthew told how wise men (he did not say how many) followed a star from the east to worship the newborn child and offer their gifts of gold, frankincense and myrrh. The early Christians decided that because the gifts were three the wise men must have been three in number; and because there was a verse in the Jewish psalter about three kings bearing gifts (Psalm 72:10), they decided that the three wise men were kings. In this form the story grew to be one of the most loved of symbols, often carved or painted by artists on the walls of churches. Later the three gifts were given special meanings, and the wise men were given names: Caspar, Melchior and Balthasar. They were shown as men of each age of life, so that every human soul from child to dotard might feel that they could bring gifts. Later still, they were shown as men of various races, so that everyone in the world could feel that they were bringing their gifts to the lap of Mary.

They put into the scene the ox and the ass, of which the Bible says nothing. One might expect that if they wished to show the animal kingdom coming to bow to the cradle they would have let the shepherds bring their sheep. Not so: the first picture of the manger that we know is on a tomb of the fourth century, where already the ox and the ass stand there benevolently. Scholars have guessed that a text of the Old Testament inspired the artists: 'The ox knoweth his owner, and the ass his master's crib' (Isaiah 1:3). But this is speculation.

They often portrayed a plaited basket as the crib, and gave it a simple roof. Sometimes it became a cave, sometimes midwives were in

A detail of Giotto's *Adoration of the Infant by his Mother*, from the Arena chapel in Padua, painted about 1305. When Jesus is given a halo it usually has a cross.

attendance. Eastern artists showed Mary weak and lying back. Western art tended to show her praying in front of her child. Through the Western tradition came a growing sensitivity in studies of affection between mother and child. The landscape was not shown as snowy until the conversion of north Germany and Scandinavia.

The first saints

Another idea that is natural in religion is a reverence for the holy person. If someone is

The Wilton Diptych; the young King Richard II of England is presented by his patron saints (from the left, King Edmund with his arrow, King Edward the Confessor with his ring and John the Baptist with his lamb) to the Virgin. The angels wear Richard's badge, the white hart. The flag of St George suggests a crusade; but the time, about 1395, was when crusading fervour had gone. One of the most beautiful paintings of the Middle Ages, and by an unknown artist.

thought to be near a god, the divine presence touches those who meet that person.

The persecuted early Christians revered the martyrs, who had the faith and the courage to face death for Christ. They began to write records of their trials in Roman courts. Some of these Acts of the Martyrs are in their simplicity among the most sublime records of Christianity. The law says that those who refuse to sacrifice to the emperor must die, but the judge sees good men and women in the dock and has no desire to sentence them. He tries to make it easy for them: such a little thing to do, a spoonful of incense. But they would not: 'The accused said "I am a Christian"; and the others said they were too.'

So the churches took the martyrs as their heroes, and did not forget to celebrate the anniversaries of their deaths. It was the start of a calendar by which brave men and women were remembered. Their graves became shrines which would be places of prayer for those who came later.

Pagans were used to saying a prayer to many little gods in many little shrines. When the Christians said a prayer at the shrine of a martyr, were they praying to God as the apostles taught them, or were they praying to the martyr in the shrine, who still lived in the life after death and might help them? As the pagans came to be Christians, it was natural for the first to pass into the second; and indeed this form of devotion was thought allowable because the saints were the servants of Christ who had died for him and must now be close to him in the kingdom of God.

The sibyl

Classical writers described many sibyls; but at first there was only one. She was a prophetess who spoke to the Greek world, and lived either on the coast of Asia Minor or at Cumae near Naples. She spoke in an ecstasy. At Cumae her words were written in verse on loose sheets, and were collected into the Sibylline Books. They were kept at the Capitol in Rome, but were accidentally burnt. The senate sent for new books from the East, which survived until the end of the Roman Empire in the temple of Apollo on the Palatine hill. In the sixth century the prophecies – with many later additions – were collected into fifteen books, but much disappeared during the Middle Ages and only eight books are now known.

It seems strange that a Greek oracle should become a Christian prophetess; but the books included writings from diverse sources. The oldest were Jewish; there were very early Christian songs, one a hymn on Christ and his cross; the eighth book had a song of mixed Jewish and very early Christian origin which threatened the fall of a godless Rome and foretold the triumph of Christ. So the

Michelangelo's sybil ('the Libyan sybil') in the Sistine chapel at Rome; the old heathen prophetess taken and turned into a Christian prophetess.

memory of the sibyl survived as a Christian seer. The *Dies irae*, that tremendous hymn of doom written by a disciple of St Francis of Assisi, began with the words:

Dies irae, dies illa
Solvet sæclum in favilla,
Teste David cum sibylla.
Day of wrath! That day
Will burn the world in ashes,
As foretold by David and the sibyl.

The early Christian Fathers used the prophecies of the sibyl in commending their faith to the Romans. In the Middle Ages prophecies about Christ were put into the mouths of the sibyls. The sibyl was mentioned by Dante and painted by Raphael, and Michelangelo portrayed five sibyls on the ceiling of the Sistine chapel in the Vatican. She had become a symbol of the continuity of faith from the old religions to the new.

THE CHRISTIAN WAY OF LIFE

The church in the house

The Jews went to a building for their prayers, the synagogue. In the earliest years, when many of them were Jews or God-fearers, the Christians were sometimes able to use the synagogue for Christian prayers. But their place of meeting was the house of one of their members; preferably a person with a large house because it would have a big room. We hear of a room so full, when a famous preacher came, that a young man had to sit on the windowsill and during the service he nodded into sleep and fell out of the window. As the number of Christians in a town grew, they might buy a house. The property had to be owned in trust; the person in whose name it was registered was known as the *episcopus* – 'overseer' or 'custodian'. He would also be the chief person in the congregation, and thus *episcopus* came to have its meaning of 'bishop'. The congregation would turn the inside of the house into a meeting room with as much space as possible. This 'house church' was the

Ornamented tombs in a Rome catacomb, that of St Peter and Marcellinus.

first sort of church. Specially built places of worship were being constructed by AD 200, when we know that one existed at Edessa on the eastern borders of Syria. A church at Antioch in Syria was reputed in the fourth century to have been built in the time of the apostles. This cannot be true; long after the apostles the congregations still met in houses.

The word 'church', and the Scottish kirk and German *Kirche* and Russian *tserkov*, come from the Greek word *kuriakos*, 'belonging to the Lord'. The adjective was first used to refer to the 'Lord's supper' – that is, the Holy Communion – and the Lord's day. But by AD 300 the name began to be used as a noun, *kuriakon*, 'the Lord's place', to mean a church. The word for the congregation was *ekklesia*, or in the more familiar Latin spelling *ecclesia*. When St Paul wrote letters to groups of Christians, he used various words: 'to you who are chosen and set apart in Rome' (or in Philippi, or in Colossae); 'to the *ecclesia* of God which is at Corinth' (or in Salonika); or,

A fifth-century mosaic in S Constanza, Rome; Christ gives the Word to Peter and Paul; probably based on an earlier mosaic, for Peter and Paul have no haloes. The water of life flows below.

where it was to several towns in a province, 'to the *ecclesiae* in Galatia'. This word meant 'the people called out', or 'chosen'. By AD 400 it also began to mean the place where Christian people met, the building.

Although in Germanic and Slavic languages the word for a church is derived from *kuriakon*, Romance and Celtic languages use words taken from *ecclesia*, for instance *église* in French and *eglwys* in Welsh.

When the meeting became too large for the house church, it might be deemed safer to meet outside the city. But Roman meetings never met in the catacombs outside the city, which were nothing but passages for burial below ground; services in catacombs were only held by little groups for burials or to commemorate the dead. At one time there was a view that congregations must have hired schools in which to meet, but there is no evidence for this. Otherwise, a congregation that grew too big to meet in the house church had to split up and meet in two places. This was the start of separate congregations in the cities. If they were asked by a pagan why they did not all meet in one spot, they are known to have replied that God is not in one place, but in all places.

There was still no accepted idea of what a church building ought to look like. Nor could

The sixth-century altar in S Vitale, Ravenna; altars at first were wooden tables; by now often stone.

there be a church which looked like one until the age of persecution was past. At first the church needed to be only the size of a chapel, which made it easier to conceal its purpose from the passer-by. But even when the need for secrecy was over it took time before churches looked churchy.

There were two models. The first was that of the temples of the gods – not an attractive idea to most Christians, much as a modern architect would not wish to build a church that looked like a cinema or a stock exchange. This was not true for all; many of the new Christians took with them into their church ideas or rites from their old faiths, and they thought it natural that a church should look like a temple. Some congregations would be happy to meet in what had been an old temple. When (about 550) they turned the Parthenon on the Acropolis at Athens into the church of St Mary, no one saw anything wrong; they were glad that so fair a temple of dead gods was again a house of prayer.

The second model for a church was the place of meeting for trade or official business – the *basilica* or town hall. Until the congregations could come above ground and build large houses of prayer they did not often call their churches basilicas, for the word suggested large size and official status. The Greek word *basilike* meant 'belonging to the king', and thus a state building. The shape of this hall soon became the common form of a church. Eventually the word *basilica* lost its former meaning and came to mean simply a church. The basilica was rectangular in plan. The original town hall would often have an apse at the far end, where there was a throne for the chairman and benches for his council. The first churches were similar, with an apse where the bishop sat on a chair in the centre, looking to the west to face the people, and flanked by his presbyters and his deacons in a semicircle. The bishop's chair was called a throne, not because they likened him to a king, but because *thronos* was a Greek word not only for a king's chair but for the chair on which a teacher sat to instruct the class.

In front of the bishop was a table with the bread and wine for use in the Lord's supper. This table was soon called *altare*, a Latin – and pagan – word for the place where sacrifices to the gods were made. An earlier Greek word was *thusiasterion*, a place of sacrifice, or sometimes *bomos*, a platform on which the sacrifice was offered; for they knew the Greek version of the Old Testament well and used its words in their prayers, so they felt it right to use its words for the table at the centre of their worship. At first the altar was often the dining table of the house where they met, and they continued to use a wooden table as an altar for a time even when churches came out in the open and the table had no other use. The first altars made of stone were the tombs of the martyrs on which the Lord's supper was celebrated on anniversaries of their deaths. For centuries any candles on the altar were put there simply to give light in the dark; the sun was the only source of light that they revered.

They did not at first have what we should call a pulpit. But since they followed the way of the Jews, in which the words of the book were read out and then explained, the hall had to be arranged so that people could hear, so they needed a raised place for the speaker. They put the bishop's chair on a dais for the same reason. The Greek word for a seat was *kathedra*, the origin of the word 'cathedral' for the bishop's church. Nearer the congregation there was a raised place from which to read, called the *ambo* – from the Greek *ambon*, a hilltop. Here the bishop, or speaker appointed by him, could read or explain the text. Soon a big church had two platforms, one from which to read the text, the other from which to explain it. The ambo was lower and simpler than the much later pulpit, but was its origin. The poet John Milton brought the word 'ambo' into the English language, to mean an early pulpit.

The apse was a place to display a work of art. It is not known when Christians first dared to depict the face of God. The commandment of the Jews, which the Christians received, said that no one should make an image, and it was particularly sinful to portray God, for God is spirit and too high and holy to be drawn without error. Early Christians seem to have been happy to allow artists to use their skills outside the church in secular art. Pagans mocked the Christians for having no likeness of God in their church. The Christians retorted that men and women are the images of God, and nothing made by an artist's hands ought to be there.

The converts who flooded into the church brought with them the desire for pictures. People would pin small religious images on their clothes. At martyrs' tombs artists portrayed the martyr's face, though some critics did not think it right. At Aquileia in northern Italy there was soon a church with a mosaic floor depicting Jonah and the whale.

Preaching

From the ambo the bishop or one of his presbyters 'preached'. Such an address was not meant to be a lecture; it was part of worship, and linked with prayer. As Paul in his letters had mingled the gospel of Christ with the moral demands made by that gospel, so the preacher was to tell of the truths of faith and apply those truths to the lives of the hearers.

We know that this frame of mind was found very early among the Christians, for from Antioch comes a strange comment on behaviour in church. This rich trading city had one of the first big Christian communities, and was the town where they were first called 'Christians'. Its bishop was as important as those in Rome or Alexandria – and of more weight than the bishop in Jerusalem, who might be expected to be the chief of bishops, because Jerusalem had been laid waste in the Jewish revolt of AD 70.

About 270 the bishop of Antioch was Paul of Samosata. He preached with such power that the congregation clapped and cheered. Some people thought it natural and fitting to applaud. But visitors from other towns, and some of those who lived in Antioch, found this noise not to their taste, feeling that it was at odds with the spirit of prayer and the

decorum of a church service. From this it is clear that the words from the ambo were considered to be near prayer, and were not meant to be a speech such as one might make to rally support for a political party. Critics in Antioch thought that the bishop's words were tantamount to a political speech, and an unfitting use of the ambo.

The use of Greek in services

At first all services, except among the Jewish Christians, were in Greek. Even in Rome or as far away as Gaul, Greek was used because the first Christians in these places were traders from the Greek world and learnt the faith as God-fearers. St Paul and St Peter came to Rome and taught and prayed in Greek. Even when the mother tongue of most of the people in church was Latin, the prayers were still in Greek; for this was the custom which they had received, and Greek was the language of the New Testament and they had the Old Testament in the Greek version. For a time there was a sense, even in the West, of the holiness of the Greek tongue. In the eastern part of the Roman Empire, where Greek was the common tongue, this feeling that Greek was sacred because it was the language of the Gospels continued through the centuries.

About AD 200 the community at Rome began to use Latin for its prayers; they wished the people to understand what was said. But there were certain Greek words now so deep a part of prayer that they were kept even while the Latin grew to be the norm. They went on saying *Kyrie eleison*, 'Lord have mercy' in Greek, and calling the feast of Whitsun by the name of Pentecost, from the Greek for 'fifty', originally meaning fifty days after Passover and later after Easter. They went on calling the feast of 6 January by its Greek name of Epiphany. When artists started to draw the crucifixion, they placed on top of the cross the letters IHS, the first three letters of the name Jesus in Greek – the H is a long E. Some Westerners could not grasp this. Consequently they sometimes spelt Jesus as 'Jhesus', or thought that the letters stood for

Iesus Hominum Salvator, 'Jesus Saviour of Humanity', or for *In Hoc Salus*, 'In this person is salvation'.

Customs and dress

The customs used in church varied according to the wishes of the group. Some communities saw no need for special dress; if a deacon or deaconess went out to bring the bread and wine to the bed of a sick person, or to give food or money to the poor, they must not be seen in the streets to wear a dress which marked them as Christians. But in church the feeling of reverence made for a slow growth in formality. They were in the presence of God. The church must be clean; there should be quiet, and times for silence; children or dogs ought not to run around the room. The feeling grew that those who conducted the prayers ought not to be in everyday clothes. They thought of the colour white as a sign of purity, or at least of a hope for purity. The Revelation told them of saints in heaven who wore white as they praised God. So they wore white; but as white was a usual colour for Roman dress, this did not mark out their clothing as a special 'vestment' like a surplice. It was not expected that the formal clothes worn in church would be different from other formal clothing.

This is shown by the chasuble, which began to be used by the bishop or president as he led the eucharist. The garment was part of the usual dress of a Roman gentleman (or indeed a lady) for a formal occasion. The clothes of the clergy gradually became distinctive because they remained the same while the rest of the world moved on; as judges in England still wear the wigs of the eighteenth century, or academics on degree days wear the clothes of the Renaissance, or English bishops wore gaiters for a century after most other people stopped using them.

Persecution

For more than two and a half centuries the churches were illegal; a long time. But they were not persecuted everywhere, every day.

It was a matter of chance whether the mob in that town was roused against the secret society of the Christians; as when the silversmiths' guild of Ephesus, angry at the fall in the sale of their statues, sought to incense the mob against St Paul. The local judge might be a Roman with a conscience, or a hard man; or an army commander might be irked by Christians who would not serve in his force; or their refusal to revere the emperor's statue might or might not be thought an act of treason. There were local reasons why a congregation was forced to face death; but this was so only as long as the Christians were few. After two hundred years they were so many, with such influence in so many towns, that emperors began to see them as a peril to the state, as a now large group with antisocial ideas. Between 250 and 313, when at last they won legality, there were three occasions when emperors determined to get rid of them, and the number of martyrs rose sharply.

The effect of persecution upon a religion is always partly good for it and partly bad. It is bad because it kills or exiles some of the best leaders. After the Bolshevik revolution of 1917 the Russian churches suffered as much from the flight westward of many of their best people as they did by the deaths of martyrs. This loss of leaders meant a narrowing of the faith, because the new leaders were likely to be less well educated. The persecution of the Jews over the centuries produced the ghetto and the ghetto mentality. As the walls of the ghetto grew higher, the mental walls against the world, the walls of the Law, also grew.

So it was with the early Christians. The martyrs were heroes; but the mind of the martyr might not be the best way of thinking if the work of the Christian was to go out to the neighbours. As persecuted Jews cared more about the Law, persecuted Christians cared more about their words or rites. They despised other communities for keeping Easter on a different date; or they might hear a preacher saying 'God the Father suffered on the cross' and consider this view outrageous, making Jesus less than a man or teaching the false idea that God can suffer. They would feel an urge to get rid of such a speaker who was leading the faith into error.

The word 'orthodoxy', from Greek, means teaching what is right and true. Christians had a gospel passed to them by the apostles and they did not wish to hear a speaker say, as though it were gospel, something the apostles could not have accepted. Persecution makes people cling to what they know, and to prayers or ideas of which they are sure. Persecution made orthodoxy more orthodox.

Persecution causes schism. During the cold war President Ceausescu of Romania treated his people with cruelty, and none more so than the Christian community. Yet the patriarchs of this time, in the wish to make their lot and the lot of their people less hard, spoke of him as a great statesman and the saviour of the nation. When he fell and was killed, could the people in church trust their patriarch any more? Some said that he helped the Church by making the bad man less bad; others that he had betrayed the Church and should be dismissed. Just such disagreements made for schism among the early Christians.

The men in the front line were the leaders, the bishops. At times they could hide and try to do their job clandestinely. But there was a feeling that the shepherd should not leave the sheep when the wolf was at the gate. Could they then find a way of conforming outwardly, while the work of the church went on? The governor would demand the Bible and the prayer books so that he could burn them. Could the bishop hand them over, or was this betrayal or worse? If a bishop handed over books that were not holy, and said that they were the books which the church used, was that a betrayal because he seemed to give up the holy books and was thought by the state to have done so? Such cases in Africa in the fourth century were the cause of a long period of strife in the Church, the schism of the Donatists, which weakened Christianity in the region. In Alexandria the bishop Peter hid during the persecution while Meletios, a brave or rash bishop from a nearby see, toured around to do his work. When Peter came out of hiding, there was a bitter dispute whether Meletios had done right, which developed into the Meletian schism. In these ways persecution split a church.

Tertullian, a North African of about AD 200, said, 'The blood of the martyrs is seed,' meaning the seed of conversion. Was that true? If the state decreed that to be a Christian was against the law and punishable by death, what effect did this have on the faith? Too many men and women through the centuries, who did as the state wished and abandoned their beliefs, proved that force can kill faith. Persecution caused Christians to say not a word to show their creed; or to argue that the pagan gods were dreams and that to say yes to them with a bow of the head, though not with the heart, was an empty rite from which no one should shrink. Once there were great Christian communities in North Africa, and Islam almost ended them. Christianity in Japan was nearly wiped out by brutal warlords. The terror of 1792–4 in the French revolution threw the French Church into a pit from which it has never quite climbed, to regain the general support of the French people. So the law of Rome hurt the Church of the apostles and of those that came after them. The claim that the blood of the martyrs is the seed of the Church is only part of the truth.

Nevertheless, it is part of the truth. Menno Simons, who founded the group which was the leading church among the earliest Baptists and which we now know as the Mennonites, was a Catholic priest who saw the police of the Netherlands kill a Baptist solely because his faith was against the law; in that moment he became a fighter for a new, radical religion.

The first Christians collected the Acts of the Martyrs and passed them round to read. If they had no actual record of a trial, they would invent one so that the people might know, or think that they knew, of the faith of this or that martyr. But they were troubled by masochists or deranged people who sought martyrdom. They would not accept the Roman belief that suicide is the noble act of a brave man; they considered those who sought out death for the faith as in a way suicides.

They also admired the 'confessor for the faith', a man or woman who faced death with courage, but then escaped execution thanks to a pardon or a change in official policy. Confessors had power in the congregation, and if they disagreed with some pronouncement of the bishop they were listened to. In every century of Christianity there were to be disputes between persons who had 'official' authority because the Church chose them to be clergy, and those who had 'unofficial' authority because the people revered them. The quality which made a martyr was not the same quality as that which made the head of a community.

The spread of the churches

Why did the faith spread so fast? The faith of the Jews in one God who made and guided the world, and who demanded that men and women do right and honour their parents; the faith that protected women by making men faithful to them, and required that the poor and the weak, the sick and the widows and the orphans be cared for – this faith of the Jews was the faith of the Christians. Its clarity cut through the chaos of religions in the Greek and Roman world, the innumerable cults of mystery and legend.

Whether the promise of a future life attracted converts is not easy to discover. The usual pagan view was that there was an afterlife of sorts, but only as a gloomy shade in Hades. The Jewish Sheol was hardly a more attractive place; but the Pharisees hoped for something better. Whether the discovery by the apostles that the tomb of Jesus was empty, and their awe at his presence among them, made the belief in a future life still more immediate is impossible to know. Religious feelings are not usually moved by a historical event; though that is not true of the Jews after the Holocaust, nor was it true of the earliest Christians because they were constantly reminded of the crucifixion by the sight of the cross in their churches. But the incoming convert must have been more drawn by the sensation of hope at Christian funerals.

If death was one fact near the soul of religion, the sense of guilt was another. Sometimes that was allied to death, for guilt is a part of mourning: 'Could I not have done more for them while they lived?' It seems unlikely that many converts entered the church for this reason alone, because the average man and woman are not often troubled by deep feelings of guilt or a need for forgiveness. But famous converts, Paul and Augustine among them, came that way.

In an unjust world, the sense of justice to be found in a future world was a belief that could draw souls. 'Come,' they prayed, 'come the future kingdom, come peace, come justice, *maranatha*' – they kept this Aramaic word in their prayers, meaning 'Come, Lord'. Later, when they no longer expected a quick end to the world, they thought that *maranatha* must mean 'The Lord has come'.

Tertullian's most famous remark was his account of a pagan exclaiming, 'See how these

From a sarcophagus, Christ seated and teaching.

The Road to Calvary, by Simone Martini, for an altarpiece
(about 1341) for the popes when they lived not at Rome but at
Avignon. By a trick of perspective, and by imagining a gate
too narrow for the crowd, as though they were squeezed out
of its mouth, he made everybody the key to the event.

Christians love one another!' This could hardly be true all the time; we have more than enough evidence of ordinary human sin, from the bribing of Judas Iscariot onwards. But the remark was not absurd, for the early Christians set up a system of care for the poor and the sick, widows and orphans. Such a thing had hardly been seen before, except among small groups of Jews. It caused surprise, and even people who otherwise scorned the Christians felt a reluctant admiration. It attracted converts; a less than pure motive for becoming a Christian. A widow might be starving; if she joined a church she would receive a dole, which might be tiny for it depended on what the congregation had, but it was something.

There would be the usual grounds for people to join societies – they might have a good friend who belonged, or marry a member.

Then there were miracles, dreams and visions. Far the most important and frequent miracle was that of healing. Galen was the best physician of Roman times, but no more than one in ten of the herbs which he prescribed could have had any physical effect; and even such expert medicine could be bought only by those with money. Faith was likely to be a better cure for the ordinary person.

Demons

Demons were a matter of observation. There were people with epileptic fits, where it seemed that a force inside them cast them on the ground, making them roll their eyes and gnash their teeth and bite their tongue. Because of this apparent presence within, the old Greeks knew the disease as 'the sacred illness' or 'the disease of the demons'. It was evident to them that this was not the choice of the soul that suffered but was the work of an evil spirit within; only the clear-sighted physician Hippocrates said it was an illness like others. It was clear too, in their

A monk exorcizes a demon; from a manuscript of Rabanus Maurus in the abbey of Monte Cassino. To the left the chapter heading, *De exorkismo*. On Monte Cassino, a hill north of Naples, was an old temple which St Benedict took and turned into the mother-house of all Western monasteries.

The Baptism of Christ, by Piero Della
Francesca (died 1492), the most serene of
the Italian painters of Christ. Notice the
baptism by Jordan water from the shell,
not by immersion in the river.

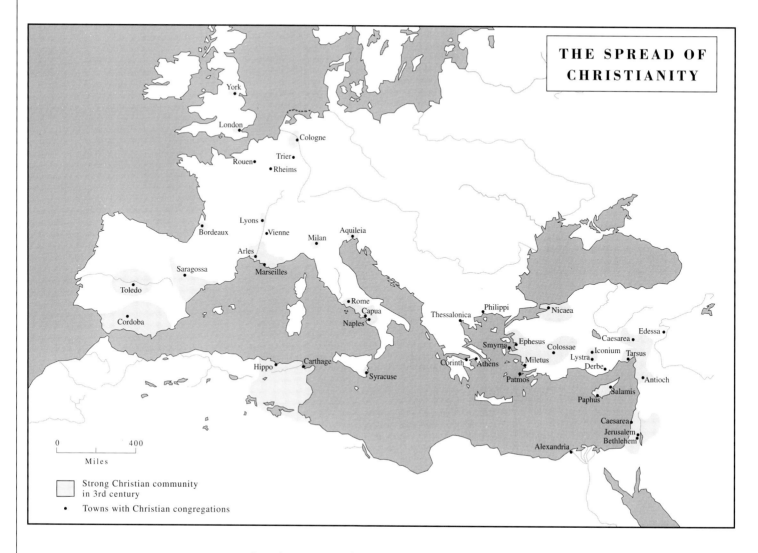

THE SPREAD OF CHRISTIANITY

Strong Christian community
in 3rd century

Towns with Christian congregations

0   400
    Miles

experience, that the power of a divine spirit could throw the demon out, making the sick whole again and restoring a sound mind to the insane. The Jews thought the gods of the heathen were evil demons, and the Christians adopted this belief. Hence there was a need, both in medicine and religion, for exorcism.

If demons existed, as was clear from the behaviour of the sick, they could be the cause of other misfortunes: floods, earthquakes and droughts, as well as the accidents of everyday life. Demons could not be seen, but it was thought that they could assume the shape of a man or woman, beast, bird or snake. They came mostly at night.

Demons had to be exorcized. Pre-Christian exorcists would frighten the demons with a shriek, or talk in a foreign tongue, or recite texts from a holy book. Amulets and charms were used; one might wear on one's body a text from a holy book or the symbol of a good god. But the best cure was found to be the laying on of hands, which soothed by bestowing the touch of the sane. Exorcists were successful often enough to make everyone sure that demons existed and could be thrown out by the power of God. Jesus accepted this power over some forms of sickness, and used it to heal. He talked of his Father as the God who was ending the power of demons for all time; the cure of those who were possessed was a sign that God's kingdom was at hand.

The Church soon added a rite of exorcism to the service of baptism; it is found in the service by AD 240. They wanted the infant to start growth with every vile power cast out of its being. One of the early forms of words was 'Accursed one, get out!' In the English Prayer

Book after the Reformation this took the less dramatic form of the godparents being asked to renounce the devil and all his works.

Eastern thought kept the sense of the victory of Christ over the powers of darkness, and had less to say about demons. Their lack of anxiety on this account saved them from falling into the worst of the hunt for witches that convulsed the West in the sixteenth century. But their monks found old experience of demonic power. The hermits went into the sands of Egypt to live alone and wage war with all the demons of the mind that fought them in their cave.

In the Latin West they inherited more of the old pagan anxiety about demons; perhaps because there was more chaos in society, perhaps because the Germanic tribes brought their own awe at the gods of the trees and springs into the Christian mentality. Thinkers asked how they had come into being when God was good and made the world good.

Therefore they told tales of the fall of Satan or Lucifer, which Milton turned into poetry in *Paradise Lost*. The chief demon was a true servant of God who in pride rebelled against his Lord and was cast out of heaven, and turned his power to hurt the earth. They based this story on the account of the fall of man in the Old Testament (Genesis 3) and the visions of the Revelation in the New Testament. There was a danger of making the arch-demon look like a hero fighting a war against the odds. But that was an idea for the educated. Most people did not care where demons came from, they only knew that they were there and worried about how to drive them off.

As the Roman empire fell apart, people in France and Italy and Spain turned to the saints and their shrines to ward off the power of evil, as well as for healing. We have to think of a world where a shrine like the modern Lourdes was in every province; those who sought to be healed did not usually have to travel far. This was not yet a rural land with parishes to administer pastoral care. The countryside was dotted with shrines, and there was more worship at these than in any church. At each saint's tomb there would be a queue of the possessed, and one might hear the howls of demons as they writhed and were cast out by the power of the saint who transmits the power of God, and see the crutches cast aside by the lame who could walk again, and see sufferers making their medicine from the very dust of the tomb mixed into a cup of water. The saint might be with God in heaven but he or she was also here to be pleased with a prayer for healing or to drive out a devil. The saint's relics were there behind their protective grille; sometimes they could be touched, even kissed. The invisible world has never been so near as it was to Christians then. Today, only some groups of Christians in Africa can feel that proximity to the divine.

Certain shrines were thought to care especially for the mad. The most famous in the Middle Ages was the shrine of St Dympna, an Irish prince's daughter buried at Gheel in Belgium. The treatment was unusual: the mad person walked through an arch beneath the saint's tomb. History is powerful, for to this day there is at Gheel an excellent hospital for treating the mentally disturbed.

The use of force

Christians were against the use of force. 'Thou shalt not kill' was a commandment from God to the Jews; but the Jews believed that it was right to fight to defend one's nation, so they made a difference between murder and killing ordered by the state. The first Christians made no such distinction. All forms of killing were banned for the disciple of Christ; war, capital punishment, private murder. Jesus had overturned the idea that the Messiah was a man of force. The Galileans were said to have wanted to make him king, and he would not be that sort of king. When Peter drew his sword to defend him at the arrest in the garden of Gethsemane, he said, 'Put up again thy sword . . . for all they that take the sword shall perish with the sword.'

Jesus drove the moneychangers out of the temple, which was the act of a policeman. He accepted that a civil government should be

The garden of Eden; from the Bedford Book of Hours. Note the two-faced God, a third face of the Trinity unseen. Prayer books had long been illustrated in margins or initials; the art at its summit in the fourteenth to fifteenth centuries. This book was made about 1420 for Anne of Burgundy who married the Duke of Bedford, then regent of England.

The driving of the money-
changers from the Temple, by
El Greco; this is his third and
most mature version.

obeyed; and civil governments cannot exist without force. St John's Gospel showed him as believing that the power of Pontius Pilate, the Roman governor in Jerusalem, was given to him by God.

In the Roman Empire the soldiers were also police. Then may a Christian be a soldier? This was not a problem while the Christians were few. Some Christians were slaves, who were not allowed in the army; and at least half the Christians were women. The army did not consist of conscripts; soldiers were volunteers attracted by the pay or the adventure. So no Christian need volunteer unless his city or province was invaded. But this could happen: a certain Maximilian was executed in Numidia in 295 because he refused an order to join the army. His body was buried as that of a martyr, and his story was recorded as Acts for the churches to read. At Caesarea in Palestine a soldier was promoted to centurion, but was then denounced by a private foe as a Christian. He was given three hours to think; he went to see the bishop, who said that he must decide between the gospels and his sword; and so he came back and was put to death. In 298 a centurion in Morocco resigned because he was expected to sacrifice on the emperor's birthday, and was put to death.

But as the Christians grew in number, doubt began to afflict them. Jobs might be hard to find; was the army an honourable way to earn a living? Men who were already soldiers were converted; must they leave the army? The question arose in the form of whether war or capital punishment is the same, morally, as murder. Around 200 there was agreement among many leading Christians that it is. Tertullian said that Christ told Peter to put up his sword, and this meant that every Christian afterwards must put up his sword. Lactantius said that human beings are sacred creatures and no one may destroy any of them on purpose.

Clement of Alexandria called Christians 'the peaceful race'. They looked for an age to come when wars would be no more, and states would not make arms, and swords would be turned into ploughshares. They were sure that nothing could do more to end war than for all the people to follow Christ. They seriously believed – and may be forgiven the illusion – that when the Gospel was accepted war would end.

Then may I start a revolution against a tyrant state? Tertullian said that Christians were treated wickedly by the state and were now numerous enough to start a revolution; but they would not, because 'our religion makes it better to be killed than to kill'. It was not till the beginning of the fourth century that we hear of a revolution by the Christians in Armenia against persecution, and we cannot be sure how far they revolted because they were Christians and how far because they were Armenians.

So if a soldier was converted it was better if he left the army – if he stayed in the army some wanted to expel him from the Church. Yet already by 174 there were Christians in the army, for we hear of a unit on campaign in Moravia in which Christian soldiers were numerous.

Origen of Alexandria, taxed with the complaint that the Christian view led to chaos and the fall of civilization to barbarians, replied that God had a purpose for the civilization of the Empire and would preserve it by his power.

May I be a magistrate? It is not wrong to judge a case about money or property. But to judge a capital case is impossible – and to perform the ritual acts of a magistrate, which then included sacrifice in a pagan temple, was also impossible. Yet near the end of the time when Christianity was still illegal there were governors of provinces who were Christians. Their fellow Christians were uneasy about this, for a synod met at Elvira in Spain and decreed that a Christian who takes his turn for a year's service as chief magistrate must stay away from church.

The churches were not unanimous; they could not be, for they accepted the state as God-given and the state's duties included the punishment of wrong. St Paul had taught that magistrates are in this way the ministers of God. Everyone agreed that criminals had to be stopped. Despite so much belief in the wrongness of capital punishment, about the year 160 we find Athenagoras of Athens speaking of a man who has been rightly put to death. But many Christians, no doubt like many non-Christians, did not have much faith in the justice of the Roman courts.

About 220 Julius Africanus wrote comments on the Bible which included a calculation that the world is 6000 years old, and the important idea that the history of the world matters to Christians. But he also wrote a handbook for generals which included useful instructions on how to wage chemical warfare.

In the fourth century, when the Christians were no longer illegal, the change of heart was general. They could praise commanders for their skill, or sing hymns at their victories. They had quite early discovered that soldiers could be honourable men — for example by treating martyrs humanely on their way to death. And if it was lawful for a Christian to be a soldier it must have been lawful for him to kill the enemy in a war. About 350 St Athanasius of Alexandria made the distinction: to kill was wicked, but for a soldier to kill the enemy was lawful and could be praised.

The early hatred of force left its mark. At all times of Christian history there have been groups who could not bear the idea that they should kill and who, though not called pacifists till modern times, would not have shrunk from that name. There was a widespread belief that special officers — bishops, priests or deacons — ought not to shed blood, either by sitting as judges who condemned criminals to death, or by serving as soldiers in the army. (This rule also existed among some pre-Christian peoples who believed that war and the sacred should not be mixed, and barred their priests from being soldiers.) The prohibition was widely broken during the Middle Ages, when bishops were natural leaders in the defence of their cities. Pope Julius II, who reigned from 1503 to 1513, twice led

armies in attacks upon cities in northern Italy. The last English bishop to command an army, in a blue coat and with a naked sword, was Compton of London in the revolution of 1688. But these warlike clerics were condemned by much opinion. A change came when Napoleon introduced conscription, so that every male, including the clergy, was obliged to serve in the army. But most Protestant states, and some Catholic ones, exempted ministers from the duty of serving in the army because the people felt this was wrong. This belief was kept alive by reading what Jesus taught about force.

Some thinkers, including Augustine and Martin Luther in their different ways, put forward the doctrine that there are two kingdoms. There is an ideal realm of which the Church is a mirror, and in that realm force is out of place and peace must reign. And there is the kingdom of fallen humanity where men and women sin and fight, and need laws that punish if harmony is to be maintained and so that they can come nearer to the true realm. As a Christian you are in the ideal world and ought not to make war. As a member of a fallen race you must take your part in making life good for sinful humanity. The doctrine of the two kingdoms had its dangers: it might be used to justify the making of an unjust law on the grounds that bad people need to be controlled or that the state cannot survive without it. Yet for every Christian the two kingdoms existed as ideal and reality.

Pictures in churches

The first Christians were uneasy about pictures; they remembered the second commandment's prohibition of 'graven images'. But after a while they overcame their misgivings and began to paint biblical scenes on the walls of their churches. By 400, pictures of Old Testament stories, such as of Abraham about to sacrifice his son Isaac, were often found. In that time even bishops found money to make the walls of churches lovely with colour; but they might still need to stand against the critics for what they had done.

They defended pictures as a help to prayer, or as an aid to help those who could not read.

Some drew back from portraying God. But if there were no picture of God, a picture of a saint could draw kisses, reverence, even superstition. Soon the *Pantocrator*, the ruler of all, was painted high in the apse with his eyes looking down at the people who prayed. He might be alone, or in the midst of a heaven with clouds and trees and angels. The artists might still avoid painting Christ, or might portray him as a lamb. Sometimes the saint of that church was painted as his companion. Santa Maria Maggiore at Rome, which was built in 432–40, was given a series of stories from the childhood of Jesus – but that was natural in a church of St Mary.

The new field of art was a challenge to an artist whether he was a Christian or not. There must have been pictures of God which were bad, and which people soon got rid of. No doubt there was a survival of the fittest; yet some of the finest works of art must have failed to survive, destroyed in the persecutions, or through war or riot, or through neglect by a poor community, or just through bad taste – or later, as we shall see, through whitewash, because many people discovered that pictures distracted their minds from prayer, and still had a feeling that any portrait of God, who is spirit, must be far from the truth and could lead to the false idea that God is an old man in the sky, and therefore it was better that the east wall of the church should be unadorned.

The canon

The Greek word *kanon* meant a ruler for measuring, and so, as a metaphor, any sort of rule or norm. So 'the canonical books' were the books which established 'a rule of faith', as distinct from other books which might be good but did not have the same authority.

When Jesus died the Jews had not yet quite settled what books ought to be in the Old Testament. Since the Christians did not yet have a New Testament, they did not use the name 'Old Testament' for the Jewish books;

The Pantocrator at the cathedral of Monreale, above Palermo, Sicily, built in 1174; in Greek letters to the left IC (= Jesus) O (= the) Panto; to the right CHR, (Christ) krator – so Pantocrator, = ruler of all things.

The sacrifice of Isaac by his father Abraham, stopped by God who gave a ram instead; a Hebrew story much used by Christians to portray sacrifice; this by Brunelleschi, a competition design for baptistery doors at Florence, early fifteenth century.

At first they did not need a New Testament, because there were still people alive who could remember what had happened, and the account was passed on by word of mouth. In this way it was distilled into words that were easy to remember — a story, a telling sentence. As the witnesses died they realized that they must collect the words in writing. The first three gospels show obvious signs of being made of a string of separate stories and sayings which those with memories had told.

To these were added letters from church leaders. For example, St Paul wrote a letter to the congregation at Corinth. Someone would read it to the church meeting there. Then a copy would be made and passed on to help the next community; so it passed into 'Scripture'.

But other people besides Paul wrote letters. And other people wrote 'gospels', lives of Jesus. The Gnostics, who wanted to show that Jesus was not a real human being, wrote gospels. Legend makers whose joy was to list unlikely miracles wrote gospels of their own. These had to be winnowed out with some care: if a 'Gospel of Peter' turned up at a church meeting, it took knowledge to see that this was not the truth that the apostles taught, and that whichever Peter wrote it, this was not St Peter the apostle.

The separation of the books which belonged in the New Testament from other books which posed as apostolic took a long time — some 350 years in the end, though most of it was settled within a century and a half. Even up to about AD 180 they still had no proper list of books which should be read in church. Because they were illegal, they could not hold a council to decide the matter. It was done by the leaders of the churches, who used their good sense. It was easy to see that our four gospels came fairly directly from apostles and were the ones which ought to have authority, though there were some differences of opinion about the gospel of St John. Several of the letters of St Paul were easy, but everything else was uncertain for a time. At least one forged letter 'by an apostle' slipped through the net and got into the New

it is first found about AD 175 in a book by Melito Bishop of Sardis in Asia Minor, who was a good literary defender of his faith. But from the first, Christians had the idea of an old covenant between God and his people, through Abraham and Moses, and a new covenant through his Son. The Greek word *diatheke* used in the gospels means both a covenant and a will or testament. Until they had the name 'Old Testament', Christians called the books simply 'the Scriptures' or 'the Scripture'. Soon they began to give them an adjective, and say 'the holy Scriptures'. Sometimes they called the Old Testament 'the Law', because the Jews considered that part of it as the most important. But whatever they called it they used it constantly; it affected their style of Greek and religious ideas.

EXPLIET VISIO QVARTA IHEPIT VISIO QVINTA :·

anno primo baltasar regis babilonis daniel somnium uidia ;

iudicium sedit   a libri apertui sua

The prophet Daniel's vision of the Four Beasts that came out of the sea; from the Silos Apocalypse: Silos was a Benedictine house in north Spain, founded 954, where later lovely manuscripts were written; the collection was sold when Spanish monasteries were dissolved, 1835–7; this came to the British Museum; Benedictines went back to Silos in 1880 and are still there.

The draught of fishes in the sea of Galilee, by Raphael; a cartoon for a tapestry. A mastery of the human figure, with no interest in the right size of the ship.

Testament as the Second Epistle of St Peter.

A manuscript of the eighth century, written in appalling Latin on the basis of a vanished Greek text, and with its beginning lost, contains an early list of books. The original was probably written in Rome about AD 200. We know the list as the 'Muratorian canon' because the historian Lodovico Muratori found the document at the Ambrosian library of Milan in the eighteenth century. It is the earliest list that shows the New Testament as a 'finished' collection, though not quite as it stands today. There are the four gospels, with twelve Epistles of Paul, the Epistle of Jude, and two (not three as now) of John; the list still lacks the two Epistles of Peter, the Epistle to the Hebrews and the Epistle of St James. The writer considers, with some doubts, that the 'Apocalypse of Peter' should be in, but not the Shepherd of Hermas, a pleasant Roman book about forgiveness; perhaps the Wisdom of Solomon, which forms part of the Greek Old Testament, should be in the New Testament; and he accepts the Apocalypse of St John, our book of Revelation. From now on there was a Bible consisting of two parts, an Old Testament and a New. The Eastern Church favoured including the Epistle to the Hebrews, the West would not have it. The West liked the Revelation, which the East would still not have. By 400 the East accepted the Revelation and the West accepted Hebrews; so the New Testament was agreed.

The intellectuals

The first Christians were Galilean fishermen and a tax collector; they followed a carpenter. They were not the sort who could frame their faith in a large view of science. They were surprised when educated Jews such as Paul discovered that they had the truth of faith for the world. The John who wrote the fourth Gospel had a good education, as did the strange and learned unknown who wrote the Epistle to the Hebrews. Paul's companion Luke was a physician, but in those early days of medicine that did not necessarily mean that he was highly educated.

A statue from the third century BC of the Stoic philosopher Chrysippus (died 206 BC): able mind, dull style. Early Christian intellectuals argued with Platonists and Stoics and learnt from them.

Gradually members of the middle class, then a few of the upper class, even some of the emperor's court, joined the congregations. If they were well read they began to ask questions of the mind. Already many of them were versed in philosophies which put forward ways of life.

The dominant name in Greek thought was Plato. Of the schools of thought which sprang from his ideas, the most helpful to the spread of Christianity were the Stoics. They taught that we can make sense of nature only if there is a single spirit that breathes life into all the world and gives it vital being. They thought that such a spirit must be 'personal' and 'conscious', rather in the way human beings are conscious. This spirit guides the movement of the world and what happens in our lives; it is very near the idea of fate. Things will happen, you can do nothing to change them; be resigned, it is fate.

The Stoics despised the myths of the old gods. They had no use for the oracle of Delphi and thought little of miracles, which did not go with their idea of the law of nature that ruled the world. They scorned the augurs who looked at the entrails of beasts to decide whether it was a favourable day for a journey, a battle or a marriage. They spurned the belief that you could make the gods kind by rites and sacrifices. 'Do you want to make the gods friendly?' asked Seneca, one of the best of the Stoics. 'Then be a good person. Whoever follows their way has worshipped them rightly.' Yet the Stoic thought that men and women ought in duty to perform the rites which were part of public life and which the people expected of them.

Their ideal was of persons with self-control; brave because they cared nothing for their own lives; upright; prompt to sacrifice themselves for those in need; ready to do the duty before them. They condemned any idea that humans should live by self-interest. They saw it as vanity to want anything in the created world, for a want puts the will into chains and the will must be free. The wise person is 'impassive', always 'at peace in the mind'.

But they looked down on the herd, for they taught a way of life for an élite. They did not expect the masses to be able to reach their reason or their virtue. Though their ideal was noble, it could be cold and aloof. To be indifferent to created things might mean being indifferent to the passions of humanity which were a source of noble acts. Stoics were kind but not tender, preferring friendship to love.

A Stoic had to aim to be a hero; a Christian did not. If a Stoic prayed he did not want to be sorry and had little use for forgiveness. He did not think it right to be humble. There was nothing in him of 'Lord have mercy on my soul'. He wished to have no fear of what might come at death. He thought that any person was allowed to kill himself, while the Christian regarded humanity as sacred and suicide as murder, even if it was to cut short an incurable disease or escape the scaffold. The elder Pliny said that it was a proof of nature's care for the world that it is filled with herbs that help men to the tomb without pain. 'If I can choose between death in torment and a quick end,' asked Seneca, 'why should I not go the quick way?' . . . 'If life is good, live on. If not, you have a right to go where you came from.'

Still, some Christians must be drawn towards the Stoics as minds which limped after what the Christians found with their heart; and some Stoics must be drawn towards the Christians. Both believed in one God who filled the world with spirit, and was a guide to men and women. Both believed in an absolute duty to try to do good and to be good; both believed it is a moral obligation to be ready to sacrifice oneself. Both believed in 'detachment' – that is, that you must avoid wanting anything in this world too much, for in doing so you turn your eyes away from what is supreme. Stoics and Christians alike believed that all men and women are brothers and sisters and have equality in the divine; that money, birth, caste or race put no one above another, but only virtue. Both believed that the best in humanity comes from the spirit that is on high. 'Without God', said Seneca, 'no one is good. . . . A God (I do not know what God) is there in every good person.'

In the world of Rome, Stoic thought grew a little more religious and a little less of a philosophy of reason. Epictetus wrote, 'When you shut the door and make the room dark, do not say that you are alone. You are not. God is there.' And this: 'I am old and lame. I can do nothing. But I can praise God. If I were a nightingale I would sing. If I were a swan I would do as swans do. But I have a power of reason. It is laid upon me to praise God. That is my task. I shall try not to stop. You should join me.'

A Christian adapted the writings of Epictetus for the use of Christians in their study of prayer. Much later, even John Calvin edited Seneca's *On Mercy* for Christian use.

In the second century, when old people could still remember those who had known apostles, the first effort began to reach out to the non-Christian educated moralist. These educated Christians started by calling their faith a philosophy. They owned that some other philosophies taught truths. Since all

truth is of God, they said, these truths must have come to Plato, or to the Stoics, by way of the Jews and reading the Old Testament, so that the truths which were common to Christianity and to the Stoics came down from the same source. (None of these pagan philosophers had read a word of the Old Testament.) Plato, they claimed, must have been taught by the prophet Jeremiah in Egypt. Pagan teachers countered that the claim of this religion to be a philosophy was absurd. But it was a sign how the first Christian thinkers began to seek common ground with non-Christian thinkers.

Despite the scorn of the pagans, these Christian philosophers felt strong because they were sure of a harmony between what they learned of God in their faith and what their reason told them. There had been a religion of human nature and it was lost, but they had brought it again into the light. Christ personified the *Logos*, the 'Word' of the opening of St John's Gospel, which was the ultimate reason of humanity and the world.

When they put these propositions to pagan philosophers, they were apt to leave out ideas from the New Testament which did not fit the argument.

Justin Martyr

Justin was that rare person, an educated man who found his faith because it seemed to him the most reasonable of the philosophies of life. He was born in Palestine and may have heard of the Christians in his early years, but he came of a family of Greeks there and was not a Jew. He described how he went out to test the philosophies of the age, questioning the Stoics, the Peripatetics and the Pythagoreans. Justin became convinced that the disciples of Plato were the nearest to the truth.

Then by chance he met an old man who was a Christian. Their talk disturbed his trust in the Platonists and drew him to look at the prophets of the Old Testament. He realized that these prophets who foretold the Messiah, and the Christians who proclaimed that the Messiah had come, possessed the truth he

On the left Eusebius, Bishop of Caesarea (died 339), who created the writing of church history; with Ammonius, Bishop of Alexandria, defender against heresy; peacocks above as symbols of eternity; from the Rabula gospels, written in Syriac in Mesopotamia about 586.

sought. He came to Rome about AD 150 and set up a school next to a public bath to teach philosophy. This was a relatively safe way to spread the Christian faith; to be found at prayers was a capital crime, but to set up a lectern, to enquire and teach enquirers, was not against the law.

Among the Christians of those days, a teacher was revered almost as much as a prophet. The famous school at Alexandria, said to have been set up by St Mark, was home to two successors of Justin: Clement and his pupil Origen. Both tried to make a bridge linking Christianity with the best in earlier philosophies. Interested pagans came to hear lectures at the Christian schools. A non-Christian queen mother summoned Origen to Antioch so that she could hear his lectures. On occasion there were public debates between the head of a school of pagan philosophy and the head of a Christian school.

Such lectures were called 'apologies' later, from the Greek legal term *apologia* meaning a speech for the defence. They tried to show the non-Christian what was true in the Christian religion. The Jews also used to argue thus with non-Jews, and Christians did not hesitate

to draw on the wealth of matter that Jewish teachers had written.

The arguments they found strongest were the old Christian-Jewish conviction that the Messiah has fulfilled the hopes and prophecies of the centuries; the power of their faith in changing men and women so quickly; the way in which their faith fitted the natural religion of mankind; and the freedom it brought from demonic power. It throws light on them that they almost never used the plea, so basic to the better-informed apologists of the eighteenth century, that the miracles of Christianity are proof of its truth.

Justin knew that much of the pagan teaching of the philosophers was good; inspired, he thought, by the Logos which is the divine reason in the world. He said that we should see the wisdom taught by a Greek such as Socrates in this light. He regarded Socrates as a Christian before Christ who, like Christ, died the death of a martyr for the truth he saw.

His school only kept him safe for a time. He was caught about 165 and killed. His death so moved his friends that he has been known since as Justin Martyr, as though that were his surname.

As the churches grew there would be three or four schools like that of Justin in a big city such as Rome. This brought what churches could consider heresy. Anyone who read books could set up a desk. Some of them loved obscure words which no one could take in, but which sounded mysterious and pious. The word *gnosis*, 'knowledge', was seen as the key to unlock the mystery of God. Teachers who taught about gnosis were apt to use the word as a label for what was not known and could not be known and had small chance of being true. Soon a teacher of this sort was known as a *gnostic*, a name which became an insult, though it only means a person who knows. But some, even if called gnostics, were able and thought hard. A knot which they spent time trying to unravel was how pain can exist in a world made by a good God.

One of these thinkers, Valentinus, who taught in Rome at the same time as Justin, thought that he had a chance of being chosen as the bishop of Rome. He had a superb command of words and drew crowds, but his words had little to do with the truth. Others of the gnostics put out myths which made no more sense than the spells of a witch. Little was known about these gnostics till 1945, when a jar was found buried at Nag Hammadi, north of Luxor in Egypt, containing thirteen gnostic books on papyrus.

Like any philosophers, these teachers did not all say the same, so that in the end bishops who cared about orthodoxy started to use the term 'school' as an insult. This was the first sign of that tug in Christianity, which has never ceased, between the people who led the prayers and the people who wished to think about God and understand him as part of all knowledge. Some of the teachers were priests, but many were lay. In the early days the people liked the teacher, lay or not, to speak in church. But the ill feeling between bishops and schools made an end of that. By the third century only a priest or bishop was allowed to speak in church.

Catacombs

The Christians called the places where they buried their dead 'cemeteries', the Greek name being *koimeterion*, literally a place where people sleep. But in Rome, Naples, Syracuse and some other towns, and on the island of Malta, the ground was suitable for digging an underground passage with shelves for burial. This was called *catacumba* in Latin, from a

A third-century wall painting in the catacomb of Priscilla at Rome, of an *agape*, 'a meal of love', which the early Christians sometimes held with the Lord's supper.

The Good Shepherd; from a Ravenna mosaic (Tomb of Galla Placidia) of the late fifth century. Ravenna, defensible in marshes, became capital of the Western Roman Empire 404–76, and afterwards of the Italian kingdom; hence great art there.

A third-century inscription from the catacombs; to a dead lady 'Romana in Peace'; early occurrence of the XP (CHI-RHO = Chr, first letters of Christ). Early lamps or pots sometimes bear a hare or rabbit, but we do not know what people understood by it; perhaps speed, and so the shortness of human life.

An ambo (early form of pulpit), sixth century, from the church of SS John and Paul, Ravenna.

Greek term for 'the place by the hollow', which suggests that the first one was made by extending an earlier tunnel.

Later the legend grew that in times of persecution the congregations were obliged to meet underground; hence the modern expression 'back to the catacombs' when a state threatens persecution. But this is not true; they met only for burials and memorial services for martyrs, and then only in small numbers because there was not much room.

What the shelves held is not easy to know because over centuries grave robbers looted things of value; even clergymen practised this thievery, and at least once a man bought a licence to hunt underground. The catacombs contain the first surviving Christian art and symbols. There are paintings and carvings on tombs dating from about 230. At first these were small works. The images are serene, not sad, confident in life after death, and full of peace. If Daniel is shown in the lions' den, or Jonah being thrown overboard, they do not look anxious. The images are roughly made, and hint at a story rather than telling it, and are hard to interpret. One of the favourite pictures was of a person standing with arms outstretched towards God, which is known as an 'orant', from the Latin *orans*, praying.

Symbols

The cross is the symbol most often seen in the catacombs. But there were others.

The symbol of a fish represents an acronym. The Greek for a fish was ΙΧΘΥΣ, in roman letters ICHTHUS. This was taken to stand for *Iesos CHristos THeou Uios Soter*, 'Jesus Christ, Son of God, Saviour'. The fish symbol comes from pre-Christian myth; one of the reasons that the legend of Jonah, who was rescued from drowning by a great fish, was so loved. The fish symbolized life in stormy waters, and the way by which a dying soul is carried over the seas to the Islands of the Blest. It was on walls, tombs, seals and rings; even lamps were made in a fish shape. Sometimes the symbols of the fish and of the water of baptism were combined.

The anchor was seen on tombs or rings, as a sign of a safe haven. A ship was used in the same way, perhaps with the sense of the Church carrying souls over to safety.

The good shepherd was the obvious symbol of Christ, used less than one might expect.

The palm tree was an image from pre-Christian art where it was a sign of victory, as in the English expression 'to bear the palm'. It became a symbol of the victory of faith.

The dove was mentioned by St Luke. Not a common symbol at first, it was used in later pictures of the baptism and also as a sign of the soul flying away to God.

X and P, the Greek letters CH and R, were formed into a monogram; the name of Jesus used as a power against evil. It became common only when Constantine, the first Christian emperor, used it as a sign of victory and had it painted on his soldiers' shields.

A and Ω, alpha and omega, the first and last letters of the Greek alphabet, were thus a sign for the beginning and the end. The Latin West turned it into A and O. This symbol comes from the Revelation of St John (1:8). To us it sounds too literary to be popular, but it was quite common from about 250 on coins, rings, graves and lamps.

One other symbol was much beloved later but is found only once in the art of the years of persecution: the pelican. There was a belief that this bird fed its young with blood from its breast – perhaps because the breast has a red tinge, but more likely from mistaken observation of a pelican feeding the nestlings from the pouch on its bill. This symbolized the suffering Christ bringing life to his people.

The phoenix was not a bird that existed. Legend told how it burnt itself to death and at once appeared again as young. In pre-Christian Egypt it was connected with the rising sun. Early Christian writers saw in the story a parable of life after death.

In the same age the peacock, which later came to be a sign of the strut, or self-display, was a symbol of eternal life. Quite often a pair (or more) were found on pictures of paradise, or near a pail evidently full of the water of life.

These symbols were the earliest Christian art. Ordinary people wore some of them as amulets, to guard against evil powers.

Peacocks, symbols of eternity, linked with a chalice of the water of life; a dove feeds on grapes; a marble relief of the seventh century, Lombardy.

CHAPTER TWO

THE CHRISTIAN EMPIRE

THE END OF PERSECUTION

Constantine

Even while Christianity was still outlawed, Christian apologists said that only bad emperors did harm to the Church. Christians prayed for the state and were glad at its strength; they knew that a strong state allowed people to lead a good life, and that power comes from God, and that to keep the law is a duty as long as that law is not wicked.

The last persecution, from 303 to 313, caused them doubts about their support for the state, but only in Egypt and the East, where many were executed. In the West the Emperor Constantius Chlorus had no interest in killing Christians. His son Constantine learnt to build his power on Christian strength. When Constantine won outright power in the West with his army, and still more when in 324–5 he won the East, he began to give presents, endowments and property to the churches. In Rome he made over the Lateran palace and built the basilicas of St Peter and St Paul, and in his reign Rome took the form of the Christian city which it has remained to this day. Christians now had no difficulty in seeing the emperor as sent by God.

It was soon clear to the state that the bishops, as influential on public opinion, should be given status; they became almost, but not quite, state officers. Augustine said that human beings are always sinners and the essence of a state's power is that it is a robber band; and though this evil is lessened by the justice and grace of God, we cannot bless the state without doubt and reserve. But in spite of this the Church and the state were soon (in theory) as one, with the state as the ruler of bodies and the Church as the ruler of souls.

The Emperor Theodosius I (379–95) banned paganism, made Christian heretics liable to penalties, and forbade sacrifices. Within seventy years the Christians, from being a persecuted though large minority, were members of the only lawful religion in the Roman state.

For centuries thinkers have argued, and still argue, whether Constantine's support for the Church helped or hurt it.

A document of about 800–850 in the legal texts of France records that Constantine made over much land to the rule of the pope of his day, Sylvester I. This came to be called the *Constitutum Constantini*, or the Donation of Constantine. It tells of how the emperor caught leprosy. The heathen priests told him that he must take a bath in the blood of innocent children; but Peter and Paul came to him in a dream and told him that he could be healed through Sylvester, who during the persecution had fled to Mount Soracte. In return the emperor decreed that the see of Rome should be the primate of all churches in the world, and its Lateran cathedral the principal building. He gave his properties in 'Judaea, Greece, Asia, Thrace, Africa and Italy and the islands' to the pastoral care of the pope, and conferred on him the symbols of empire – the diadem, the purple robe and the sceptre. He raised the clergy of Rome to the rank of senators and, as a sign of respect, he laid it down that the emperor should lead the pope's horse by the reins in procession. He gave the pope secular power over Rome and all the provinces and cities of Italy and the West; and he decided to found Constantinople and live there because it was not right that a secular emperor should rule in the city of the head of the Christian religion. That all the pope's successors might keep this gift, he laid a copy of the decree at the tomb of St Peter.

An Eastern Nativity; in the East, Mary usually
lies by the manger which is by the cave.
Below, Constantine and his mother Helena;
from Greek gospels of the eleventh century.

So said the document first found in France, five hundred years after Constantine. It may have been written by a cleric in Rome, or by one in western France. If the object was to win property for the pope or to put power into his hands, it was badly framed. Anyone capable of making it up must have known enough to realize that no such thing could happen. The forger must have known that to make the pope into the king of Spain, France, the Rhineland and Britain was a wild dream. Those opposed to papal power considered that this gift was the base of the claim of the pope to rule the Church; and that when it was proved to be a fake – which did not happen till the fifteenth century – popes would fall. This discovery of the Donation's falsity was to have an effect on the reformers of the sixteenth century.

But the Donation was hardly used to claim any power for the pope, at least not for two hundred years after it was forged. Popes did not use the Donation much, and it is clear why. Their power must be seen to rest on God's gift, which had descended to them through St Peter, not on a gift from the state. What a state gave, a state could take away.

In 305 you needed courage to be a Christian; in some lands you were still at risk of death. Ninety years later there was still in the churches a large minority of determined people, notably the monks and nuns; there were also people who knew little about their faith but said and thought that they were Christians; there were those who knew nothing about the faith but said and thought that they were Christians; there were some who were not Christians and knew they were not but said that they were; and there was still quite a number of people who were not Christians and knew they were not and said they were not. When a bishop had power, did it make men wish to be a bishop for the wrong reason? When the see of Rome chose a bishop in 366 and there were two candidates, rival mobs fought in the basilica and left 137 dead on the floor. What had happened to the Church of quiet and peace?

It is easy to see the Church before Constantine through a haze that veils what was not peaceful. But the case for Constantine is plain. A society has a moral influence on men and women who by their nature are not very religious. It affects the laws that are made, the schools and what they teach, the accepted rules of family life. One man or one woman can convert another; one society can affect other societies. Sub-Saharan Africa would not now be the Christian continent it has largely become unless it had received its faith not only from individual Europeans acting alone, but by the sharing of a whole culture which went back to Constantine. During the four hundred years after Constantine the Germanic tribes from Gibraltar to the Baltic were converted to Christianity and changed the face of the Christian Church. For the most part they were converted not by men or women working alone – though the fame of saints played a part – but in whole groups, as the conversion of one tribe led to that of another; and the prime mover was the magnetic power of a Roman empire, where to be civilized and educated was also to be a Christian.

Not many Christians knew what it meant to be civilized or educated. Some three-quarters of the inhabitants of the empire during the fourth century must have been illiterate. Their 'doctrines' would be very simple. God rules. He is like light. He can defeat demons. He can heal the sick. He can grant us a good harvest. He promises us heaven after this life.

But the oddity is that simple men and women were not always simple about Christian doctrine. They could demonstrate in the streets against someone who, they were told, was a heretic, by singing psalms or shouting holy phrases. They were supposed to receive instruction before baptism, as 'catechumens' (*katechein* is Greek for 'to teach'; St Paul had used this word for teaching religion, and *katechumen* for someone being taught religion). Some of them did, but it was more likely that they would be baptized first and then expected to come for instruction; usually they failed to turn up. Those who administered baptism had faith that God worked in it to change a person's character for the better. They thought the sacrament far more important than the instruction. So there were instructed people; but far more people who thought and said that they were now Christians knew little of what this meant.

Intellectuals were still troubled about faith. Still we find the 'philosopher's quest', like Justin Martyr's – the educated mind testing teacher after teacher, and sometimes finding Christianity difficult or repellent. The common people were going Christian, but that did not mean that the educated person's search for truth was over. The way certainty came, if it did come after so much doubt, was difficult to describe. Basil of Caesarea spent much time in study, then suddenly looked at the Messiah; the sight was full of light and he felt his study to be a waste of time. Hilary, the future Bishop of Poitiers, was educated as a Platonist and persuaded by reasoning that there can only be one God, an eternal creator. Then he read the Old Testament with its creator God, and the New Testament with its Logos as the rationality of the world; and felt that he had found what he sought. The process sounds serene, put like that, but he was tormented in mind. Marius Victorinus taught the Platonic philosophy in Rome and translated some of Plato and Aristotle into Latin. One day about 355, Rome was astonished to find that this famous Platonist was a Christian. Augustine had a Christian mother and a pagan father but he was repelled by Christianity, partly because of its moral code (such as the command to put away one's mistress) but more because he read parts of the Bible and did not like it. For a time he followed the Manichaean doctrine of two opposed gods. In Milan, through Bishop Ambrose and his own study of the Platonists, he reached an intellectual sort of Christianity – but again, not at all serenely, indeed in agony of mind. In 386 he had a non-rational moment of crisis when he heard a child's voice in the next garden saying 'Take it and read it'; and he opened the Bible and hit upon a text which exactly addressed his condition

(Romans 13:12–14). Then in Ostia, the port of Rome, came an experience which he felt to be a vision of God and the truth. He remained so grateful, and yet so puzzled by how it had all happened, that he had to write a book, the *Confessions*, explaining himself to himself.

These were highly educated people; two of them were professors. Their road to faith was not typical. No doubt we know more about such famous converts than we know about philosophers who rebelled against Christianity and remained hostile to it.

The structure of the state was different now. Constantine gave the Christians in the army (though there cannot then have been many of them) time off on Sundays. That did not make the army a lot of Christians: a quarter of a century later they cheerfully fought for the non-Christian emperor Julian, and it has been calculated that about half the army commanders during the century after Constantine were still pagans. This mattered, because in the past the army had been the maker of new emperors and it was soon to have that function again.

Still, privileges began to come the way of the Christians. Their churches were exempted from taxes. Where a new church was built it was easy for the community, at least in some regions, to get a state grant or bricks or stone for building. The church welfare system for destitute virgins, widows and the sick found that the state was willing to help. As the temples began to empty, the state declared their treasures public property.

It was now possible for church leaders to meet. In the time of persecution they had devised a system of local meetings of bishops, known as 'synods' (Greek *sunodos*, 'assembly'). This could now go on safely and it was possible to have a general synod, such as that at Nicaea in 325. So many new questions came up for decision that these synods needed to be frequent. They were one of the first systems of government by committee in the history of Europe; and they proved the truth since accepted, that committees usually quarrel even if they are composed of well-

The vision of St Augustine, by Carpaccio, *c.* 1500. Note the bookshelf, well lit; no halo; a collection of bronzes; the prie-dieu (prayer-desk) already the shape of a modern prie-dieu; the bishop's crook and mitre, though he was not yet a bishop. Here he is the scholar, struck by a sudden light and listening.

In the Bible it was said that all God's Law was burnt by enemies and God told Ezra to write it again at once; here Ezra is at work. Notice the cupboard for books, a rare example so early; seventh to eighth century, from Jarrow, Bede's monastery near Durham.

state is a friend, is it in any way part of the state's job to make sure that the Church does its job well? Can we ask for the state's force to make a synod agree, or to banish a heretic, or to order a temple to be destroyed? In 384 the first heretic to be executed by a Christian state, the Spaniard Priscillian, was killed by the Western emperor at Trier near the Rhineland. But to some extent heretics escaped the more rigorous edicts of the emperors because the state had difficulty in enforcing its laws.

It was now possible to publish and circulate Christian literature. That was not as important as it sounds, because so many were illiterate; but books could go far. Athanasius, or someone who called himself Athanasius, wrote a life of the first hermit, St Antony. Copies turned up in Trier and Milan. The copying of Christian manuscripts began to be an industry. One sign of this was the introduction of the book. Old documents were written on long scrolls. The *codex*, that is a book with pages bound together, was invented during the second century AD. But most still preferred scrolls to read – until the churches of the fourth century realized how compact and easy to read a codex was; so books conquered the world until the coming of the computer.

Now a church could be built in a city centre, in the market square, and preaching could be carried on in the square itself. This coming of churches into the open offered a great challenge to builders and architects. At first the basilica was simply a rectangle of stone walls with a wooden roof; then it was made wider by side aisles, with the roof above the central part supported on stone columns. Then the walls rising above the side aisles were opened to the light with a series of small windows, either open to the air or glazed with selenite, a translucent stone – for at that date glassmakers, very skilled already in vases and ornaments, had difficulty in making sheet glass and this was rare and costly. There had to be a semicircular apse behind the altar at the east end where the bishop sat on his throne with his presbyters; at first this was constructed

meaning people. They did many good things; settling points of church order or doctrine, the second of course with far more difficulty. They were by no means enjoyable occasions, and some bishops were reluctant to attend. Normally the government paid their fares. The bishops liked government to shut the mouths of the minorities on the committees.

There was danger ahead for the churches. They felt all other gods to be evil and a danger to the state; and serious heresies to be destructive of truth and the Church alike. Obviously we can ask for police to stop a riot at the election of a bishop. But, now that the inside the rectangle of the hall, but later built on to the outside. The side aisles were dark in comparison to the main aisle, lit from above. Outside, the walls were without ornament. But the interior of the earlier house churches had already been decorated, and decoration became more elaborate in the new bigger spaces; there were mosaic floors, but as yet no pictures. At the entrance, town halls usually had three doors, and the new churches had the same.

A city church might need more than three aisles. The first great church to be built in this new world was the cathedral of Rome, the Lateran. It had five aisles and was as big as the biggest state buildings. Its style affected other cathedrals at Tyre and Antioch, and the Holy Sepulchre at Jerusalem.

The cemetery was outside the city; here martyrs were buried. Many of the finest early churches were built not within the city but outside it, over the tombs of martyrs. Constantine built five 'cemetery churches' around the walls of Rome, though these were probably in part for members of his family rather than in memory of the martyr. The chief of these martyr churches was that built over the tomb of St Peter. Ever since, the most important church in Rome has been not the cathedral at the Lateran where the pope then resided, but instead St Peter's, which was outside the walls.

St Peter's

The site of St Peter's is a former heathen cemetery at the foot of the Vatican hill, not one of the famous seven hills of the city proper. It is likely that Peter was buried here. His grave became a goal of pilgrims, and after a short time a small memorial was built there. When Christianity became legal, Constantine founded over the memorial a church of which the west end cut into the hill and the east end had to be supported on an embankment. The slope prevented the church from being built with the altar at the east end, for the porch had to face down the hill, with steps leading down from it to the open space in front.

A hundred years later a covered way was built along the street to the bridge over the river Tiber. The church was bigger than the Lateran, but nothing like as large as the modern cathedral. It had five aisles and an apse like the Lateran. But because of the tomb it had a new feature — a well-lit cross-piece to accommodate the numerous pilgrims. This became a common feature of later churches, especially those built over martyrs' tombs. Its two wings were known as 'transepts', from the late Latin *transseptum*, 'a place fenced in'.

Soon the church was furnished. The memorial to St Peter was topped with a raised altar, and the walls were embellished with colour and mosaics which were much admired. In the eighth century frescoes were added, with pictures of biblical stories and portraits of saints and popes. Other tombs, richly decorated, were added. So were other precious relics; a chapel held the handkerchief with which St Veronica was said to have wiped Jesus' face as he carried his cross to the crucifixion, so that a portrait of the face was stamped on the cloth. The story of Veronica in its present form was framed in the thirteenth century; but in one form or another it went back much earlier. It was said that a handkerchief stamped with the face of Jesus was sent to King Abgar of Edessa in Syria; and that Veronica (in Greek, Berenice) was Abgar's daughter. She became one of the most beloved of saints as a lady of pity, and is still remembered every Holy Week in one of the stations of the cross. Many pilgrims in the time of Dante and for four centuries after looked upon this handkerchief as the most important of all the treasures of St Peter's.

Because St Peter's was one of the goals of Western pilgrimage, it had an effect upon church building all over Western Europe, as far as Scotland, Ireland and Scandinavia. But by the beginning of the sixteenth century this relic of historic Rome was no longer spacious enough for the multitudes of pilgrims, and the structure was in poor repair. Pope Julius II therefore instructed the architect Donato Bramante to draw up a design for a new

A rare picture of the old Lateran, original cathedral of Rome; shown because the pope (Innocent III) was said to dream that St Francis propped it up. By Giotto or a pupil at Assisi.

in the Quirinal Palace until it was seized by the Piedmontese army during the unification of Italy in 1870, when it became the palace of the kings of Italy, and later of the presidents. So popes lived in the Vatican only from 1377 to 1580, and from 1870 onwards because then they had nowhere else to live. In 1929 Mussolini set up the Vatican city as a state separate from Italy, and put into it Castel Gandolfo, the estate in the Alban hills used by popes from the seventeenth century as a summer residence to escape Rome's heat.

Coping with crowds

Soon there was a need for a porch to shelter the crowds of pilgrims, or a place where penitents could worship without entering the nave; and so at the door might be built what was called variously an *atrium* (originally the central open space of a Roman house) or *narthex* (literally a fennel plant, because it was long and thin) or *galilee* (origin unknown, probably as a symbol for the outer Holy Land from which one goes up to Jerusalem). Around 500, stone altars began to replace the wooden tables such as had been used in the house churches.

Christenings were at special seasons, usually Easter; this meant that a lot of catechumens were baptized together. So some churches had a separate building known as a 'baptistery', circular in plan with a central font. Other buildings soon clustered around the church: a hospice for pilgrims, a hospice for the sick, houses for the clergy, poorhouses, even baths.

The clergy had trouble with the behaviour of the people who came to these big new churches. They had not been used to the need to control crowds. Some of the people had been accustomed to dance inside non-Christian temples and thought it natural to dance in their new churches; the clergy felt this to be an irreverent and pagan habit. Some worshippers felt it natural to clap speakers, others thought applauding a sermon to be irreverent. Some brought bottles of wine into the church, and this went down too well for comfort. Preachers had little idea how a

cathedral, which was to be the largest in Christendom. Later Raphael continued to develop the design, and after him Michelangelo and the best of the Italian architects of that generation. It was long in building: the foundation stone was laid in 1506, and the cathedral was not consecrated till 120 years later. The circular colonnade of the piazza before the entrance was made by Bernini 35 years after that, from 1657. The only part not altered was St Peter's tomb, which is now slightly out of line with the newer building.

The cathedral church of the bishop of Rome was the Lateran, and the pope lived in the Lateran palace. Soon after the first St Peter's was built, the pope built himself a house nearby; later popes kept it up for convenience but did not live in it until 1377, when it was enlarged. The Lateran palace was burnt down in 1308. From 1580 the pope normally lived

**Veronica with her cloth;
by the mature El Greco, *c.* 1580,
Toledo. A beloved legend of
the way of the Cross.**

The entrance to the church of the Holy Sepulchre at Jerusalem.
Constantine saw to it that the sites of Calvary and the empty tomb,
already visited by pilgrims, were given a church. It was burnt three
times by raiders and in 1808 by accident, so that much of this building
is from 1810; the bell tower on the left is from the crusaders.

crowd could turn into a mob. Say from the pulpit that all non-Christian gods are demons and you might see your people streaming out to burn down the nearest temple.

The new space in church brought a flowering of art, not always religious in nature; we know of a presbyter, Nepotian, who was skilled at painting flowers on the church walls. For another century after Constantine's reign the catacombs remained in use, and the best works of art there date from this time. But whether digging became too expensive, or the wishes of families changed so that they no longer wanted to go down into the dark to see their beloved, they stopped using the Roman catacombs in the fifth century, and henceforth religious art was kept for churches. But it was slow to develop. The old Jewish tradition in Christianity was still powerful.

Fifty years after Constantine, the portrait – whether picture or statue – began to touch the people's devotion. They used to have statues of household gods in their rooms; now they liked to have a Christian image as the religious centre of the home. This change came to the home before the church. But churches needed ornament, and paintings of Christ and the saints became common; the people started to feel about these pictures or statues what they felt about the little statue in their room at home – a religious presence which blessed and had a power for good.

A quarter of a century after Constantine died, one more ruler of Rome who was not a Christian came to the throne: Julian, who reigned for a year and a half from December 361. He was brought up as a Christian, but in his later education under pagan masters he left the faith secretly at the age of twenty and was anti-Christian. As soon as he became emperor he opened the old temples and went to them to sacrifice in the old way. Trying to bring the old rites back to life, he pretended to revere the mother goddess Cybele with her taste for bloody sacrifice. He favoured the cult of the sun, and himself acted as acolyte at services. A superstitious man, he believed that at night he was visited by spirits. He removed the Christian symbol from the Roman standard, taxed Christian priests like anyone else, and after six months of his reign banned Christians from teaching in schools. Many of his soldiers cheerfully cast incense onto the pagan altar in return for a bit more pay, so it is clear that their faith did not touch their conscience.

But his religion was oddly half-Christian in that he also aimed at the high ideals of the Platonists – a desire to share in the perfect being of God; trust in the providence of God; an attempt to purify the body of its lusts; restraint in food and drink; a quest for light in the mind; hope in the life to come; belief that power is entrusted to a ruler by God; and greater value put on the soul than on the body. His instructions to his new pagan priests on the moral life were drawn from the ideals which were taught by those who trained Christian clergy.

Yet Julian's plan did not work. At Antioch and elsewhere there were riots when he tried to restore a pagan temple and was thought to have dealt wrongly with the tomb of a bishop. The emperor could hardly understand what was in the minds of the people. When he arrived at Aleppo he preached a non-Christian sermon to its senate. The words were heard coldly if politely by the senators, most of whom were Christian. And they were not displeased when Julian was killed in battle in Mesopotamia. Never again was there a non-Christian emperor of Rome.

For thirty years after Julian, Alexandria's most prominent building was still the temple of Serapis, high on its mound; valued by those who loved books because it housed a good library, and even by some of the Christians because old ideas did not die fast and there was an idea that its cult was linked to the rise and fall of the river Nile by which Egypt lived. By 390 the temple had become a fort, liable to attack by the zealous and defended by its servants. The city asked the government what to do; and the emperor, now Theodosius I the Great, ordered the cult of Serapis to end. The temple was pulled down without resistance and a church was built on the hillock, while

Memento mei amica dei

A Benedictine paints the Virgin and Child; from a manuscript of the Book of Revelation in the Lambeth Palace Library, London, written *c.* 1260; a manuscript probably from St Augustine's monastery, Canterbury; an abbey founded by Augustine of Canterbury, it lasted till the Reformation.

the library and the other buildings were left. In the circus a fire was lit on which the huge statue of Serapis was burnt amid the shouts of the crowd.

The best Christian leaders would not permit the mob to burn temples. St Augustine considered such an act wrong. Convert the pagans, he said, and then they will join us in ending their old idols.

Theodosius made it high treason to kill beasts at altars; he went further and banned the little gods in the house, and the pouring out of water or wine or incense to the gods. But many country people did not know of the decree or did not care, and kept up their old observances. If it was their custom to drink a lot on the day sacred to Bacchus, the god of wine, they would not abandon their drinking or forget the god. Most people kept a shrine in their house, and it was only slowly that the figure in the niche changed from an old household spirit into Mary or another Christian saint revered by that family.

Pagans of the ruling classes could still hold high office, safe from disqualification for not being Christians. In some cities, though not all, pagan writers could still publish their books without fear – crowds did not read books. Their houses still had pagan motifs, the old ceremonies mostly went on, they still did not like to sit down thirteen to dinner (a Greek superstition, nothing to do with the Last Supper), they still called the days and the months by non-Christian names, they had a good time on New Year's Day ('That is sacrilege,' said the Bishop of Ravenna when he saw the rites), and their manuscripts were decorated with symbols taken from the old cults. But Christian symbols also appeared in many places: in mosaics and wall paintings, on table knives and plates, even on milestones.

MONKS AND NUNS

In the Dead Sea Scrolls we find a Jewish sect for whom it was a condition of the perfect life that a man should live without women. Not all the group followed this rule, only the élite.

Their souls fought a war, and they must not turn aside and seek the ease of comfort in the home or the arms of a wife. They may have been kin to the Essenes, Jews who lived like monks, ate in silence and dressed in white.

In the faith of the apostles there was no idea that refusal to marry was a requisite of holiness. No one said that Jesus was perfect because he did not marry. Peter, the chief apostle, was married.

The first groups of Christian celibates were women. There were more women than men in the world, and the Church was fiercely against the habit of 'exposing' unwanted babies, who were usually girls – that is, abandoning them and leaving them to die. The congregations used some of these unmarried women to help the ministry of the church. They were numerous in towns. They started to order themselves, coming to pray in the church at set times, and to see that it was clean and its cloths not soiled, and to care for the sick and help children. Their rules developed into a way of life. Some of them gained fame as teachers of girls, others as guides to souls.

They were not yet nuns, for they did not share a house. They lived at home and helped their mother, or lived with another unmarried girl in a room in the town. But their way of life was turning into that of the nunnery, and they had the same work as the later active sort of nuns. At church services they walked in a procession, or sang psalms as a choir; female choirs were known, though not everyone thought this a good idea. At first they did not dress differently from other women; but soon they began to wear the same form of dress so that they looked alike, and in that way became distinctive. They sought advice from older women, or from a priest.

If their local church was threatened with force, their fate was not likely to be happy. Like other women of that day they could not travel far alone without the risk of rape, so their world was a small one. If they went on pilgrimage to a distant shrine, as many did, they went in a band and with an escort. Later,

some women travelling alone dressed themselves as monks to be safe. A holy woman was quite often found sharing the home and the love of a holy man without a sexual relationship; this heroic temptation of virtue brought hard words from the bishops who called her a *subintroducta*, that is, a girl brought into the house in an underhand way. The practice caused more fury than was fair, for sometimes she was just the priest's housekeeper. But it was for this reason that bishops pressed for unmarried women to live in a community – the future nunnery – and also why, in the Greek East, bishops began to prefer parish priests to be already married.

As women gathered into communities, more of them learned to read and write, for a community needed members who could read the Bible to them and could talk about it. They were not under vows, but they were seen by the people as committed to serve God in this way. Girls could leave if they were bored, or wanted to marry. After a time the Church became opposed to this natural behaviour, taking the view that they were dedicated persons. It was said that in truth they were married, but to Christ.

Later in the fourth century such women began to go through a rite like that of marriage in which they 'took the veil', an act which, like baptism, was carried out at high feasts of the Church. The veil for a bride was pre-Christian; it was not white but red. The Latin word for 'to marry' was *nubere*, 'to cover up', from which comes the English word 'nuptials'; so the veil made the name for marriage. The Christian bride followed the pagan custom of wearing a red veil, and so did the unmarried girl dedicating herself to God.

Some girls could not marry because there were not enough men. The number of men to marry grew fewer as men too started to think that the unmarried life offered them more time for God. They would live alone and pray. Soon they began to be called in Greek *monachoi*, people who are single, from which comes our word 'monk' though these men were not yet monks.

Before AD 300, still in the age of persecution, people felt drawn to the sands of Egypt as a setting for this solitary life for God. This strange happening is still hard to explain. Hundreds of people found that they could move out into the desert, not too far from an oasis for water, and live alone in a cave or cell, and plait mats or baskets – which they sold for the sparse food which they thought it right to buy – and try to pray all day. These hermits were the first monks. Ever since, the hermit's life has remained a part of the Christian tradition.

This rush to flee the world perpetuated the spirit of the martyr standing up against the Roman state. Without the earlier martyrs, later monks would not have happened in the way they did. There may also have been a wish to get away from the rat-race – and from the taxman, for the Roman government had such large needs and so few resources that taxes were oppressive. But this is only a guess at a reason for this rush into the desert; there is no evidence for it in documents of the time.

The hermit's life was not possible for women because they would not be safe. Even for men the rate of death by violence was not small. (The most famous hermit of the twentieth century, Charles de Foucauld, who said his prayers alone at an oasis in the Sahara desert south of Algeria, was killed by tribesmen in 1916.) Therefore hermits gathered in groups, though they still lived separately. The first groups were at Nitria (Wadi Natroun) and Cellia in the desert outside Cairo. The most famous is that which collected on the rocky peninsula of Mount Athos in northern Greece during the tenth century, and made it the holy mountain it has remained to this day, where no women are allowed to come, and the remoteness, the rocks and the numbers make for safety.

But hermits needed to band together for other reasons than safety. They grew old and in need of care. They wanted to go to church on Sundays. And they soon found that their way of life attracted thieves on the run, or proto-hippies who had spurned the world for reasons other than the will to pray, or mad folk for whom there were no asylums. They found that the ideal could be followed only if there were rules.

They discovered that hardly anyone can pray all the time; and that you do not get rid of lust by going where you will never meet a woman; and that you do not escape greed if your only needs are water, a little bread and some beans, a rug, and a pen and papyrus. They found that endless leisure brought not peace of heart, but boredom and melancholia. It was soon clear that to be alone all the time endangers sanity. These were the motives which turned the early hermits into monks.

There were two types. The first were groups of hermits under a common rule and an abbot, who met together for Sunday worship and other needs, but who for much of the week were still alone; and this ideal remains that of many monks in the Eastern church to this day and of certain orders in the Western church, especially the Carthusian order founded in the foothills of the Alps at the place now called the Grande Chartreuse, that is, 'the big house of the Carthusians'. In the Eastern church the Greek word for an alley, *lavra*, referring to the links between the cells, became used for a loose grouping of monks under a common superior.

The second type was the monastery as generally understood in the West – a group of single men living together as a community, with common prayers and common meals, obeying a written rule and governed by an elected abbot. They would earn their living by a common work, which at first was farming or copying books; they might also teach children. Later they might look after the needs of a nearby village; later still, some became scholars. The Greek word for this kind of community was *koinobion*, 'communal life', in Latin *coenobium*.

In religion the chief difference between these two ways was in their prayers. Those of the hermit group were the quiet, incessant prayer of the lone man. The coenobium held church services which were said or sung together, several times in the day and night. Because most men and women cannot pray all the time, to bring them to church often and let them join in the prayer of a group could uplift their souls for the whole day. They might suffer boredom as much as a hermit, and become melancholy, and even yearn for the freedom of the world; but in a group such discontent was helped more easily. Aged monks could be looked after.

The record of moral collapse among young hermits who went into the desert caused the authorities to order that no young man could become a hermit until he had served for long years in a coenobium.

This communal way of life was the model for the groups of unmarried women who became nuns and lived in a cloister – in Latin *claustrum*, originally meaning a lock or bar and derived from *claudere*, to shut. The idea of shutting oneself in came first from the need to keep out unwanted visitors, and second from the need for safety in an unsafe land. The

nunnery was also known as a convent, from the Latin *conventum*, a gathering of people. The Latin name *abbatia*, 'abbey', applied only to groups with an abbot (from the Aramaic *abba*, 'father') as their head. Originally an abbot was simply any holy person who gave counsel. There were no abbesses till the sixth century.

The monks looked back to St Antony as the first hermit in Egypt, where he fought wild battles with demons. After surviving this terrible mental experience he created a group of hermits with a rule. Then he went back to the solitary life; but he could not be fully alone because by then he was known as a guide to souls, and his work was to advise visitors. St Pachomius was said to be the first to create a monastery with a common life, at Tabennisi in Upper Egypt; the rules he drew up are the earliest to have survived. His house had a wall with only one gate.

Others, too, drew up rules of life. In the East St Basil, born in Caesarea in Asia Minor,

The three Fathers, Gregory, Basil and John Chrysostom; from the royal chapel at Palermo, built 1132–43 with splendid mosaics; in multicultural Sicily, their names are in Greek and Latin.

and who died in 379, spent a time as a hermit in Egypt. He is better known for his later life, in which he was busy as a bishop, but before this he built monasteries at Caesarea and wrote rules for their conduct. These rules were very loosely followed by his successors in the East, but the monks of the East always looked upon themselves as Basilians; in contrast to Western monks, whose rules came from St Benedict.

What was common to Basil and Benedict was common sense. In the early years some hermits behaved oddly, sitting on top of pillars (these were called 'stylites') or loading themselves with chains. Their principle was to beat down the body so that the spirit will be free to seek eternity. Both Basil and Benedict wrote their rules to be fairly easy for ordinary people to follow, and so made monasteries a normal part of life.

The critics

This wave of idealism was not without critics, who were fearful for the good of the world when so many people left it. Vigilantius was a Spanish priest who served just on the French side of the Pyrenees. He did not like the cult of the people to be centred on the tombs of the martyrs, and disapproved of rites formerly used in the worship of idols but now seen at Christian tombs. He said that these bodies were nothing but dust and ashes, and the souls

A fourteenth-century picture imagining the first hermits in Egypt, out in the sands west of Cairo, at Nitria and Cellia; the first origins of Christian monks, with loose rules to allow each to go his own way in devotion. Despite the picture, they were not near the Nile.

that we revere are up in heaven; and was doubtful that the miracles at the tombs were real or that they did good. Nor did he like so many to vow to give up sex for ever, for he thought that some would not be able to keep the pledge; nor that so many people should give up all their money and be poor for Christ's sake, because he thought they could do more good if they kept what they owned and used the interest to help those who were poor. We need good men and women, he said, to help us bring the pagan to Christ; is it right that so many of such people should go away to be monks or nuns, and how then shall we convert the heathen? He thought it odd to light candles in broad daylight, and his experi-ence of what the young did in the dark of vigils made him want to keep the night watch only on the eve of Easter. He was against the custom of sending collections of money to Jerusalem when there were so many poor people in his own land. To his foes, who said that to go into a monastery helps because you do not meet harlots and you do not rub against men with whom you may quarrel, he said that this is the act of a coward; a Christian can stand up to the devil and put on the armour of God.

These arguments were accepted by Vigilantius' bishop and some others, but they put no brake on the way the devotions of the people were going.

A critic who caused more anxiety – to judge by the number of prominent people who wished to prove him wrong – was Jovinian. He had been a monk, but gave up the solitary life – though not his habit nor his celibacy – and came to Rome. Here he wrote a book against the monastic way of life; it was written in pompous Latin and hard to follow. He did not condemn women for choosing to be nuns, but talked much of liberty instead of life by rule; in the eyes of God it is no better to be a virgin than to be a widow or a wife. He praised the unions in marriage that are blessed in the Bible. He cited the *Song of Songs* and its praise of sexual union. He condemned other forms of abstinence: in the eyes of God it is no better to eat very little than to eat well and give thanks. The Creator made the earth full of plants and meat so that we should have enough to eat. There is work to do in the world and that needs strength.

He had more influence than Vigilantius; some girls who had decided to be nuns changed their minds and married. People in Rome and in Milan and a few other towns said that he was right. Two church councils declared that his teaching was wrong. He had little influence on what was happening.

Unmarried priests

If it were accepted that the unmarried life is higher morally than the married, there was bound to be a movement to prevent priests from marrying. Already at the great Council of Nicaea in 325 someone proposed a ban on the marriage of bishops, priests, deacons and subdeacons. The proposal collapsed when Bishop Paphnutius, who was listened to because he came from being a hermit in Egypt and had been brave in the late persecution, said that if it were passed the result could only be immorality and that it was enough if clergy did not marry after they were ordained.

But sixty years later it took hold of Rome. All through that century the idea grew that priests ought not to be married, or at least not to have children. St Ambrose, the Bishop of Milan, was an advocate of this opinion,

though he knew that it would not happen easily. In the big cities it might be possible to find enough clergy who were single, but there were certainly not enough for country parishes.

In 385 it did not seem absurd for Pope Siricius, claiming that St Peter was present in him, to lay down rules on church discipline. He ordered that no bishop, priest or deacon should engage in sexual intercourse. During the following century this Western rule was enforced in theory, but proved unworkable in the country and scarcely workable in towns. In the texts of councils, which by often restating the law showed that it was not being observed, a bishop's wife was called *episcopa* and a priest's wife was called *presbytera*. The East followed it to some extent, by requiring that bishops must be drawn from the ranks of monks; a parish priest might be married (though he was not allowed to marry after he became a priest), but a bishop would be unmarried. In the West the clergy remained married in most parts for some centuries and no real effort to enforce the law was undertaken till the eleventh century; and even this, so far as it was successful, only helped to produce the Protestant movement, with its conviction that the right to marry is a freedom which the priest ought to possess like any other Christian man or woman.

This demand for celibacy was the most surprising by-product of the wave of idealism which sprang out of Egypt and swept over the churches during the first age in which they were no longer persecuted.

Cassian and Benedict

The Egyptian ideals spread westward, to North Africa and Gaul and Spain. Their chief guide was an exile in Marseilles who had studied with the hermits in Egypt. John Cassian, who died about 432, was the first serious student of the morality and psychology of the life of the monks and nuns. The *Conferences* are lectures on prayer and the contemplative life and all that went with that, put into the mouths of Egyptian hermits whom he had

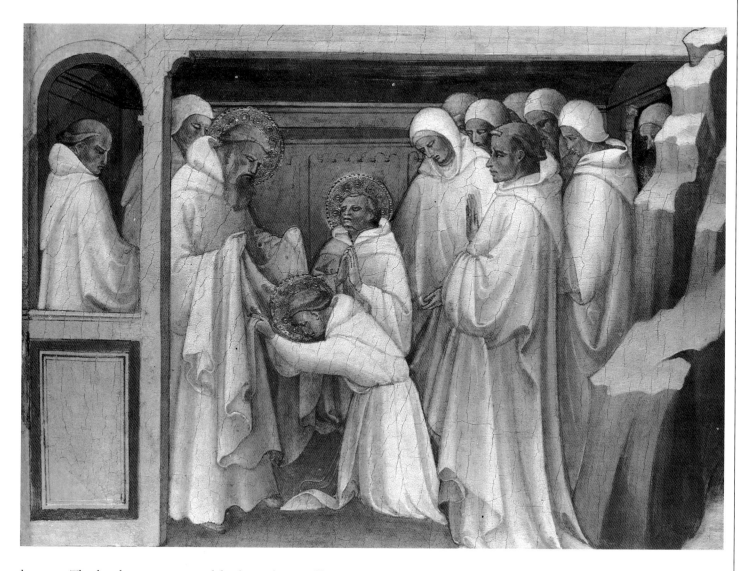

known. The book is very inward-looking; but it is also the most penetrating psychological study of purity of heart and prayer that was written in the ancient world. It was taken up by the rule makers who succeeded him. An unknown man, whom we know from his first words as 'The Master', wrote a rule for Latin-speaking monks; this rule was in good part taken over and made better by Benedict, who died about 545. Benedict settled first at Subiaco, not far from Rome, and then at Monte Cassino near Naples.

The Benedictine rule is plain and down to earth. He regards it as 'a little rule for beginners', which in comparison with the heroic deeds of the early hermits it was indeed. He wanted them to read John Cassian, to go to the heights. But it became the classical rule of all Western monks. Orders of monks which made their own rules were still conscious of it as a base.

Despite its sense and restraint, the rule enshrined the early ideals. We need men and women who pray much, who will bring all our needs before God. This is the first aim of the monk: *opus Dei*, the work of God. To do this, monks must be apart from the life of the world. They need to be in a group because life alone endangers the mind of most people. They should not claim their bed or their pen; all the needs of life are met by things which are there to use but not to own. They put away their own will, and give it to another to decide, by electing an abbot whom then they are bound by the moral law to obey. They need to eat, so they must work in the fields at

St Benedict clothes two of the earliest Benedictines, Maurus and Placidus; by Lorenzo Monaco, c. 1420. Maurus was said to have followed Benedict as abbot of Monte Cassino. Monaco was teacher of Fra Angelico, and a Camaldolese monk. The order of Camaldoli, founded 1012, was of the hermit type.

77

A bejewelled early
medieval reliquary, ninth
century, in Vienna, of
an important saint, said
to be Stephen.

times outside the set hours of prayer. These ideas were put into the vows that the monk made when he dedicated his soul to the monk's way: to be poor, to obey, and to remain chaste.

For the sake of safety nunneries were put in or on the edge of a town, or if in the country next to a community of monks. This second sort was called a 'double monastery'. The plan caused doubt, as people fancied that one sex would be disturbed by the other. But if nuns were to have the peace of fields and woods and not to live in a town, it was the sole way they could be safe. In the West the abbess, not the abbot, was head of the whole monastery; this shows how the monks lived there to help the nuns and not the other way round. The reform of the ninth century in France abolished these twin houses. Before long they appeared again, for they met a need; orders of monks and nuns were founded to use the plan. They were not quite banned in the West, but the people were not fond of them and, when at last the roads were less beset by bandits, they faded away.

The coming of the monks and nuns made a big change in the life of the churches. In AD 200 the churches were groups, most of them small, holding their prayers in house churches, caring for the sick and poor; and hidden from the police, with church members liable to be seized, tried and killed. The centre of their prayers was the church. Three hundred years later, many of the best people were no longer part of town or village life, but hidden away in houses of prayer.

SAINTS

The early Christians called all the members 'saints'; and the Church was called 'the communion of saints'. They did not at first think of Paul or Peter as saints in the modern English sense of the word. The Greek word *hagios* means both 'saint' and 'holy'. Everyone was a disciple, so everyone was *hagios*. In the pagan world they had observed a cult of heroes, but they were not quickly drawn to it;

there is no early evidence for a cult of saints. They looked on Christ as the single person through whom it was right to pray, and from whom one could ask for an answer to prayer.

Soon they had martyrs; the first, Stephen, as early as AD 35. Polycarp, Bishop of Smyrna, was arrested about 155 at the age of about 90 – he must have known some of the apostles. He refused to recant and so was burnt. The congregation of Smyrna recorded that they gathered his bones, 'which are more precious than jewels or gold', and placed them in a decorated tomb; 'and at it we shall by God's grace, and as we can, meet together in joy to celebrate his birthday, that is, the day of his martyrdom.' This record is the first sign of a celebration of saints by Christians.

Teachers of doctrine said that the saint is in heaven but God is everywhere. Yet the people, like the Jews who revered the holy or the Greeks who revered heroes, felt that the tomb was a place where they could still touch the one who had gone to God, and that somehow the spirit was still to be found there. They took the sacrament by the tomb, and often a meal as well. When in the end they emerged from persecution and could meet in the open, it was natural that traders should bring goods to sell to the crowds who came on the day of the martyr's death, and a market grew around the holy places.

A child who had loved a mother and lost her found it natural to go on asking her to help in death as she had helped in life. The first sign of this is in the messages on graves of the third century, asking for the prayers of the dead person; in the catacomb of San Sebastiano in Rome is a graffito dated August 260: 'Peter and Paul, pray for me in eternity'.

At first the only saints were martyrs. It was claimed all the eleven apostles were martyrs, although there was no evidence for most of them. They hunted for the bones of martyrs – the chief discovery, in 415, was of the body of St Stephen, the first martyr, not far from Jerusalem. But by then martyrs and confessors were not the only saints. The flight to the desert, the coming of monks and hermits and

St Jerome, in a cell at Bethlehem, translates the Bible into Latin, later called
the Vulgate translation because he did the work well and after a time every
Latin speaker used it. He usually has a pet lion. He would not have had an
hour-glass, nor a crucifix, nor a hat in that form. (The first known crucifix
was nearly two hundred years after him.) This is by Dürer, 1511.

nuns, made for a new sort of hero, who like a martyr suffered for the faith.

This reverence for the monk and the nun took a hold on Christianity which has lasted until now, and made monks or nuns the largest class of good men and women who have been thought to be saints. They did not feel a need for a record of the life of a saint at first. They needed three facts only: the name, the day and month of the execution (the year was unimportant), and the place where it happened. When they began to write Lives of Saints (as distinct from Acts of the Martyrs) these documents were more like sermons than history; some of the earliest were sermons. Jerome made up imaginary lives of people of whom he knew almost nothing. Lives often included events from after the saint's death – healings at the tomb, or whether the body had been moved ('translated') from the scene of death to a church. In the sixth century they at last began to use the word 'saint' in the way we do, as a prefix to a person's name. The first short form was SCS, for *sanctus*, 'holy'.

In the early centuries saints were made because people came in such numbers to their shrines that bishops consented to approve prayers there; these were saints by the memory of a people rather than by edict. After martyrs, the people had most love of monks or nuns, then (trailing by a long way) of bishops. But even the people started to ask, as the bishops asked urgently, whether some persons were such that they ought to have prayers said at their tomb – that is, whether the cult of the people was always informed. It was under Charlemagne that Western bishops made the first effort to find a way of 'approving' a saint. About 1000, the pope started to authorize certain cults. Two hundred years

later the pope's right to decide became the law of the Western Church. The people went on making their saints without paying any attention to what Rome decided.

In later centuries monks and nuns were still made saints more often than any other type of person, but for a different reason; less through folk memory, and more because there had to be a long test of their quality before the cult could be made lawful. Communities of monks and nuns did not die and so could campaign for the sanctity of their candidate for a long time – and afford the expense of doing so.

In the harsh centuries after the civilization of Rome was broken in the West, there was a difference between Eastern and Western saints. The East, fairly settled, went on in the old way; the saints were monks who renounced the world, the prayerful in their quiet sanctuaries. In the unsettled West, great leaders, powerful men, were revered and came to be saints; such as Pope Gregory the Great, or the Emperor Charlemagne (who was not a saint by any modern standard), or Edward the Confessor of England – they were men of action who stood for peace or were

A reliquary said to contain the arm of Charlemagne, with what is said to be his portrait outside.

unreadable medieval Latin manuscript text in the illustration

The painter of the shrine is not approved, so the devil approaches. It is a law book of the early fourteenth century, probably not written but illustrated in England; in the fifteenth century owned by St Bartholomew's in London, a priory already attached to the hospital.

symbols of a peace that had gone and was longed for.

The people expected all saints to be the same. They had an idea of a saint, and all their saints were supposed to fit it. Monks wrote lives of the saints; with small variations they were all the same life and told of the same virtues. We possess very few lives of saints which are 'lifelike', a piece of real history, until we reach St Francis of Assisi in the early thirteenth century. Then at last saints could cease to be flat – though the boring view of saints went on.

People liked their children to be christened with the name of a saint. Each church was now expected to have its relic of a saint under its altar. That was not too difficult; for example, the emptying of the Roman catacombs to protect bodies from thieves was a source of memorials.

This brought a change in the interior layout of churches. If the saint must be at the altar there was no room in the middle of the apse for the bishop; he had to move out to a throne at the side. The saint was the 'patron' of that church, the guardian of that congregation.

Particular professions or times of need got their special saints; St Nicholas was patron of children and of sailors, St Margaret of midwives and women in childbirth. One form of this patronage of a saint was fostered by heads of the Church. A pagan god might have a shrine where his help was invoked, and such a shrine might draw crowds. Bishops realized that the best way was not to let a mob destroy the shrine, but instead to keep it and to put into the altar a saint whose gifts were much the same as those of the god.

Asklepios was the Greek god of healing, and had temples to which non-Christians, and even some Christians, took themselves or carried their sick in the hope of healing. To sack Asklepios as though he were a demon felt like pulling down a hospital where longed-for cures happened. So a bishop saw that the right way was to replace Asklepios with a saint or

St Christopher, never without a
staff, carries the Child across the
ford; from a French prayer book
open at his day, 25 July.

saints whom the people believed to have the power to heal. Then the same people went on going to the old temple, which was a new church, to find healing. They now looked for the cure from a Christian power.

Here, as in the cult of the sun, was a piece of 'natural religion' which the converts did not so much get from the churches as bring into the churches with them.

Christians felt themselves (at their best) to be pilgrims, part of a vast army of men and women who walked before them towards heaven; their prayer was a small piece of a purer praise that went on in another world, and in this way they linked earth to heaven. They thought, or tried to think, of death as a gate, and the grave as a sacred place; they also thought of a presence which in idea was everywhere in the created world, but in fact was met at special points in the world of matter — the sacraments, the tombs of the martyrs, the pictures and stories not to be separated from the cult of prayer or from their common memory, and the meetings of the people.

Let us consider three special saints with names much valued through the centuries. Of all three, they knew, at first, only the three basic facts: that they were martyrs, where they died, and the day of the year when they died. On this small base grew stories.

George, the soldier's saint, lived in Palestine. The earliest picture of him is of the sixth century; here he is a footsoldier with no horse and no dragon. The Greeks revered him as the patron of soldiers, and by 1100 some Western churches were dedicated to St George. The crusaders who fought in Palestine met him and brought him home with them. King Richard Coeur de Lion of England took George as his patron, and in 1222 he became the patron saint of England. Knightly orders usually adopted him, as did the Order of the Garter in England in 1308. By now he was shown slaying a dragon, symbol of the forces of evil; a patron not of any war but of war for a just ideal.

Christopher is the traveller's saint; his Greek name, Christophoros, means 'Christ-bearing', and the story about him grew from this name. But it was a thousand years before anyone much paid him reverence. Then we first find the story of how he was told by a hermit to carry travellers across a ford; and how a child asked to be carried, and on Christopher's shoulders the weight grew so heavy that, by the time he reached the other side, he knew that this was the Christ child. In all pictures of him he bears a staff to support the weight. Because he carried his Lord safely over the river, he became the patron of anyone on a journey. His image was painted on the outer wall of churches, or sometimes inside, facing the porch, so that passers-by might see him. In modern times motorists hang his medallion in their cars.

Cecilia is the musician's saint. From about 500 she was connected with music, but at first she was said to have rejected it. The story told how, while the organs were playing, she closed her ears and went to die. By the Renaissance she was considered a lover of music and she began to be shown with an organ; Raphael painted her thus at Bologna. As everyone is inspired by music, the name of Cecilia still evokes affection. The poet John Dryden in 1687 wrote his *Song for St Cecilia's Day*, a lyric to the place of music in creation:

Orpheus could lead the savage race;
And trees unrooted left their place,
Sequacious of the lyre:
But bright Cecilia raised the wonder higher:
When to her organ vocal breath was given,
An angel heard . . .

It did not matter that she never played an organ; what mattered was the story and its link with a divine gift.

Mary

During the fifth century the bishops came to a verbal war over Mary, the mother of Jesus. Was it right or wrong to speak of 'Mary the Mother of God?' This was really a war about how we should look on Jesus rather than how we should look on Mary. Some said that God

St Cecilia with her organ, by Carlo Dolci,
a detail, mid-seventeenth century.
Dolci loved to portray gentle heads.

St George, by Paolo Uccello, about 1450; Uccello loved to paint animals and tried to choose religious subjects with animals in thcm. He was fascinated by perspective.

cannot be born, so the right words are 'Mary the mother of Jesus in whom God dwelt'; and if you call her the Mother of God you talk as though Jesus was not truly a man, and strike at one of the most important parts of the Gospel. Others said that by speaking of Mary as the mother of Jesus in whom God dwelt, you make Jesus into two, God with a man, rather than God-in-man who is one. The people wanted the phrase 'Mother of God', which fitted their love of her as a saint. The bishops cared more about how we should look on Jesus, the lay people more about how we should look on Mary. In 431 at the Council of Ephesus the bishops approved the words 'Mother of God'.

This debate showed the people's desire to bring their affection for Mary into shrines and prayers. At Rome the church of Santa Maria Maggiore was built, and soon embellished with the mosaics that make it one of the most wonderful churches of Christendom. By the seventh century there were feasts of St Mary in the calendar: the Annunciation, when the angel told her she would have a child who would be the Son of God; the day of her birth (which like the birthday of Jesus no one knew); the Purification, a usual ritual after childbirth; and the day of her death – but no one now liked to think of her as dying, so in the East the day was called the Dormition, or falling asleep, and in the West from the eighth century it was called the Assumption, when she was taken up into heaven.

Something in natural religion was missing in Christianity: God was Father, and Jesus and the apostles and all the bishops were male. The mother goddess had no counterpart. But now her place was taken by the mother of Christianity; she was at the heart of everything that linked human instincts with religion – birth, motherhood, suckling, simplicity, and the deepest of natural affections between two human beings. As reverence for her spread across the world it took various forms and names. For a time the Christians did not try to baptize natural religion by taking the shrine of a mother-goddess and turning it into a church

Leonardo, the cartoon of the Virgin with
St Anne. Anne's name as that of Mary's
mother comes first in the *Protevangelion*,
a legendary life of Mary but very early,
perhaps even late second century.

The church of Santa Maria Maggiore in Rome, built 432–40. It has superb mosaics. There was a later legend that one night snow fell in summer; Mary left her footprints and so the place was chosen. About 600 AD pieces of wood were found, believed to be struts of the cradle at Bethlehem and were revered.

of the Blessed Virgin, but by the fifth century church leaders began to find this a good step on the road to Christianizing a people. Some converts came from cults where the supreme being was a goddess, such as the Egyptian cult of Isis or the old cult of the Great Mother; and there was a continuity in art between the old pictures of the Great Mother or of Isis and the Christian pictures of the Madonna and Child. This was the same instinct which in America of the later twentieth century caused some feminists to call the Christian God 'She' although Jesus had called him Father, and other feminists to use Mary as their symbol. From the sixth century this instinct took shape in names: Mary was known as the 'Mother of Grace', 'Mother of the Church', 'Mother of Mercy'. The Greeks even called her *Panagia*, 'All-holy'. In the Council of Constantinople of 553 the bishops ruled that she is ever virgin; that is to say, she bore no brothers nor sisters after Jesus was born; she was mother to God and to him alone.

These instincts inspired lovely works of Christian art. They also evoked the desire to free her from the experience that all men and women sin; in some of the thought of the later Middle Ages they spoke of her 'immaculate conception'; that is, she was conceived unlike the rest of us, not doomed to sin. After a debate which lasted centuries, in 1854 Pope Pius IX declared that all Christians ought to believe this.

As there was no body, pictures must take its place. Mary was served by the people's affection for her portraits and icons. For a time the bishops worried: do we pray to Mary and the saints in the same way that we pray to God? The second Council of Nicaea, in 787, ruled that we should give 'adoration' or 'worship' to God, but to the saints we should give 'reverence'.

Mary was important because they could use her to educate people in the ideals of virtue; in her, goodness was enchanting, not boring; she embodied the virtues of self-sacrifice, compassion, affection, duty, humility and purity. This moral function of Mary is clear

Michelangelo's *Pietà* in St Peter's, Rome; the most famous *Pietà* in an age when many churches wanted to have one.

Middle Ages had a painting or sculpture on this theme. In the twentieth century it was often used, with reason, on war memorials.

The angelus – the reciting of the Ave Maria three times a day at the ringing of a church bell – dates from the twelfth century. The rosary is a few decades older: a string of beads which the wearer touches one by one, and for each bead says an Ave Maria or an Our Father, so making a 'chain of prayer'.

In the modern debate over sex equality, argument raged around Mary. Was this devotion to her a way of elevating the female sex because a woman was the god that mattered? If so, did the Reformation hurt the female sex by weakening this symbol? Or was the devotion to Mary such a cult of the mother and the home, of humility, of the mourner, of the excellence of chastity, that she was the wrong model for women to follow? Whatever the truth of this, no one can deny that she is the type of the gentler virtues.

The halo
Pagan artists used to mark the chief men and women in their pictures with a ring of light round the head, usually of a gold colour. The Greek word *halos* meant, among other things, the disc of the sun or moon. Latin speakers often called the halo *nimbus*, 'cloud'. It was reserved for the illustrious: gods or demigods, and later for the Roman emperors. Its use was associated with the cult of light as a special gift of God, and was found in the East among Hindus and Buddhists. When artists started to make pictures of Christ they almost at once gave his head a halo; if they used the lamb as his symbol, because out of reverence they did not want to draw his face, they gave the lamb a halo. It was only during the fifth century that the halo started being given to others, to Mary especially but then to other saints and angels. Later still they started to give it to anyone big in the church, such as bishops or abbots, even while they were alive; for this purpose it was usually not round but square. When others gained the halo, the halo of Christ was marked out by a cross.

from the sermons preached and the hymns sung about her in that age.

Soon after 1100 the use of the *Ave Maria* (Hail Mary) as a prayer began to be found. When devotion to Jesus took the form of fellowship with the sufferer, Mary followed; we have the image of the *Pietà*, Italian for 'compassion' – the mother holding in her arms the dead body of her son brought down from the cross. We do not know of this from the New Testament, but it seems likely that it happened. Originally the Pietà was not sad but a moment of ecstasy, and Mary's face was shown full of joy. But soon it became the supreme example of the mother suffering at the loss of her child. This image first appeared two hundred years before the most famous example, by Michelangelo in St Peter's at Rome; most Western churches of the later

The Flight into Egypt, by Juan de Borgoña, about 1525; one of the artists who understood about children.

TIME

During the third century BC, the Greeks decided to date events from the first year in which the name of the victor of the Olympic Games was known, that is 776 BC. The Romans took as their starting point the year the city of Rome was founded, which was said to be 753 BC. This was the system used by the first non-Jewish Christians. The Jews had a more reasonable system: the Old Testament gave them a good idea when the world began – in our reckoning 3760 BC – and they dated time from then. Many early Christians used the Jewish calendar. Soon after 1253 years from the foundation of Rome – that is, AD 500 – there was argument between Rome and Alexandria on the right date to celebrate Easter. Rome had a learned monk, a native of what is now Romania: Dionysius, but he was nicknamed Exiguus, 'Tiny'. They asked his advice about Easter. In 525 he made a list of the dates of Easter in future years, and in so doing started a new way of counting: from the birth of Jesus. From this come the letters used in dates, BC for 'Before Christ' (in Latin AC, *Ante Christum*), and AD, *Anno Domini*, 'in the year of the Lord'. He got the date of the birth of Jesus wrong by a few years.

The churches did not take to his system quickly. The English were the first, and it was used by chroniclers. In the early eighth century the Venerable Bede used it; France started to use it about a century later. In modern ages dictators who wished to weaken Christianity thought that the BC-AD system helped to diffuse Christian ideas in society and tried to replace it – the French revolutionaries set their 'Year One of the Revolution', and later Lenin in Russia and Mussolini in Italy tried to enforce their own systems. All these new schemes were unpopular, and impractical because they did not go back far enough. And it is far from certain that Dionysius the Tiny's system did much to diffuse faith, because it was two or three centuries before churches as a whole used it.

Dionysius made a change to the time when the year began. Most Romans began the year on 'the calends of January'; that is 1 January, hence the word 'calendar'. Dionysius reasoned that the start of a Christian year should be not the time of the birth of Jesus, but nine months before, on 25 March, the day of the Annunciation. This timing was much used in Europe and survived even into the eighteenth century, in Pisa till 1745 and in England till 1752; it still confuses historians who need to work out which year it was when something happened between 1 January and 25 March. But the use of 1 January had become a habit and never died out, and in the end was reinstated.

THE CONVERSION OF THE NORTHERN TRIBES

The Germans

From the third century onwards, Germanic tribes from the North began to settle within the bounds of the Roman Empire. Families moved across the borders in search of a better home. More often they came as troops, whom Rome took as mercenaries and rewarded with a gift of land within the borders. Why the tribes needed to migrate is still not known, but probably they were displaced from their lands by Tartars or Magyars from the steppes of southern Russia. In 406 the Roman frontier on the Rhine finally broke; soon there were kingdoms ruled by German chiefs: Vandals in Africa, Visigoths in Spain, Franks in much of France, Angles and Saxons in Britain, Ostrogoths in Italy, and later Lombards in much of northern Italy.

The sack of Rome by Alaric the Visigoth in 410 was seen as a turning point in history, for Rome was revered as the 'Eternal City' and people could not imagine a good state which did not have Rome at its head. The catastrophe did not weaken the Church in the West for, with political power gone, the Church was the place where old ideas of order might still be found. But the countryside was now a more dangerous place, so churches were reasonably safe only in towns, and in monasteries, which now had higher walls.

The Germans who were allowed to settle

inside the frontiers started to receive the religion they found in the people among whom they now lived. To the Germans the name 'Rome' meant education, peace, roads, villas. They accepted the axiom that those who were not barbarians were Christian. Ulfilas (the usual Greek form of his name; Ulfila in Latin; and in German probably something like Wölfchen, 'wolf cub') was a Goth who lived north of the Roman frontier on the Danube. His mother had been captured from Asia Minor in a German raid; she was a Christian and brought him up as one. He went to Constantinople, became a reader in the Church and then, about 341, was made Bishop of the Goths. He served north of the Danube for seven years until a persecution broke out; then, with many Christian Goths, he fled south across the border. His group settled in what is now Bulgaria, where he continued as a bishop for thirty-three years, preaching in Greek, Latin and Gothic; the main part of the services was conducted in Gothic. He was also recognized by the emperor as secular ruler of the Gothic tribe. He made an alphabet for the Goths and translated the Bible into Gothic, omitting the Books of Kings so that his Goths should not think it good to shed blood. Of Ulfilas' translation, only the four gospels survive today.

The faith as Ulfilas taught it spread across the Germanic tribes; the Goths when they came into Italy and Spain were Christians, so were the Vandals when they conquered North Africa; so were the Lombards when later they moved into northern Italy. Their Christianity was crude and let them keep many of their folk customs.

The tribes farther to the north were not at first touched. The Angles and Danes who invaded Britain were heathen, and so were the Franks who came into northern France. In 498 King Clovis of the Franks, moved (though not easily) by his Christian wife Clotilde, was himself baptized in the cathedral of Rheims, which was the chief see of his part of France. At this conversion Bishop Remigius of Rheims is said to have remarked, 'Adore what you burned and burn what you adored.' Even if he

did not say this, it became famous as a dictum of conversion. It also shows how the Romans thought of the conversion of the Germans as in no way a bettering of any religion they had before, but as a rejection of it.

The Germans invented a form of church organization not known before: the private chapel or *Eigenkirche*. The lord, usually a German, at times a Roman, set up a squire's estate in remote country, with his private chapel and chaplain. He had no idea that this chapel and chaplain ought to be under the control of the bishop of the nearby town; they were 'his'. This private chapel slowly grew into the parish church of the village because it was all the church that the villagers had, but although it was the villagers' church it was ruled by the squire and not by the bishop.

Constantine's mother Helena commended this convert to be baptized and here the bishop baptized him. Note the bishop's stole and his headgear; this manuscript was copied at Wessobrunn, an early Benedictine house in Bavaria which was in later times a seat of learning; suppressed in 1803; its library went to the Bavarian State Library.

Iona abbey, off the west coast of Scotland; settled by St Columba from Ireland about 563; from here he brought Christianity to the Picts and Scots. Though unsafe from pirates, it remained till the Reformation. The church was restored in 1900; later the Church of Scotland (Presbyterian) re-established it as a community and place of pilgrimage.

Some squires had odd ideas about the best way to run a church; but so, in those anarchic days, had some bishops.

The king was the owner of many estates and so of many private chapels. He issued laws for the Church; new bishops could not be appointed without his choice or leave. But synods of bishops still met and decided rules. They were more educated than the kings and squires, so had influence in the state. They were also powerful because the people gave them more and more money and land. The rules enacted by their synods are valuable evidence of what the Church was like in a young German kingdom with Roman subjects.

Despite so many Germans' conversion, there were still more Christians in the East than in the West. The empire was stable in Constantinople, and Greek was still a more common Christian language than Latin. The West's weight only became evident to everyone at the beginning of the ninth century.

The Celts

In Christian history there appears from time to time an air of freshness, of mountains and open skies and breakers on the water. We find it among Russian sages, and among the early Greek and Coptic monks. But in the West we sense it as we read of the earliest Welsh, Irish, Scottish and Northumbrian hermits and pilgrims, members of what are commonly called the Celtic churches.

From Roman Britain a few foundations of churches, and Christian symbols on old silver or on fragments of mosaic, are still left. Then, as their empire weakened, the Romans went away and left Britain at the mercy of the Angles, Saxons and Danes. Of the British people some stayed and served under the new masters, and kept up their religion at places such as St Albans or Lichfield. Others sought refuge westward, in the marshes of Somerset around Glastonbury, or the Cornish peninsula, as at Tintagel, or the Isle of Anglesey where they made a shrine, or Whithorn in Galloway which was the see of a bishop, or farther west to Ireland or north to Scotland. We know

them from rough inscriptions, remains of cemeteries, and a few carved crosses and other objects for worship. Because these Britons were fighting pagans, religion was a binding force for them; this helps to explain the flowering of Celtic churches in a time when law and order had broken down and any homestead might be at the mercy of raiders from the sea.

Patrick was a Briton of Christian family living near the west coast, probably in Cumbria. At the age of sixteen he was seized in a raid by Irish pirates, taken to Ireland and enslaved. He escaped, but resolved to go back and tell the Irish about his faith. Patrick is important because his two little writings, a short letter to a chieftain called Coroticus and a brief defence of his own life which we know as his *Confession*, are the only literary evidence we have of Irish Christianity at its origins. It is very possible that he set up the centre of his Irish work at Armagh, which was the chief see of Ireland even though it was never the most important town. Often the chief see of a country today dates from a time before the present capital of the country had been Christianized. Jerusalem was not the most important city in the Levant; even before the fall of the empire Rome was not the most important city in Italy; Canterbury, not London, is the centre of the English Church, and St Andrews, not Edinburgh, of the Scottish; it is the same with Uppsala in Sweden and Trondheim in Norway.

In the nineteenth century there was found in an old manuscript at Dublin a hymn which we know as 'St Patrick's Breastplate'; in its most famous translation it begins:

I bind unto myself this day
The strong name of the Trinity . . .

The manuscript goes back to about the tenth century, and it appears that then the hymn was widely used and believed to be written by Patrick.

In the early Celtic kingdoms there were no towns and life was insecure; people gathered in settlements clustered around monasteries. The ideal of the monastic life was evident in the way they organized their churches: abbots were as important as bishops or more so. A unique religious practice was a 'pilgrimage', which they understood as a holy man going out into unknown country in a quest to find solitude and quiet and God.

One such quest ended at Iona off the Scottish west coast, where Columba landed when he sailed from northern Ireland, not knowing where he was going. Another quest by one of Columba's men, Aidan, this time by invitation of Oswald, King of Northumbria, ended in the shrine at Lindisfarne off the Northumbrian coast, later called Holy Island. Another Irish monk, Gallus, founded the famous Swiss monastery of St Gall.

These Celts had an astonishing desire for learning. One would have expected people with a simple ideal and a hermit's way of life to care little for books. On the contrary: they helped the churches of the West to recover what little knowledge of Greek survived. They made books for use in services, of which the Irish Book of Durrow, dating from about 700, and the slightly later Book of Kells, now in Dublin, are the best known. The illuminations to the Gospels in the Book of Kells are done with a skill and taste which makes it one of the most delicate examples of early Christian art. The Celts' love of learning affected others. It was quite remarkable that the best historian for at least three centuries in all of Europe, Bede, should have lived in a monastery at Jarrow, so far to the north in a country troubled by tribal war and by pirates from the sea. He was accorded the unique title of the Venerable Bede only a century after he died.

The Celts had trouble with the customs of the Latin churches; they kept an old-fashioned date of Easter, and priests or monks cut their hair an unusual way. The tonsure, or shaving of part of the head, had long been a custom in various Eastern religions. Hair was associated with the religious instinct; it is enough to think of Samson, whose strength depended on his hair. Eastern Christian priests wore beards from the beginning, and still do; the monks at first shaved all their hair. Latin priests shaved their faces and made a circular tonsure on top of their head. The Celts shaved the front half of the head but conformed to the Latin usage later. The Protestants abolished the tonsure, and in modern times it fell slowly out of Catholic use; in 1972 the Roman Catholic church dropped the custom, though some monks still keep it.

The synod of Whitby in 664 seemed to have won agreement on adopting Latin ways; but for more than a hundred years afterwards some Celts kept Easter on their old date and cut their hair as before. The Welsh were isolated, probably because they did not want to agree with what the English had just decided to do – as so often, religious customs were a sign of a people's independence. The Welsh went on using the older text of the Latin Bible long after other countries had accepted the Vulgate, St Jerome's much better translation. They had a special saint in Dewi or David; he was associated with St David's because this became a goal of pilgrimage. They remembered him as a hermit. No one knows how the leek became associated with St David's day; his *Life* does not mention a leek.

Because the politics of the Celtic countries were unsettled, the churches were centres of little kingdoms or broad estates which were really independent. Despite civil unrest, they had enough money to buy good vessels for their worship, bronze for bells, and silver for reliquaries and bishops' crosiers. The bishop's staff was first used in Constantinople, and by 700 Spanish bishops were using it as they processed into churches. By 1000 all Western bishops were given a staff in the ritual when they were made bishops. Later in the West, it was supposed that this staff was a sign of the bishop being a shepherd to his flock, and it was made in the shape of a shepherd's crook. No Celtic bishop, nor any bishop anywhere, then wore a mitre. Its use was due to pilgrims in Rome who saw a pope wearing a hat of that shape. It became universal for

bishops and some others, such as important abbots. The Protestants thought it pomp and stopped its use until it was revived in modern times.

This rare Celtic world, still with old Roman ideas such as prophecy by studying the flight of birds, slowly changed as Europe moved in – the French into Brittany, the Normans into Cornwall and then Wales and Ireland, English influence into Scotland. There remained a memory of an 'age of the saints', with legends of their lives, and lines of poetry which were thought to go back to them, and a half-forgotten tradition of holy men who lived in the forest or the mountains and healed the sick who came to them, and praised their God in the quietness. It could not be a memory of holy women in the forest, because life was too unsafe in the wild; and unsafe enough for men. It was necessary for a nunnery to be part of a 'double monastery', with a male community next door. But there were memories of abbesses, the chief of whom was Brigid, abbess of Kildare, who was venerated by the Irish although they knew nothing for certain about her. There was even a story that she had been made a bishop. She may have inherited the praise of a pre-Christian god.

Bells

The Celts encouraged the use of bells. These were invented in the Far East, probably in China, long before Christ, and came westward to Egypt and then Rome. Small bells could be used to warn, as on the collars of sheep, or to call out the watch, or to summon the family to a meal, or as an ornament on horse harness; larger bells in temples had magical associations, a pure sound which helped to keep away demons.

In cults such as those of Bacchus or Mithras bells were rung violently to stir worshippers to ecstasy; therefore early Christians did not like bells linked with religion. But when the empire became Christian this mattered no longer, and by 380 bells summoned people to church. But they were not common in the West until the Celtic missionaries used them.

The portrait of St Matthew in the
Book of Kells (about 800), a masterpiece
of early Irish art now in Dublin.

In Dublin there is still a bell known as St Patrick's bell.

These early bells were usually quite small; some were cast in foundries set up by the early Benedictine monasteries of Germany. The people loved to have bells in their church tower because the sound was believed to protect the building against lightning and fire; when a thunderstorm approached they rang them. Pastors found them useful to tell people who could not come to prayer that a service was about to start, so that they could join with it in spirit though not in body; or to warn them that someone had died and was about to be buried (the 'passing bell'), so that they could say a prayer for the soul that was on its way to God. From the Celtic era onwards, church bells were blessed in a special ritual.

The English

King Ethelbert of Kent married a wife from France, and she was a Christian. This gave a chance to Pope Gregory the Great to send an abbot, Augustine, with four monks 'to convert the English'. With the memory of a Christian Britain under the Romans, and with the Celts coming down into Northumbria and Yorkshire from Scotland, and the messengers sent by Rome pushing northward from Kent, it was only a few decades before the Anglo-Saxons accepted Christianity.

The way in which Christianity brought the Northern nations into an international Europe was illustrated here. The Church in England was organized by a Greek monk, Theodore, from Tarsus in Asia Minor, who was sent to be Archbishop of Canterbury; he died in 690. This was the time when Greek influence on the see of Rome was at its highest. Just as the converts of Ulfilas had worshipped in Gothic, so the English soon used Anglo-Saxon in their devotions. Bede wrote in Latin; but he told a moving story about an illiterate cowherd at the Whitby nunnery, Caedmon, who was discovered by the abbess to have the gift of religious verse. If he were told stories from the Bible he could make them into Saxon poetry. Thus Caedmon had created the first

St Cuthbert sails with two companions; from 664 he was with a Celtic group of monks at Lindisfarne off Northumbria; later a hermit on the Farne Islands; revered in north-east England; from a manuscript of the twelfth century.

Edgar, King of England 944–75, offers worship. He was crowned
at Bath only two years before he died; his is the first known rite of
coronation and leaves traces in the British rite today. At Glastonbury
he was revered as a saint, but they had to overlook things.

English poetry, about the making of the world, and Adam and Eve, and Moses' escape across the Red Sea, and how Christ was born and died and rose; and how judgement and heaven or hell await all mankind. We possess only a small fragment of Caedmon's verse from the manuscripts of Bede.

Some of the early English religious poetry, metrical versions of Bible stories, was very dull. But an unknown created a poem of genius, which was only discovered during the nineteenth century in an Italian manuscript: *The Dream of the Rood*. The manuscript is of the tenth century but the poem is earlier. It has a claim to be the most enchanting meditation upon the cross ever written in English.

The Saxons

The Saxons occupied north-west Germany between the Rhine and the Elbe. They were heathen and raiders, and the Franks under Charlemagne waged a long border war with them. Whenever Charlemagne won, which was often, he made them take a pledge that they would give up their gods and become Christians. Some of them were baptized, and some showed penitence at what they had done; but as soon as his army went away they went on as before. After severe Frank losses in a Saxon raid, Charlemagne said he would kill all the Saxons unless they became Christians. He founded sees, issued a decree banning the rites of the heathen gods, and ordered the Saxons to be baptized and to pay tithes. The only result was another large raid on the Franks, after which the emperor beheaded 4000 Saxons at Verden. The war went on, with Saxons burning new churches, killing Christian priests, and rebuilding the shrines of the gods.

Charlemagne killed many Saxons not because they refused to be Christians but because they killed Franks; yet he had the idea that if they became Christians they would be less likely to kill Franks — which proved correct. He was himself a pious Christian, had influence in Church synods, and was sure that his power came to him from God; though he was not fond of popes and other clerics. Slowly he settled southern Saxony and took young Saxons into France where they were educated as Christians. There were nine Saxons sees by 847, and at Corvey and Fulda were two abbeys which were the centres of Saxon higher education.

The old Gallican liturgy of the seventh century in France had a prayer: 'Let us pray for the most Christian kings, that God may put all the barbarian peoples under their power, so that we may have lasting peace.' A hundred years later a synod at Frankfurt prayed that 'Almighty God will put the barbarian peoples under our king, and so they will come to see the truth and know that the living God is their creator.' Even in Rome they prayed that the emperor might conquer all barbarian peoples.

The conversion of the Saxons was enough of a success to make the later Saxon chiefs mainstays in the German kingdom, which became a buttress of the new Christian Europe as it extended from the Mediterranean. It enabled the northern Saxons to start bringing Danes and Swedes into Christianity. Yet the axioms 'No one can be given faith by force' and 'Put up thy sword' still stood. The question that had arisen in Rome during the fourth century now applied to the German peoples: should you use law to make everyone a nominal Christian, and then trust that the social effect will in time make many of them real Christians? Or must you admit that this method is a sure way to corrupt the churches?

The bishops sent to Saxony to guide the converts were also officers of the emperor; they were like later German prince-bishops, who had secular power as well as spiritual authority. The popes of that age also began to be secular rulers in Italy, the origin of the papal state which, after an interruption from 1870 to 1929, is with us still in the Vatican city.

In Saxony there were real missionaries, headed by Boniface and other Anglo-Saxons sent from England. Boniface was killed by the Frisians, and Kilian was murdered in Würzburg. These were not the only deaths.

As Anglo-Saxons, these missionaries could

The baptism of King Harald of Denmark near Mainz in 826. He wanted military help from the Frankish emperor to get back his kingdom. Note the shape of font for an adult baptism. The king wore a white robe, was baptized in water and anointed with oil. The emperor stood godfather.

judgement that is to come, and the use of fasts and of giving money to the poor.

One effect of their work was that German became a written language. The finest work of this time was a poem called *Heliand*, 'The Saviour', which turned many of the Gospel stories into Old Saxon verse. The Germans found the humility and non-resistance in the Gospels difficult to accept; the unknown author of *Heliand* could not believe that Jesus rode into Jerusalem on an ass.

Anskar was a monk of Corvey who in 826 went north from Germany into Denmark and then Sweden, far out of reach of any help that could come from the swords of the Franks. But he found a few Danish traders who had been baptized when they travelled south. He built a church in Schleswig, and brought money to buy back Franks who had been taken prisoner and made slaves. Anskar made a few converts, one of whom built the first church in Sweden, and brought back a few Danes to Saxony for religious instruction. He founded the see of Hamburg to look after the mission to the North, and then sent the first bishop to Sweden. All this was ruined in raids and murder; Hamburg was sacked with its church and library, though Anskar did manage to rescue the relics. But archaeologists have discovered many signs of Christian churches in Denmark and Sweden during that age.

Sweden's conversion came in the eleventh century through missionaries from England. In the twelfth century the Danes began to remember Anskar as a saint. Nearly two hundred years after that, the Swedes laid relics of him in the chief church of Sweden at Uppsala.

Bavaria had been much nearer than Saxony to Roman law and culture. By early in the eighth century Western missionaries had created some monasteries and churches. A missionary, Emmeram, set up a monastery at Regensburg; another, Corbinian, founded one at Freising. Both these houses were pillars of south German Christianity. Charlemagne conquered Bavaria and added it to his empire and appointed the first archbishop at Salzburg. But he hardly needed force to make the land

make themselves more or less understood in the language of the people. Boniface's 'laws' survive, and show what he expected the newly converted people to understand. The rite of baptism must be in Latin, and properly said. The language was incomprehensible to most Saxons then, but for Charlemagne Latin was the sacred language of the Bible and the mass and the prayers. The priest must also explain to the convert in German that they must renounce the devil and must make their confession. German was also used for the Lord's Prayer and the creed, for sermons (of which some were written down and survive), for hymns, and for some readings from the Gospels. The missionaries tried to explain the creed and the cross, the need to do right, the

The garden of Eden from a ceiling in
an early Norwegian church (Stavkirke),
late thirteenth century.

The imperial crown, said later to be 'Charlemagne's crown' but of the late tenth century; on left, 'by me kings rule'; right, King Solomon, as a type of wise government; now among the crown jewels in Vienna.

fourteen Czech chiefs to Regensburg, where they requested baptism. But most of the Slav peoples lay in the Greek sphere of influence, and became Christian as the churches moved northwards from Constantinople and Salonika.

Coronation

Power had to be seen to be lawful, so some rite of recognition of a new king was needed. The Germans lifted him on the shields of his warriors, and put a spear in his hand and a diadem, or headband, around his head. When the people became Christian the new king needed prayers for his office. He was still raised on shields and given a spear, but he also went to church.

The Christians were used to the idea that the head of the Roman state, the emperor, was called by God to keep the peace and defend what was right; and so the emperor was thought to have a holy calling. In the Byzantine state he always kept this touch of the sacred about his person. The

Christian. The result was a flourishing set of abbeys where many manuscripts were copied and libraries built.

A Christian Saxony and a Christian Bavaria pushed out towards the Slav peoples. The Bavarians, before they were conquered by Charlemagne, had planned a mission to the Slavs and for this purpose founded two abbeys. From Regensburg they went towards the Czechs in Bohemia, and from Salzburg towards the Slovenes, and from Passau towards the Slovaks. In 845 Charlemagne's grandson Louis the German welcomed

Bible recounts that when King David was dying there was a dispute as to which son of his various wives should succeed. One son, Adonijah, decided that he was the one, and collected armed men for a coup. So, with David's assent, 'Zadok the priest took an horn of oil out of the tabernacle, and anointed Solomon' as king (1 Kings 1:39). This was evidently what a people should do to make a new king. So the Germans kept their raising upon shields, but added to it a rite in church in which the chief bishop anointed the new king and put a crown upon his head. This gave the king some of the holiness of a priest.

The oldest known rite for crowning a king is English, in the *Pontifical of Egbert*, a prayer-book of the eighth century. In the middle of the service a bishop prays for blessing on the king and his reign, and then pours oil on his head while a choir sings an anthem, 'Zadok the Priest', still sung at coronations though not with the same music. Then the bishops and lords put a sceptre in his hand and a helmet on his head, and set him on a throne. A little later there were small changes: a crown instead of a helmet, and a ring for his finger, and a crowning for the queen as well. This ritual was considered so important that in both England and France there were legends that the oil came down by a miracle. It was brought to France by a dove carrying a sacred vessel, the *Sainte-Ampoule*, (Latin *ampulla*, flask), which was kept at Rheims. All French kings were anointed from the *Sainte-Ampoule* until it was smashed by revolutionaries in 1793. In England the sacred oil was supposed to have been brought by the Virgin Mary to Thomas Becket.

In 800 both the pope and Charlemagne the Frank wanted to revive the Western Roman empire. The empress in Constantinople saw this as illegal, a usurpation. A coronation was essential to both Westerners if what was done was to be accepted by the people. So on Christmas Day at St Peter's in Rome, Charlemagne was crowned by Pope Leo III. First the Pope set a crown on his head, then the people acclaimed him emperor, and then the Pope did homage to the new emperor. It was the last time a pope did homage to an emperor.

Not only was the coronation a sacred ritual, the crown itself was holy. The oldest and most hallowed of all crowns is the Iron Crown of Lombardy, with which the Lombard kings were crowned and then anyone who claimed to rule Italy, even Napoleon. It is kept in the cathedral at Monza, near Milan. The iron band was later said to have been beaten out from one of the nails used to pin Christ to the cross, so that the crown is a sacred relic as well as a

sign of power. The Holy Roman Emperor was usually crowned by the Pope, the last to be crowned by the Pope was Charles V in 1530. Germany accepted that the coronation added nothing to the emperor's lawful right, which was made by his election.

Kings and queens might be overthrown and republics set up; yet still sovereigns were crowned and the ritual was felt to be right. In the Hundred Years' War between England and France, it was Joan of Arc's supreme achievement to ensure that her king was crowned in Rheims. In countries where the constitution was not overturned, the consecration of power was still valued; though everyone knew it to be a symbolic act.

Joan of Arc, in the register of the Council of Parliament, 10 to 11 May 1429. Flag with IHS, first three Greek letters of Jesus. Joan, a shepherd girl, had a vision telling her to save France from the English. Aged only seventeen, seven days after this entry she led the French army to raise the siege of Orleans, the first English defeat. They made this flag at her wish. Later she was captured and burnt as a witch/heretic. She was made a saint in 1920.

CHAPTER THREE

EAST ROME

CONSTANTINOPLE

When the emperor Constantine founded his new capital in the East, he chose the ancient town of Byzantium because of its strategic site. Here he decided to build a Christian city which would bear his name, with Rome as the model for its architecture and works of art collected from other towns to adorn it. The city grew rapidly in size – 20,000 when it was founded, half a million in the sixth century. Because it was the capital, its bishop was ranked above all others. One might have expected the bishop in Jerusalem, goal of pilgrimage for all the Christian world, to be the most important cleric in the East; or if not, the bishop of Antioch, where the Christians were first called Christians; or the bishop of Alexandria, where St Mark the Evangelist was believed to

have been the first bishop. But between 636 and 642 Jerusalem, Antioch and Alexandria fell under Muslim rule and left Constantinople the only great see of the East that was under Christian government.

It was a city full of churches, so many that when the first crusaders arrived they were awed. It was also a city of many monasteries, some of which did much for higher education, or ran a school for manuscripts or collected a good library. They were enough to exert a powerful political influence in times of stress.

St Sophia

Constantine began to build next to his palace the first church of St Sophia, 'the Holy Wisdom'; his son Constantius finished it. Forty-five years later it was rebuilt, but a century later, in 532, it was burnt to the ground in the Nike riot, one of the worst

A fresco from a Coptic church at Asyut, Egypt. The two big saints are Cosmas and Damian, brothers, physician-martyrs, who in life gave medical services free and after death helped in epidemics. The three saints below are their three brothers. Remarkable are the three above, in Phrygian caps, who were thrown into the burning fiery furnace but not burnt.

The Emperor Justinian; from a sixth-
century mosaic in S Vitale, Ravenna.
His great influence was to cause the
codification of Roman law, restated under
the influence of Christian principles.

St Sophia in
Constantinople, the great
dome above, with
Muslim hangings.
Built by Justinian as his
cathedral, turned into a
mosque by the Turks in
1453 and into a museum
in 1934.

disturbances ever to afflict a European city. Then the Emperor Justinian built the church of St Sophia which we still know; the biggest church in Christendom and one of the most beautiful. In 1453, when the Turks captured the city, they turned the building into a mosque. The mosaics, which contravened the Muslim ban on portraying living creatures, were covered up. In 1934 the government of Turkey turned it from a mosque to a museum, and the surviving mosaics were uncovered. It had continued to be a place of Christian pilgrimage even while it was a mosque. A pope said prayers in it as recently as 1967.

The churches of the fourth and fifth centuries were still rectangular basilicas with aisles and an apse, and sometimes transepts especially if there were a saint's shrine. Towards the end of the fifth century the idea of a dome to cover the crossing of transepts and nave is first found; sometimes this was built on a circular wall, sometimes on four arched segments at the tops of the four pillars of the crossing. St Sophia took the latter plan; the result was so astounding that ever afterwards the basilicas of the Eastern Church were built with domes. This was the first great church of which we know the designers' names: Anthemius of Tralles and Isidore of Miletus, both Greeks from Asia Minor. They were scientists by profession, not architects, one a geometer and the other a physicist.

In the days when it was a church, or later a mosque, the worshipper would have been overwhelmed by surprise at the sense of space, with a feeling of calm, which may still be felt today despite the thronging tourists. The light streams in from the upper domes, which look as though they are floating. The giant dome is between 31 and 33 metres (102 and 108 feet) in diameter, its crown 56 metres (183 feet) above the floor. The fairest marble, porphyry and basalt, brought from all over the empire, were used to colour the walls up to the level of the lower domes. Many of the old mosaics, which must have been exceptional for they were made in a time when the art of mosaic was at its height, were

later destroyed; and we can only form an idea of what they were like by going to a Western church decorated under Byzantine influence, such as the churches at Ravenna, Italy.

From time to time the church authorities — or the taxpayers — had to pay for repairs, reinforcements and ties to keep its glory in being. Throughout the centuries more and more external buttresses have had to be added. It was dedicated in 537; only 21 years later the dome collapsed. Isidore's nephew, Isidore the Younger, repaired it, reducing the outward thrust of the dome by making it meet the walls at a steeper angle. The new dome stood for 426 years despite earthquakes. Then it fell again; this time an Armenian, Trdat, repaired it. In 1204 the soldiers of the fourth crusade sacked the city and looted the church of its treasure and relics. The dome fell again in 1346 and was rebuilt once more. In the last decades of the Byzantine empire the church was allowed to dilapidate.

The last Christian service in this greatest of all cathedrals was held all night on 28 to 29 May 1453 as the Turks burst into the city; and the first Muslim service, with the fittings turned to face Mecca and the walls covered hastily with yellow wash, four days later. The Turks kept it up with pride as their finest mosque. Museums cannot guard objects as easily as when they are revered in a church where many pray, and the imperial monograms on the heavy doors, placed there by Justinian's architects, vanished during the 1960s.

The question must be asked whether the creators of this magnificent structure aimed at the glory of God or their own glory. Cynics reported that on the day of its dedication Justinian, overwhelmed to see what he had done, exclaimed 'King Solomon, I have outdone you!' The tale is not reliable, but shows how even at that time some were uneasy about ostentation. For posterity there could be no such doubt.

There is a story that about the year 987 Vladimir, Prince of Kiev, wanted to be religious but was not sure which religion was

A sixth-century mosaic of the
four evangelists from Ravenna.

true. He sent envoys to see the Muslims on the Volga, but they were not pleased with what they found. Then the envoys went to Germany and on to Rome, and found Christianity better, but said that the services were not beautiful. So they came home by way of Constantinople and were present at the sacrament in St Sophia, and felt what others have felt: 'We did not know whether this was heaven or earth. We never saw such splendour or beauty. We cannot tell you what it was like; except that we are sure that God dwells there among men, and that this is the best form of worship. The beauty is unforgettable.'

The story might have a foundation in the experiences of actual Russians who visited Constantinople; St Sophia makes it credible. The name 'Holy Wisdom' was not uncommon for churches in the Greek East, Russia, and the parts of Italy and Sicily under Byzantine influence.

It was the beginning of an age of mosaic, fresco and icon which is as unique in Christian civilization as the Western flowering in the Renaissance. Of necessity mosaic was a formal art, unsuited to the depiction of gaiety or emotion. But it compensated by stature and solemnity, harmony and symmetry; colours were limited by the materials, but placed so variously that they could not be dull. It was an art perfectly fitted to express religious ideas. The *Pantocrator* who looked down from the dome of St Sophia, and afterwards from many domes of Byzantine churches, evoked the unity in God between power and compassion. The artists loved to dwell on the links between the Old Testament and the New, and often showed an Old Testament story on one side of a building matched by a New Testament story on the other. They had a few simple pieces of scenery – trees, snow, or a flight of birds. But mostly they showed figures of apostles, saints or angels. All was splendid and serene; the art of a society which might be tortured, but from the walls you could never know its agony because it showed no fear about what was ultimate.

THE LAW

The law of Rome had fallen into chaos. There were collections of laws, but emperors kept adding to them without care for consistency; all was confusion in the courts and among those who studied the law. The change to a Christian empire cast doubt on laws passed by pagans; but the laws of the Christians were in an equal mess. Only thirty years after the first Christian emperor died, lawyers demanded that something should be done at once.

The Emperor Theodosius II appointed a committee of lawyers. They drew up a code which was put into force on New Year's Day 439; it is known as the Theodosian Code. They were given power not only to list laws, but to adapt them to modern needs or to drop them if they were obsolete. The code was consciously a Christian body of law, and was supposed not to include any law passed earlier than the time of Constantine; actually some pre-Christian law got in, partly because they could not do without it and partly because of a useful legend that the great legist Papinian, who came to Britain when the Emperor Septimius Severus invaded Scotland and afterwards was foully murdered, was a Christian. This idea was helpful, because the basis of Papinian's attitude to law was a conviction of its moral purpose. The code also included laws from the time of Julian the Apostate, but not those hostile to the Christian religion.

The lawyers did not think the new code comprehensive. The laws and their commentaries were still so voluminous that not even a big library had all the books courts needed; some laws still contradicted each other, and even experts were confused. Ninety years later the lawyers were at the Emperor Justinian for a new code. The result was a second edition, which we call the *Digest* or the *Pandects*, which came into force in 534 and is still the basis of the laws of many countries. It was much more complete, for it drew on pre-Christian law. It was careful of the standards of the clergy – for example, it forbade them to gamble, insisted that monasteries be apart from nunneries, and required bishops to supervise the marriage of clergy; it did more for the disadvantaged and gave the Church the duty of caring for prisoners and babies abandoned by their mothers; and it empowered the bishop to ensure that the finances of his town council were not embezzled. Outwardly this was a more Christian code than that of Theodosius, invoking the name of Christ at the beginning of each law. In this way the religion and morality of the state affected the structure of society.

TRADITION

Because Greeks were among the first converts of the apostles, and because the language of the New Testament is Greek, the Orthodox churches of the East kept a sense of life not broken since the age of the apostles. They were aware that they were the source from which Western Christianity flowed. When other peoples were converted – whether Slavs, Armenians or Georgians – they thought it right that church services should be in the language of the people. But they still felt Greek to be the language not only of the New Testament, but of civilization. For several centuries they considered Latin a barbarian tongue.

The word 'orthodoxy' showed their value of tradition: 'We kept the faith which the apostles of Jesus taught.' In 843 the final defeat of the iconoclasts, who wanted to banish icons and pictures from churches, was celebrated with the introduction of an annual holy day called 'the feast of orthodoxy', which reminded the Church of its pride in the truth of the apostles and its duty to cling to it.

The Eastern services had their early example in the Liturgy of St James, which was believed to go back to the earliest services held in Jerusalem by the apostles. In the age of Justinian, a Syrian named Romanos came to Constantinople and wrote hymns. He proved to be a true poet in the Greek language and won the name Melodos, 'the master of lyrics'.

The Serbian monastery of Gračanica; the greatest of the Serbian monasteries of the Middle Ages, built 1313–21; it housed the first printing press in Serbia; only the church, with five cupolas and fine frescoes, and not the monastery buildings, survived the sacks of wars.

The east end of the Armenian cathedral at Jolfa, in Isfahan,
Iran, built 1606. The Armenians were converted by Gregory
the Illuminator in the third century. They celebrate Christmas not
on 25 December but at Epiphany on 6 January. The King of Persia
(Iran) forced thousands to settle in Jolfa where they prospered
as a Christian community. Some are still there.

He created a musical form known as the *kontakion*; the word means 'stick', in this case the rod around which a scroll of choral music is rolled. It was a short sermon cast into stanzas for singing as a hymn. Some have survived; English hymnbooks contain an adaptation of the solemn Russian *kontakion* for the dead: 'Give rest, O Christ, to thy servant with thy saints where sorrow and pain are no more.' But many of the earlier *kontakia* fell into disuse and were replaced by a *kanon*, which here meant a verse of poetry sung between the verses of a canticle from the Bible; a custom said to have begun in Crete. Then the poetry began to be sung by itself, without its Biblical frame.

Orthodox churches would not allow musical instruments, other than the voice, in services. Nor did the Latin West at that time, but later it accepted instruments – at first only to help the choir to strike the right note. In recent times some Orthodox churches in America have allowed the use of instruments.

The icon

In the Byzantine East the picture of a saint turns into the icon; that is, a picture which is not a mere portrait or ornament but, like a tomb or shrine, makes the saint 'present'. Early icons had something of the status of the picture of the king or queen on the wall of a public building – not only a likeness, but a symbol of the unity of the nation. By the seventh century the people's love of saints made the icon into something more than a picture on wood. It was seen to have a kinship in spirit with the person painted on it; it could receive the veneration and prayers addressed to the saint, and transmit his or her blessing to the person praying before it. It presented a saint to the soul. Icons were not portrayals of scenes, like some of the stained glass windows of the West. They were of one person, a holy portrait.

They were not kept for the church only. An icon would be hung over the front door of a house to guard all in it from ill; a little icon could be worn on a journey to protect the traveller. An icon hung in a monastery cell, a prison cell, a ship's cabin. A church icon would be borne in processions; candles were lit before it. Like some relics in the West, it could transmit power. A person might be cured by touching it – the healing power was that of the saint, but the icon passed it to the sufferer. No one who damaged such an icon would escape punishment. There were stories of icons which had been painted by no human artist; these were called *acheiropoietes*, Greek for 'not made with hands'. In Jerusalem was found a picture of Mary said to have been painted by St Luke. This made Luke not only the patron of doctors (in one of the earliest pictures of him he has surgical instruments) but also of painters.

The iconostasis

This is a screen that divides the altar and sanctuary from the rest of the church; it is present now in almost all churches of the Eastern Orthodox tradition. It is hung with icons, which churchgoers go to kiss. At first it was no higher than a Western altar rail, but was then made higher with columns and lattice-work, still much like a Western screen. The need to hang icons before the people made the screen more of a wall for hanging icons; and by the early fifteenth century it had become so tall that it hid the altar. A pair of 'royal doors' in the middle were kept closed except when the priest came out at the most solemn moment of the sacrament; there was also a door at each end for use by deacons, sacristans and nuns. At each side of the royal doors it was usual to have an icon of Christ and Mary; other icons were hung in a regular though not invariable order. Handbooks gave instructions to designers of churches on the best order in which to arrange the icons. The early schools of icon painters, in Constantinople, Salonika, Ochrida and later Moscow, developed this art form into one of unique beauty.

The arrival of a high screen to divide the church made a big difference, at first sight, between the form of worship in the East and the West. It added greater mystery to the rite.

The Romanian painted churches are unique in Christendom, many of the frescoes being on the outside walls. The monastery of Sucevitza was the last to be so decorated, in the later sixteenth century. This is the outside of the apse.

Western visitors often felt that it divided the clergy too sharply from the lay people. But better knowledge of the Eastern way of prayer shows this is not so; the choir and the vergers move freely in and out of the sanctuary through the doors at the side of the screen.

Iconoclasm

One of the serious arguments in Christianity was about pictures. This is part of the Jewish heritage, for the Jews did not allow pictures in a place of worship. The ordinary folk of the later Roman empire wanted religious pictures and did not see why they could not have them. Epiphanius, a tough-minded bishop who died in 403, saw a picture of Christ woven into a curtain at a church in Palestine and pulled it down; but already this was old-fashioned. Bishops not only believed that the ordinary people were helped by pictures, they wanted their churches to be full of colour and rich mosaics. They believed that icons helped the illiterate to understand their faith.

From 726 the Eastern Orthodox churches were divided between the *iconoclasts*, breakers of icons, and the *iconodules*, reverers of icons. In Armenia the debate led to a schism.

At first the emperors were on the side of the iconoclasts. God is impossible to picture; therefore it must be wrong to attempt a portrait of Christ. Mary and the saints are surrounded by divine glory, and no one can paint glory.

But the people, among them the monks, wanted their holy pictures; and in the end they won. They were defended by at least one excellent divine, John of Damascus, sometimes thought to be the last of the early Christian Fathers, who died in 749. He held that by becoming man, God made it possible to paint a portrait of that man; and God has made the painter's art. If God can be upon an icon then those who owe their glory to him can also be on icons. God made wood and paint, and there is nothing wrong in using them to his glory.

The effect of this fierce argument was to make the icon a necessary part of the devotion

The Armenian church on the island of Akdama on Lake Van, Turkey. A cathedral built in 931 and flourishing for centuries; until in the First World War Russia fought Turkey, and Armenians (as Christians) were suspected of being pro-Russian. Massacres followed and Akdama was left empty.

The Pantocrator icon in the cathedral of the Dormition
(= the falling asleep of Mary) in the Kremlin. This cathedral was
built 1475–9 and was where the Tsars were crowned. In it were
collected the greatest icons of that age of great Russian icons. This
icon is thought to come from the still earlier cathedral on the site.

The Coptic abbot Menas with Christ; Egyptian, sixth or seventh century;
notice the CHI-RHO between the haloes. Coptic was the original language
of those Egyptians who were not Greek. The Copts became Monophysites
(for whom see p. 288). They survived far more strongly than any other
Christian body in Muslim North Africa and are still influential in Egypt.

The Coptic Church of the al-Mu'Allaka in Old Cairo. Probably seventh century. The pictures stand above the thirteenth-century iconostasis, not on it.

The struggle over images at Constantinople. Bottom, iconoclasts pull down an icon. Bottom left, two saints blame a patriarch who wants to be rid of icons. Half way Nicephorus, left of the two, Patriarch of Constantinople 806–29, deposed for resisting the emperor's iconoclasm. From the Studion or Theodore Psalter.

of Eastern Christianity. There came to be a pattern of paintings in churches: Christ as the Pantocrator in the dome; Mary in the apse; and on the iconostasis a varied pattern of icons which often included St Michael, St George and St Nicholas. Without the presence of the icons the church was not thought to be a holy place.

MOUNT ATHOS

If we were to seek Christian communities that today are most like the congregations of the fourth century, we perhaps might go to some Congregational or Methodist chapel in the deep Midwest of the United States. But we should also go to Mount Athos.

Other monasteries of the Orthodox East had the same quality not long ago, such as the monastery of St Catherine founded by Justinian on Mount Sinai, and decorated with the most superb mosaics that still exist from that date – they survived because in the time of the iconoclasts Sinai was under Muslim rule. But in modern times these have been perturbed by planeloads of tourists. A few monasteries have kept the old quality of retreat, for example the house on the island of Patmos off the Turkish coast where St John wrote his Revelation.

Athos is the eastern of the three peninsulas of northern Greece, a long finger of high ridges and rocks. Most of it is still to be reached only on foot or by mule, or by climbing the precipitous cliffs from a small boat. It was a natural place of refuge for people fleeing from their enemies, and monks started to use it as a remote place for their life and their prayers. By 1000 the mountain contained a monastery and many hermitages; fifty years later it was known as 'the Holy Mountain'. The monks were under no government, though the promontory had leave from the emperor (later the Turkish sultan, and then the Greek government). They elected a council of elders. Raids by bandits and incursions by nomad shepherds led them to fortify the houses. Men came not only from Greece but all over the Christian world: Russia, Georgia, Serbia, Italy. By 1912 more than half the monks were Russians, though numbers fell after the Russian revolution five years later. No women, nor female animals, nor beardless youths, were allowed on the mountain.

Their ways of life were not uniform. There were the hermits; the monasteries with a common life; the 'idiorhythmic' houses where monks lived in the same place but each went his own way in prayer and rule of life and the one common act was the service on Sunday; and the so-called *skiti*, which were little groups of hermits in huts around a chapel with a superior. Today there are twelve monasteries with a common life and rule, eight are

ΨΑΛΜΟΣ :

Κρῖνόν μοι Κ(ύρι)ε ὅτι ἐγὼ ἐν ἀκακίαι
μου ἐπορεύθην :
καὶ ἐπὶ τῷ κ(υρί)ῳ ἐλπίζων, οὐ μὴ ἀ-
σθενήσω :
δοκίμασόν με κ(ύρι)ε καὶ πείρασόν με :
πύρωσον τοὺς νεφρούς μου καὶ τὴν
καρδίαν μου :
ὅτι τὸ ἔλεός σου κατέναντι τῶν ὀ-
φθαλμῶν μού ἐστι :
καὶ εὐηρέστησα ἐν τῇ ἀληθείᾳ σου :
οὐκ ἐκάθισα μετὰ συνεδρίου μα-
ταιότητος :
καὶ μετὰ παρανομούντων οὐ μὴ
εἰσέλθω :
ἐμίσησα ἐκκλησίαν πονηρευομέν(ων)
καὶ μετὰ ἀσεβῶν οὐ μὴ καθίσω :
νίψομαι ἐν ἀθῴοις τὰς χεῖράς μου :
καὶ κυκλώσω τὸ θυσιαστήριόν σου κ(ύρι)ε :

ὁ Νικηφ(όρος) ὁ πατριάρχ(ης)

ὁ Σωτήρ

ὁ Σωτὴρ ἐλέγχων μετὰ τοῦ
πατριάρχου τὸν εἰκονομάχ(ον)

οἱ εἰκονομάχοι

Χ(ριστό)ς

St Nicholas, a Russian icon of the
sixteenth century; Christ offers him
the book, Mary offers a stole.

idiorhythmic, and every *skite* or hermit is attached to one of the big houses.

After years of decline through the era of communism in Eastern Europe, it began again to attract men who wanted to say their prayers in quietness. The mountain is not quite free from the tourists who afflict modern monasteries, absolutely free from the urban and the industrial, with mountains up to 1800 metres (6000 feet) surrounded by the glory of the Aegean Sea. These communities represent one of the deep inheritances of the Christian culture and devotion of the eastern Mediterranean and the Slav world.

THE MYSTICS

Mysticism is an experience of direct communion with God. It is not, for example, reading about Jesus and saying that is what God must be like; but kneeling down to say a prayer and suddenly feeling God there, facing you or beside you or in you. Early Christians had such experiences. When they tried to describe these moments they could find no words that were adequate, and knew that they could not.

But those who read the Platonists and the Stoics found that the experiences were not only Christian, so they described them in the terms that the old philosophers had used – for instance, 'the contemplation of God'. St Augustine, who had read many works by the disciples of Plato, had a vision of God at Ostia, the port of Rome, and used words from the Platonists to describe it.

An early photograph (1869) of St Catherine's monastery on Mount Sinai, one of the two most historic monasteries of Christendom. Sinai was an early goal for pilgrims and the place has been almost continuously occupied with Greek monks; but it has needed these fortifications.

In St Catherine's monastery, high on Mount Sinai, the Transfiguration; Moses and Elijah appear to Jesus, and the three apostles Peter and James and John are overwhelmed by the vision; this picture is very rare because Sinai had no iconoclasts and so it goes back to the time of the Emperor Justinian. In other parts of the East most pictures were destroyed during the eighth century.

Rock churches and cells cut from cone-shaped volcanic rock in Cappadocia, Turkey, some as early as the sixth century, later a flourishing religious centre; some were occupied even until the expulsion of Greeks from Asia Minor in 1923.

The Grigoriou monastery on the western shore of Mount Athos on the north Aegean coast; coenobitic, that is, with a communal life; fortified against raiders from the sea; one of the twenty houses of monks on the Holy Mountain.

In Justinian's century the use of Platonic language was given support from the Bible, in an odd way. When St Paul preached at Athens one of his few converts was Dionysius, a member of the high court of the Areopagus. Soon after AD 500, books appeared purporting to be written by this Dionysius. Everyone, Greek or Latin, accepted them as authentic writings by one of St Paul's most educated converts. We do not know the real name of the author; we only know that he drew on one of the late Platonists, Proclus, who was not a Christian. Proclus was one of the last heads of the once famous but now dilapidated academy at Athens which was still debating philosophy, some lecturers opposed to Christianity some influenced by it, until Justinian closed it in 529.

The books of Dionysius made a starting point for the way the mystics were going. He taught thus: between God and the world is an ordered world of angelic spirits. God is perfect, and unchangeable except that he is a force always creating. He is not being, for he is beyond being; so the human mouth can never describe him. Yet he shows himself out of the darkness as present in Christ, so that we

can truly speak of the 'God-man'; and also in the Bible, though this can be understood only with the help of his grace; and in symbols, the sacraments of the Church, which bring cleansing and light. But when we meet him directly we meet him in what Dionysius calls ecstasy — that is, not by our senses but by being taken out of them. Yet still the God we meet there cannot be known. Faith is darkness.

These ideas made Dionysius one of the most influential writers for several hundred years. In the ninth century he was translated into Latin, and then the Latin thinkers used him constantly.

The monks of the Orthodox Church were accustomed to long prayers and to much use of psalms. Most people apart from hermits and the unusually devout said their prayers in church, but did not think of saying them out of church. Then, in the mountain monasteries and in Constantinople, there appeared a movement for private prayer, continuously in one's room. They were encouraged to sit instead of stand, so that they could go on longer and think less about the body; to lower the head and to breathe quietly; and then say in a rhythm, and in time with the regular breath, over and over again the 'Jesus prayer': 'Lord Jesus Christ Son of God have mercy upon me.'

This was a revival of the teachings of Cassian and some of the early monks, and it was now carried through ardently. But it was not only a way of repeating prayer. It was linked to the purifying of the soul from the eight deadly sins. (There were eight in the original list drawn up in the Egyptian desert about 390: vanity, arrogance, melancholy, accidie [torpor and indifference], covetousness, lust, gluttony and anger. The later list of seven drawn up by Pope Gregory about 600 fused the first two into 'pride' and the next two into 'sloth', and added envy.)

This movement is known as Hesychasm, from the Greek hesuchos, 'quiet', because these people chose the prayer of quietness. But soon doubt arose. When the monks prayed in this way some saw a spiritual light,

illuminating the soul; a vision of the truth about the world and humanity. Some of them claimed that this was the very light from God, like the rays from the sun. When Jesus went up on the Mount Tabor he was 'transfigured' in light, witnessed by three disciples. To the Hesychasts the feast of the Transfiguration, and Mount Tabor, became very important. The light which came in their prayer must surely be the same light as the light of Tabor, and it was a light that they not only felt with the soul but saw with the eyes of the body. The movement spread fast, all over the Balkans and into Russia, and flourished until the sixteenth century — we see traces of it even in the novelist Dostoevsky in the nineteenth century.

Opponents of the movement said that no one could see God, and that this talk of the eyes of the body was absurd, and that people were being misled. But the councils at Constantinople backed the Hesychasts.

The best known of them was Gregory Palamas, who died in 1359. He had learnt the way of quiet on Mount Athos, and then had to flee before a Turkish raid. He became Archbishop of Salonika, but his see was again and again troubled by Turks and he spent a year as their prisoner. He was a persuasive defender of Hesychasm against its critics. God cannot be known in his essence. But he can be known through his working powers (his 'energies'), and these are himself, not something distant from him, and are what we know in the pure prayer of quiet. Although after the sixteenth century the ardour of the Hesychast movement faded, in the end of the eighteenth century two Greeks collected all the old texts, from Cassian to Gregory Palamas and after, that were to do with the Jesus prayer. The leader of the two, Nicodemus, a monk on Mount Athos, was made a saint by the Orthodox Church as recently as 1955. He called his anthology *Philokalia*, 'love of beauty'; it was published at Venice, where many Orthodox books were printed while the Turks occupied the Balkans. Soon it was translated into Slavonic, and then into Russian, and was valued in Russian devotion. In modern times those who practise this way of prayer often use a rosary. In the West the rosary is a chain of beads. Among the Orthodox it is normally of knotted cord and is known as a *kombo-schoinion* (*kombos*, a band; *schoinion*, a cord).

THE EFFECT OF ISLAM

In the century after Justinian's death the assured Christian world, expanding fast among German and Celtic and Slav peoples, suffered its first dramatic losses. About 600, Arabia was viewed much like Ireland or Scotland, as soon to accept the faith. The peninsula contained historic Jewish communities and scattered Christian congregations.

Muhammad had visions that convinced him he was a prophet of God and called him to write a holy book, the Koran, for the Arab peoples; it dealt with belief in one God, the coming judgement, the resurrection, mercy and the rule of law. In the century after his death in 632, Arab soldiers of Muslim faith conquered historic Christian countries: Egypt, Palestine, Syria, North Africa, Spain.

Since the time of Julian the Christians had lived under Christian governments, except for those who had spread eastwards through Persia to China and southern India, and the few who had gone to the still unconverted lands of the Far North. After the Arab conquest many of them lived under non-Christian rule, and these lands contained the

The Dome of the Rock; built within the precincts of the old Jewish Temple. The rock which it enshrines was believed by the Jews to be where Abraham sacrificed Isaac, and by the Muslims to be the place whence Mohammed went to heaven. Built by the Muslim conquerors about 700.

The Church of the Nativity at Bethlehem. Constantine ordered a church to be built over the place of Jesus' birth; Constantine's mother Helena encouraged the work when she came on pilgrimage. Two crusading kings were crowned here. Equal to Jerusalem as a shrine for pilgrims.

seedbeds of the Church: Bethlehem, Nazareth and Jerusalem, Antioch and Alexandria.

In the Muslim states the Christians and the Jews were given a special place because they were 'people of the Book'; that is, they shared in the Old Testament. The Christians were often accused of tampering with it, making it mean what it could not mean; and, because they talked of God as Trinity, of not really believing in one God. Their habit of putting pictures in church was thought shocking. But they shared much of the truth. All three religions had a common ancestor in Abraham, who had taught the world that there is only one God. They were seen as preparing the world for the coming of Muhammad. Their founder Jesus was a great prophet. So, in return for a tax, Christians in Muslim states had a right to be protected and could practise their faith; except that their churches must not be prominent on the streets, and any attempt to convert a Muslim was a crime, and a Christian male could not marry a Muslim girl.

Muslim governments did not always practise such tolerance; but for long periods there was nothing to stop Christians from holding high office in Muslim governments. They knew little about Islam. An able Byzantine theologian, Nicetas, published a *Refutation of the Koran*, and this was much used by scholars, though it was of no concern to ordinary folk.

At first this tolerance did not work the other way round. Christian kings did not allow their Muslim subjects to practise their religion; they must convert or leave the country. Yet between diplomats in Christian Constantinople and in Muslim Baghdad there was friendly talk, which produced some understanding. During the eleventh century Western kings in Spain and Sicily started to win back the lands the Muslims had conquered. Here, for the first time, they allowed Muslims to remain without giving up their own faith. Such a broad-minded attitude was too good to last: at the beginning of the sixteenth century Spain ordered every Muslim to become Christian or leave. This act only reflected what the Christian peoples really felt.

Some Christians looked for truth in Islam, considering that the Koran was a mixture of what was true with what was not. They did not like some of the rules, especially the liberty to marry more than one wife. But they admired Islam's unbending faith in one God. Some saw Islam's conquests as punishment by God for the sins of the Christian people.

It was pious to go on pilgrimage to the holy places, to Jerusalem and Bethlehem and Sinai. At first the Muslim rulers of Palestine were happy to let this continue. But in the eleventh century their goodwill waned, and the pilgrimage became more dangerous. Western Christendom retaliated with the crusades, to recover Palestine and place it under Christian government. Motives were mixed. Italian seaports wanted to open trade with the East, the French government wanted to be rid of knights who fought each other, adventurers saw a chance of gaining wealth in the East. But without the religious motive to make pilgrimage possible, the crusades would not have happened.

When the crusaders set up Christian states in Palestine, Lebanon and Syria, these states had to trade with their Muslim neighbours. So out of the crusader states came the first sign of real Christian understanding of Islam, notably by William of Tyre. He was an exceptional person: a graduate of two Western universities; archbishop of Tyre from 1175, and the author of the best work on the crusades of his century, which is also one of the best books of history written during the Middle Ages.

Even at the time of the early crusades, Peter the Venerable, the abbot of Cluny in France, wanted people to recognize that the right approach to Islam was not with the sword but with the word. This gave rise to a Western effort to find what Muslims really believed. An English scholar, Robert 'of Ketton', was living in Barcelona, studying Arabic and astrology. He made the first translation of the Koran into Latin in 1143; it was used for seven hundred years afterwards. Yet Robert believed his translation to be trivial work compared with his astrology.

The friars encouraged some of their members to learn Arabic. Both in the fourteenth century and in the nineteenth centuries Western knowledge of Arabic and the Eastern languages was fostered by the drive to find Christian missionaries equipped for the East. The friars did not achieve much. St Francis of Assisi sailed to Egypt to convert the sultan, but failed. Yet their writings did spread knowledge of Islam in the West. About 1310 a friar of Florence, Ricoldo Pennini of Monte Croce, who had travelled in Iraq, Palestine and Armenia, published a *Confutation of the Koran* which was important to Western knowledge, and was later translated into German by Martin Luther. Dante thought the faith of Islam a heresy of Christianity.

The chapel at Crac des Chevaliers; the impregnable fortress of the crusading kingdoms in Palestine and Syria. It was given by the king of Jerusalem to the Knights Hospitallers. It held out for more than eighty years after Jerusalem fell to the Muslims.

CHAPTER FOUR

WESTERN SOCIETY IN THE MIDDLE AGES

POPES

The Greek word *pappas*, originally meaning 'daddy', was used in the Eastern Church for abbots and for bishops, and later for parish priests. Its first known use to describe a pope is on the tombstone of Pope Liberius, who died in 366. The word came into use in the West during the fifth century.

Soon the West found it fitting to use the word only of the bishops of Rome. But there were other titles. The Patriarch of Constantinople called himself the Ecumenical Patriarch – the term meant 'universal', from *oikoumene ge*, the inhabited world. Pope Gregory the Great found this pretentious and, to set a humbler example, called himself *Servus servorum Dei,* 'servant of the servants of God', a name which has remained in documents to this day.

The occupants of the see felt that because St Peter was the chief apostle, and because there was a tradition that he was the first bishop of Rome, they inherited his authority; that is, Rome was not only the chief see of Italy but had a wider authority. When Constantine transferred the capital of the empire to his new city on the Bosporus, that left the bishop of Rome as the most important person in Italy, not only in affairs of the Church but also in politics and social welfare. Pope Gelasius I, who had difficulties with the emperor in Constantinople, and who did a lot to help the poor and sufferers from famine in Italy, in 495 was the first pope to be addressed as 'vicar of Christ'; but it took six hundred years for this title to become usual.

Meanwhile the German tribes, from Bavaria to Northumberland and Norway, and the Celts, and then Slavs on the German border, adopted Christianity in a Latin, Western form. They looked to Rome as the centre of the Church; the city stood not only for the truth about God, but for education and civilization. The bishop of Rome, at first only the head bishop in Italy, was now asked for rulings on disputes in France, England, or Germany. Gregory the Great strengthened the Western Church by his mission to convert the English. The Englishman St Boniface converted the Germans to the idea that the centre of Christianity lay in Rome. Charlemagne made a new Latin-speaking empire in the West and needed a pope to crown him. The advance of Islam weakened the power of the Eastern emperor and his bishops.

To get a good man as pope – that is, to stop villains controlling the election – and when you had got him, to protect him from brigands and make sure he was free to do the good that he wished – needed the protection of the state. But the collapse of Charlemagne's empire in the hands of his grandchildren left Italy in anarchy. Where there was no state to protect, the city and the office were at the mercy of gangs. The power of the popes remained low for the next 150 years. Some of the popes of this time were good men all the same, and took decisions which affected France, Germany and the Slavs. The first pope in history to be murdered (as distinct from martyred), John VIII, was killed in 882; but he personally commanded a papal fleet against Muslim raiders. One pope was strangled in gaol by order of his successor. From 962,

Pope Sixtus IV with Platina, the historian of popes, in the Vatican library. Sixtus encouraged scholarship and art and used the resources of the Renaissance to help make the Vatican library one of the very few first-class libraries that then existed. He made Platina librarian in 1475.

when the German Otto I 'the Great' recreated the Holy Roman Empire, peace was briefly restored.

These events had consequences which persist to this day. The humiliation of being dominated by gangs in Rome, beyond the protection of the emperor, made popes realize that they could never do their work properly unless they were independent of a secular government. They must be their own master, politically as well as spiritually. The idea of a 'papal state' had been growing since the eighth century, as the forgery of the Donation of Constantine shows. It became an axiom that the pope had land in Italy of which he was the political sovereign. Without it, he now thought, he would not be free to do what he should for Church or state. The existence of Vatican City as a tiny state is due solely to the refusal of popes to accept that they could ever be the secular subjects of Italy; and that refusal is due to the memory of the bad years so long ago.

The early popes used their own names; the first one not to do so was Octavian, a bad pope elected in 955, who called himself John XII. Nearly twenty years later a man called Peter was elected, and to avoid using the apostle's name called himself John XIV. The next pope really was called John but his successor, a German called Bruno, felt that his name did not sound papal and called himself Gregory V. After this it became normal for a pope to change his name unless it was already a common one for past popes, such as John or Benedict; and soon it became the custom always to take a new name.

SOCIETY AND RELIGION

Gregory VII (who reigned from 1073 to 1085, and is often known as Hildebrand, his name before he was pope), set standards for the clergy which have made historians talk of 'Gregorian reform'. They did not get far in his lifetime, but in the hundred years after his

A mathematician monk, Luca Pacioli,
1495, by Jaco Bar. A Franciscan, Pacioli
was the first to print mathematical
textbooks and to propagate a system
of double accounting. He was backed
by Duke Federigo of Urbino, who
is in the picture.

death there was a steady improvement. It was agreed that priests must be educated; they must not have wives or mistresses; they must not bribe their way into posts; and they must obey their bishop who in turn must obey the pope.

It was hard to raise the standards of the clergy, most of whom could hardly read although they had the job of leading prayers for those who could not read at all. But now there were signs of success. If the clergy were not to have women they would be lonely, so the bishops brought many of them into groups – orders of canons. Here they could work as a team, with the support of a common house.

The name 'university' was first used by teachers in Paris, to mean the corporation of teachers and students. But long before that, some colleges had been behaving like universities, attracting students from other countries; Paris for theology, Bologna for law, Salerno for medicine.

These places of higher education were Church institutions. They needed to be free from interference by the city council or the government; or, if that was impossible, as free as could be managed. The only way to secure this was to extend to all university members the exemptions enjoyed by the clergy. Everyone still assumed that if someone was educated he must be some sort of cleric. A degree, which in effect was a licence to teach, was given by the university as representing Church authority.

A monk, Amalric of Bène, lecturing. The chronicler speaks of the beginning of the university of Paris. Amalric was an early teacher there of Aristotle (from Latin translations of Arab translations). He proposed that God spoke by Greek wise men as by Christians; heaven is a good conscience, and hell is remorse. Amalric was condemned as a heretic and recanted.

mal talent a aucuns des Barons qui estoient souspeconeus de traison.

parole. comment lerese des amoriens fu attainte et punie.

En celi temps florissoit a paris philosophie et toute clergie. et y estoit lestude si grant et en si grant auctorite: que len ne tenoie pas que

monde. Si nestoit pas tant seulemet pour le delitable lieu ne pour la plente des biens qui en la cite habundent: mes pour la pais et pour la franchise que li bons rois loys avoit tous iours portee. et que li rois phelippes ses fiu

An English medieval village church:
Sompting in Sussex. The rectory belonged
to the Templars, and after their suppression
to the Knights of St John. The unusual
tower is Saxon and has some Roman bricks.
The Templars rebuilt the nave.

them; what mattered was that they could be saved through Christ. When they painted pictures of the future life, they showed paradise. They were sure that heaven awaited them.

The two who did most to make the fires of hell an ever present fear in the Middle Ages were the greatest of the early popes and an unknown faker of the fourth century. The second of these wrote a *Vision of St Paul*. At first the churches took little notice of this work; it was not part of the scriptures, and Augustine said it was false. But between 800 and 1300 it was copied countless times and had a profound effect on ideas of the future life; ideas which were taken up by Dante in his journey to the future world. The *Vision* painted hell with an intent to terrify.

The pope was Gregory I; a practical man, a good administrator, rational in the way he spread the faith and developed the ideal of the Christian pastor. But he also wrote a book, the *Dialogues*, full of strange miracles but not of good sense, and so unlike the rest of his works that some critics have tried to prove that he did not write it. It contains a vision of the punishments that we shall suffer at once when we die.

By the beginning of the thirteenth century the vision of a future hell had become frightening. It made for tremendous sermons to the crowds by friar-preachers, and perhaps did some good in preserving moral standards in an age with few policemen, though that cannot be proved. The social necessity of the doctrine of hell was widely believed into modern times; without the prospect of hell, we would refrain from crime only because of the police, and no police force is capable of stopping us all. Some of us must want to do good because it is good, and not because doing evil is against the law. The threat of hell was considered the main safeguard against social collapse. This was one reason why for so long atheists were thought to be immoral. They did not believe in God, so they did not believe in hell, so they corrupted society.

There was difficulty in reconciling the vision of a merciful God with that of God as a stern judge. That severity was part of the Christian idea of God, but if it was seen as the single quality of God that mattered, it was non-Christian. To preserve the idea of God's mercy it felt necessary to allow another kind of punishment: purgatory. The early Church had no idea of such a place; Christians went to heaven. When it became all too clear that not all Christians could go to heaven because some of them were criminal, it also became evident that there must be a way to make bad people better after this life; not the hardened bad, but most were not that. There must be a purging where the Church and its faith could still help by its prayers.

God's wrath at sin was described in sermons; but in country churches sermons were not common. It was also shown in the church porch or the chancel arch which often portrayed, in stone or fresco, a vision of judgement; good people being gathered up by the angels to the joys of heaven, bad people being pulled down by demons towards the torments of hell. If folk believed that at death there were only two prospects, glory or pain, they found a God without pity towards themselves or their dear ones. The idea of a future discipline after death — that we die not yet ready for the glory of God, but we may be cleansed afterwards and so come to see God with pure eyes — was slow to form. This state of cleansing was, from the eleventh century, called purgatory, 'the place of purging'. A poet such as Dante took it for granted; but in visual art it only began to appear later, about 1450. It is hard to know whether purgatory

Heaven and hell on the ceiling of the Florence baptistery, thirteenth-century mosaic; women saints curiously in the second row.

137

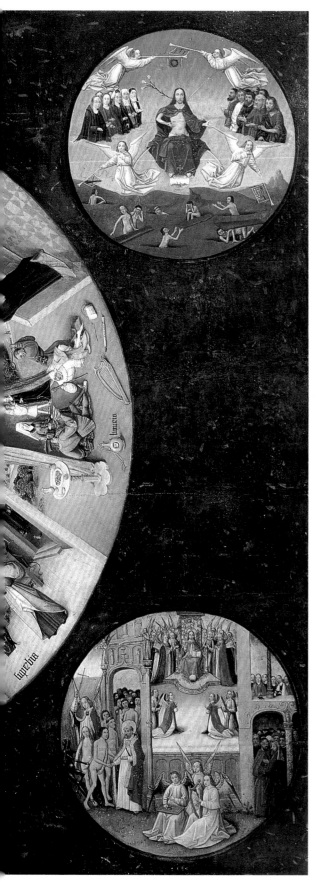

was a moral support to society; but for two centuries it helped the peoples of the West to preserve their faith in the mercy of God.

It made possible the idea of an 'indulgence' – that is, a way by which in this life we can help our dear ones who have died, and can lessen their time of cleansing and pain. We buy a certificate from the church authorities stating that we have done something good — even if it is only paying for the certificate. The money thus given was needed for all sorts of good purposes, such as building cathedrals or bridges. And thus there came to be a motive for preaching purgatory which was neither a desire that people should not do evil, nor a love of the pity of God, but simply the wish to raise money like a modern bazaar. There was trouble in store for the Church.

Dante

The ideal of the Western Middle Ages was summed up in the genius of Dante. He was important in the politics of Florence, then a city full of culture and prosperity. A city coup overthrew the governing party, of which he was a prominent member, and sentenced him first to exile and then to death. He was never able to go home; for twenty years he moved through northern Italy from city to city, spending most time in Verona and in Ravenna, where he died. He wrote in Latin a good book on political science, *On Monarchy*, which made his name in the rest of Europe. For two hundred years readers outside Italy thought of him as a political thinker, not poet.

About the same time he wrote, in Italian and in verse, the first part of his *Divine Comedy*, the *Inferno*. He called it the *Comedy*; a later printer added 'Divine'. Comedy meant simply a story with a happy ending, for Dante described a visit to the realms of the life after death: first hell, then purgatory and lastly paradise. His purpose was to teach. Society, he said, is in a shocking state — he had personal reasons for thinking so. What powers are there to mend it, and how may this be done? Individuals are bad, and cause society to be bad. What power can induce them to do

The seven deadly sins; by Hieronymus Bosch (died 1526, he enjoyed drawing sin); from the foot, anti-clockwise – anger, pride, lust, sloth, gluttony, avarice, envy.

William Blake's fantasy of Beatrice addressing Dante from the car. Blake dedicated his last years to illustrating Dante. A gryphon draws the car; Beatrice in a white veil on the platform rebukes Dante for being late in coming this way; Dante (at the right) looks ashamed.

Durham cathedral, the most virile piece of church architecture, with its great Norman columns. The Anglo-Saxons made a cathedral here especially as a shrine to St Cuthbert (see p. 99). The Normans started to rebuild it in 1093.

right? Both questions are at the heart of his poem. These were earthy questions; the glory of the poem is that while they are seen to be earthy, they are answered in the light of eternity. What judgement will fall or does fall on villains? What will cure villainy? How can the structure of politics be changed?

In his youth Dante fell in love with Beatrice and worshipped her as his ideal. He could not marry her; then she died. So in his mind she became an imaginary person, the goal of all that was best in him, the personification of love, the human example of what it is like to sit at God's right hand. In the poem she symbolizes the redemption of the individual under God's power. She has passed into the spiritual world, but his love for her still has passion.

As a young poet he was moved by Virgil's *Aeneid*, and thought of the poet as his master.

So it was Virgil who guided him round the lower realms of the departed spirits. Thus the social message is framed: against the iniquities of our age stands the ideal of the society that is perfect because it is under God's law and obeys him. For Dante, Virgil was in the long line of Roman imperial greatness, the possibility of government at its best. Beatrice is like a saint, drawing out of him all that is best in his own character.

With most poems the person of the poet does not matter; we know little enough about Shakespeare. The *Divine Comedy* is all about the feelings and experience of its author, it is uniquely personal; even the author's experience of exile is taken up into the wandering of the soul, here and there, to and fro, passing danger after danger, but despite appearances not on a haphazard course, because it moves

The Bell Harry tower of Canterbury Cathedral; some of the earliest fan vaulting in Britain; by the mason John Wastell who also finished King's College chapel at Cambridge. Augustine, when he came to convert England, built a church; rebuilt by Norman architects, the choir and nave were later rebuilt again. Always the chief church of England and later of the whole Anglican Communion.

towards an ultimate destination. This soul is lonely on its journey, it has a guide but no friends except a distant beloved ideal. It is not humble, because the poet is aware of his poetic genius and is sure of the rightness of his moral judgement. This is a person with a complicated inner life, who circles in dark sayings which even now we can hardly understand. The writing, tortuous at times, even grotesque, has offended some readers.

For all this personal quality, like an allusive and mysterious autobiography, there is in it no pushing of the self, because everything is seen in the light that streams down from outside. No poem ever had a more unearthly subject. No great poem was fuller of the dirt of the earth, the crimes and follies of mankind, many

of which we should know nothing about but for Dante. He had no use for the legends of the Middle Ages, the cult of dubious saints. He moved among real people, and had a terrible sense of evil: Italy was chaotic, the popes without standing, the emperor a nobody, justice polluted, monks and friars corrupt, bandits in the streets, cruelty rampant, religion unable to cure and only able to console. Yet, though he felt horror, he was certain of the providence in the world, that law and good government and liberty were there to be found and would one day be found. This view of what is foul in the world is lightened by the sight of nature. He loved nightingales singing, geese squawking, eagles soaring, frogs leaping, pigs pushing, ants hurrying down their track

and goats on the mountainside; the light at dawn and sunset, the rainbow and the storm; light which reflected a source of light not found on earth.

ARCHITECTURE

The Church was rich; it built soaring abbeys and churches. That opened a career to architects, and the shift from the massive bulk of the Romanesque style to what we know as the Gothic. There was a desire for tall churches with soaring columns, and with roofs of stone as a guard against fire, and this twin need was met by the new style, with its pointed arches and daring vaults. Churchmen asked themselves whether a building can lift the soul towards God by its structure and its ornament. Some doubters, including that most popular of saints the austere Bernard of Clairvaux, blamed monks and bishops who sought magnificence in masonry and ritual. Motives were mixed: a town was proud to build a noble church which exalted visitors, a village competed to make a higher or longer church than the next village. No one thought of posterity in these acts of faith or civic pride, or of how future generations would keep these vast structures standing.

A few spoke out against this splendid display. They were puritans who thought the money better spent on the poor, or townsmen who resented being asked for money, or conservatives who loved their cramped old church. Most approved. Some felt that they were helping in an act of God. There was a moving scene at Chartres in 1145 when people of all classes, from nobles to the poor, pulled the carts of stone to the building and sang hymns as they went. If the church had a shrine, as Canterbury Cathedral had the tomb of Thomas Becket, or Rome had St Peter and Veronica, or Compostela in northern Spain had St James, money was not hard to get; pilgrims poured it into the chests.

There were seats only for the clergy and the very infirm. So the new churches, though big, were not big so that they could hold a lot of

St Barbara, by Jan van Eyck of Bruges. She was, in legend, shut in a tower by her father when she became Christian. She became the saint who helped people to die well and her symbol was a tower, with three windows because she persuaded the builders to make them as a sign of the Trinity. Another of her symbols was a long feather pen, it is not clear why. Because she had a tower, she is also patron of builders and fire brigades.

A demon from the abbey of Vézelay in Burgundy; they used the capitals of pillars to tell stories. Vézelay (Benedictine) was first famous because it was said to have the body of Mary Magdalene and so was a chief shrine for pilgrims. St Bernard preached the second crusade here; Richard Coeur de Lion met the French king here to go on the third crusade. A supreme example of a Romanesque building, the monastery lasted till the French Revolution.

Pilgrims to Canterbury; from a Canterbury window of about 1280.

145

A pilgrim's medallion, found in the ruins of St John's church in Ephesus.

seated people. On a feast day, such as the day of a church's patron saint, hundreds stood tight packed, as they still do at the feasts of saints in the Eastern Church. There were also processions, and there had to be room for movement inside the church.

Processions

These began in the early churches as the solemn entry of those who were to lead the prayers; a tradition borrowed from pagan festivals. There were more formal processions in which family and friends bore a corpse to the grave; and also in what was called the 'translation' of a saint, that is, taking his or her bones from the grave to a shrine that had

been made ready in the church. In Jerusalem at Easter they began to follow the *Via Dolorosa*, the way of the Lord to the cross, and this form of procession was copied in the West. People liked processions. When the church was safe in the world and so strong that no policeman could object if its pious work stopped the traffic, processions moved out into the streets on big days; through the town with an ass on Palm Sunday, or with a statue of the Virgin on her day, round the fields to pray for the harvest, round the city walls if an enemy came near. The custom grew until every Sunday saw a procession in the cathedral or abbey church, or in the big parish church; this called for a spacious nave, and hence for the skill and expense of building a roof that would not fall on the people's heads.

All other processions were put in the shade by that of the feast of Corpus Christi, 'the

Body of the Lord', which was founded at Liège in Belgium in 1246 to honour the sacrament of the Lord's supper. Within thirty years the Corpus Christi procession at Cologne was already elaborate. The priest or bishop bore in a silver vessel called a monstrance (meaning that it was for showing to the people) the bread of the sacrament, called the Host (from the Latin *hostia*, a sacrificial victim). Few monstrances are known from the first hundred years of the ceremony, but there are many examples from the fifteenth century. The Reformation abolished nearly all these processions in Protestant lands, and Catholic Europe stopped many of them during the eighteenth century.

Stained glass

The new high walls had tall windows. From early times churches had brightly coloured frescoes or mosaics on the walls; but now there was a wonderful new art. Early churches had windows of translucent stones or of glass, which was not clear enough to see through. Coloured glass was used as early as the seventh century, though this was not 'stained' with painted designs bonded to the glass by heating. The earliest true stained glass that we still possess is of about 1100: four windows depicting prophets in the cathedral at Augsburg. (They are not the four principal prophets that might be expected, but Daniel, Hosea, King David and Jonah.) The skill developed over a long time, but during the twelfth century it became a partner to the building. From the years after 1140 come some of the loveliest examples, as at Chartres and Canterbury.

Not everyone approved. St Bernard's order of monks, the Cistercians, who cared for

The Ommeganck (Flemish for procession) in Brussels; by Denys van Alsloot. That shown here was of 1615, but it went back two hundred years before, to celebrate the translation of the image of the Virgin of the Sands from Antwerp to Brussels. The whole town took part – magistrates, religious orders and clergy escorting the image of St Mary.

A painted processional banner, fourteenth century.

figure of God on his throne, or the Virgin or the saint of that church. Some artists loved to make their patterns so intricate that the story was not to be understood without a guide. Stained glass probably did little to teach those who could not read, but its best defenders pleaded for its effect on their hearts. Durandus, who was the chief student of ways of worship in that age, said of it, 'The glass windows of a church are scriptures of God because they let the rays of the sun, that is of God, into the church and the church is the hearts of all the faithful people.'

THE PARISH SYSTEM

Everyone belonged to a parish: an area served by a church whose priests were supposed to look after his or her spiritual needs. The system developed from the private chapel belonging to a squire and attended by his workers. The bishop might try to take control of the chapel from the squire, usually without much success. Then monasteries founded chapels on their estates and the bishop had the same fight. Both kinds of chapel often grew into parish churches, under the bishop's administration but with an element of local control; in some parishes to this day the squire retains the right to choose the vicar. How well the parishes covered a land depended on its people and its wealth. By 1100 much of France was covered in churches and parishes; in England the south had many but in the north the parishes were much larger and more widely spaced; in the Rhineland there were a lot of parishes but in eastern Germany and Scandinavia there were few. The big towns were at first one parish, but soon this became too large and had to be split up. In 1215 the Lateran Council at Rome was able to take it for granted that everyone had a parish when it ordered that all should make a confession at least once a year to his or her own pastor.

The parish church and its priests were supported mainly by tithes — a tax of a tenth part of the produce of land or stock, or a cash sum in lieu of this. There was a less regular income

simplicity, banned the pictures; but after a few decades they relented. Stained glass was defended against its critics by the plea that it is the gospel of those who cannot read; they could learn the stories of the Bible from the pictures. Others knew that the aim was like that of the whole building, to give glory to God through beauty. Windows were often too high on the wall for the eyes below to 'read' a story, but there would be a majestic

The south rose window at
Chartres cathedral, north-west
France; some of the loveliest
glass ever made; from the
thirteenth century. A cathedral
was built there originally
on the site of an old Druid
sanctuary.

A mass at St Denis, chapel of the kings of France near Paris; the priest elevates the Host for the people to adore. King Louis XII prays. Denis was said to be the first missionary to Paris and a martyr; in the ninth century he was identified with Dionysius the Areopagite. It is a painted wooden panel, *c.* 1500, by the Master of St Giles.

Sunday. The central act of the mass was no longer the consecration of the bread and wine, because that could not be seen by the people, but the elevation of the bread and wine above the head of the priest so the people could see and adore the divine presence. The people's role was now mostly a silent one.

The result was that the priests were freer to do as they liked with the form of the service. They could make it more elaborate, for it was no longer necessary for the people to follow it. It was not even necessary to say the prayers loud enough for all to hear.

The miracle play

One way of teaching the people about religion was with plays. Scenes from the Bible were acted, often with music – the fall of Adam, or the shepherds and the three wise men at the manger, or the parable of the wise and foolish virgins, or the women at the tomb of Jesus.

The theatre sprang from four roots. There were clowns – strolling players of the street, lewd and funny with slapstick and songs, satirical and therefore anticlerical. Our word 'pantomime' comes from the Greek name for such an actor (not the play itself), who performed a comic dumb show. Second, there were the tragedies of the ancient Greeks; but these were hardly known at this time. Third was the 'school play', used as an easy way to teach Latin, for example a comedy by Terence; this piece of Roman education was recovered as the schools grew better. As early as 970 Roswitha, a canoness at Gandersheim in Germany, who had a sense of humour, wrote drama to teach Latin in schools, aiming to replace Terence with Biblical themes. Fourth were explicitly religious plays, which may have developed from narrative songs forming part of a church service, but were later staged by town guilds on carts in the open. They were called 'miracles' as they were often about the marvels done by saints.

from bequests and donations, for example payment to have a certain number of masses said for the soul of a deceased person.

People were now taking a different view of what went on in church. In the early churches the service had been an act of the community; but now lay people did not understand the words because these were in Latin. Nearly all came to mass every Sunday because it was compulsory. They did not receive the communion more than once or twice a year, but would watch the priest celebrate it every

In this way stories from the Bible became well known, as did legends of favourite saints such as George, or events of Church history like Constantine's mother Helena discovering

**Giotto's crucifixion from the
Arena chapel at Padua, 1305;
still no attempt to portray pain.**

the true cross at Jerusalem. They acted out the Passion as, in a rare survival, they still do at Oberammergau in the northern Alps. There were also plays written expressly to give moral instruction, such as *Everyman*, in which a man in his dying hours discovers that the salvation of his soul depends on the virtues he has neglected; the most significant work on this theme until Marlowe's *Doctor Faustus*.

The rood

With the high new churches and so much air above the heads of the lay people, there was a need for a symbol of the faith that could be seen by all. This was supplied by a rood – a tall crucifix. In early days Christ had usually been shown not on the cross but as a ruler or a lamb. From the fifth century the image of the crucified Christ came to be loved; but here he was not shown as one who suffers but as triumphing over pain, the Saviour who rules the world from his cross. In Northern Europe from the tenth century they started to show him as a dead or dying man. The Italians did not like it; a cardinal even said that this was blasphemy.

The change was caused in part by St Bernard. He wished people not to be afraid of God as judge but to love him in return for his love; and so it was not the king that they wanted to see on the cross, but the poor man who suffers for humanity. It was affected also by the growth of devotion to Mary, for the people were moved by a mother's suffering as she stood under the cross of her son. Giotto portrayed the idea at the limits of beauty in the Arena chapel at Padua, about 1305. The most tragic portrayals of suffering are found in Northern Europe for the next century and a half, with a crown of thorns, and a head sunk upon the breast, and Mary torn with grief at the foot.

The usual form this image took in Northern Europe was a large wooden crucifix set above the screen which divided the nave from the choir. By 1200 most churches in Northern Europe had such a rood. In old English the word 'rood' meant a wooden beam, then a gallows; the 'Holy Rood' was therefore Christ's cross; and then it came to mean this crucifix, the most visible thing in the church to the eyes of any lay person saying a prayer.

The brotherhood

Lay members of a parish might belong to a brotherhood: a guild or club whose members dined together and helped each other in time of sickness or by paying for a funeral. Some brotherhoods ran hospitals. The modern city companies of London, with their mixture of dinners and charitable work, developed from

brotherhoods organized by trades – for example drapers, skinners (leatherworkers) or goldsmiths. A brotherhood would have an altar in the parish church, and pay for its upkeep and for masses to be said. In a big city it might have its own church and pay the priests.

The first such brotherhoods, or 'confraternities', were found in the East, and very early, as groups of friends to remember the dead. But it was in the West that they were specially liked. They could be weighty in a town's management and in effect be guilds. Often they had special insignia. In processions they won precedence in the march and might carry flags or a float. They were the really important organizations for the piety of laymen in the parish churches of the Middle Ages. At Paderborn in Germany was a Brotherhood of Refugees, which took the duty of caring for these incomers. This brotherhood still exists. Whether they learnt anything in religious education is in doubt but they shared in a big way in the life of the parish. Sometimes they ran a hostel on a route for pilgrims – to Rome or Compostela or Jerusalem or some other

The Hospital of St Matthew in Florence, by Pontormo, early sixteenth century; served by nuns, not by nurses hired by nuns. Notice the little shrine in the midst of the ward. The building is now the seat of the Florence Academy, but the portico of the old hospital is still there.

The Hospital of the Knights of St John at Rhodes in the Aegean; begun 1440. It is thought there were thirty-two beds, each with a canopy; and two surgeons always at hand. The Hospitallers began with a hospital for pilgrims in Jerusalem; then a military order to protect the Holy Places; when the crusaders were driven from Palestine the knights made their headquarters in Rhodes; forced out by the Turks after a heroic defence, they came to Malta, where they were based from 1530 until Napoleon.

shrine. But more of these hostels were run by a house of monks.

The sick

The Church was expected to care for the poor and the sick, widows and orphans, and could afford to do so. To those who asked why the Church owned so much land, the answer was that the income from its property was used to look after the unfortunate.

The bishop was supposed to order what was done for the poor and sick. In fact this duty fell to the monks. Their houses often had a hostel for poor old men, or a home for lepers. There was a monk in charge of alms for the poor – the almoner. Monks gave out broth at the monastery gate. At feasts such as Christmas, crowds assembled at the door of a big monastery because it was known that then the monks would distribute food or clothes. In a time of famine, the abbey might run short of funds or food; the best of the religious houses would sell off silver, even some of the sacred altar vessels, to get the means to help.

The trouble with all this (apart from the corruption of monks who used the wealth of their abbey to have a good time) was that it did not help enough. Most monks were in the country and many of the poor were in the towns. There the brotherhoods helped, but usually attended only to their own members.

Hospitals

'Hospital' or 'hospice' first meant a place where men and women who needed help were given a home, much like a modern hostel for the destitute (all these words come from the Latin *hospes*, 'guest'). Those who lived there were not necessarily sick; and if there was room, passing travellers could be housed. At first the nurses were often nuns, the porters often monks; but as time passed the nuns hired women to nurse and the monks hired men to carry. In the unsettled centuries there were never anything like enough of these hospices. It was not expected that doctors would visit sick inmates; nor that they would do the patients' health as much good as God might do through the hospice chaplain. There was a not unreasonable contempt for what doctors could do, and a healthy belief that nature has its own healing powers.

When doctors acted, there were three areas where good might be done. First, centuries of trial and error with healing herbs had discovered a small number which worked; many other herbs did not help at all medically, but at least persuaded the patient that some good was being done. Second, midwives had acquired real experience. They worked in people's homes; childbirth hardly ever took place in hospitals, and the only women professors in Europe were in the medical faculty at Salerno. Third, surgeons did know something about anatomy. On religious grounds, Westerners shrank from carving up flesh with a knife; for a long time most surgeons were Greeks or Jews.

In Constantinople a big monastery, the Pantocrator, ran a large hospital with good surgeons, a separate ward for women, and annexes for lepers and the old.

From 1100 onwards many more hospitals were founded by rich men, or by cities, or by monks. They were seen as houses of religion; in France the chief hospital in a town was known as the *Hôtel-Dieu*, the hospice of God. Fighting in Palestine to keep Jerusalem out of the hands of Islam, the crusaders created orders of knights, who were required to be unmarried and keep rules like monks, but whose calling was to fight in the Christian cause. One of them was the Order of the Hospital of St John of Jerusalem. The first business of these Hospitallers, or Knights of St John, was to protect pilgrims; then they looked after the sick and founded hospitals for them; seen at the best, still, in the hospital in the near-impregnable Hospitaller fortress on the island of Rhodes in the Aegean.

Marriage

Before 1100 the peasants and workers did not bother much about marriage. They were taught the commandment 'Thou shalt not commit adultery'; but if a man and a woman chose to live together without formalizing their union at the altar, they were considered by law to be married. With the upper classes it was different because money and property

were at stake. Marriages were arranged between families. Often the partners were still children; the adults signed the deeds, and brought in priests to bless the pair so that eventually they might have children of their own. Such a system of arranged marriage naturally led to adultery by those not content with the spouses their parents had chosen for them; then state and Church acted without too much zeal against the unfaithful. If the pair were important and had no children, it was so vital to produce an heir that most people condoned a new union.

When is a couple married? Evidently not at the church service, because there need be no service. If the partners say 'I take you as my wife' and 'I take you as my husband', those two sentences are the moment of marriage. It is a sacrament made not by a priest, nor by the law, but by two lay people. If children, or

The marriage feast of Cana; by Veronese, 1563; a marriage more like those of Venice than of Galilee. Cana was a crux in resisting moralists who held that the married state was morally lower than the unmarried.

bigamists, or persons of the same family, said the words, they were invalid.

The giving of a ring as a sign of betrothal was a pre-Christian custom. By the sixth century AD the ring was sometimes used as a Christian symbol; four hundred years later we find the first prayers for blessing the ring; sometimes each partner gave the other a ring. Its first meaning was that of a seal, because men used rings to sign documents; the ring said, this is a contract I bind myself to keep. The fancy that the ring is a symbol of eternity, because a circle has no end, is much later.

From the end of the western Roman empire, both the Church and the lawyers wanted witnesses to the couple's consent. The priest was well placed to act as a witness, as he was the most responsible person in a community, the one who could be trusted to ask whether these two were too closely related, or whether they really wished to marry each other, or whether one or both of them were already married. His religious function was an additional asset; couples wanted children, and so the union should be blessed by God. Sometimes the actual marriage bed was blessed. From quite early there was a form of service in church for a marriage, but it was optional and not many of the poor sought it.

The system of consent led to abuses, with one partner claiming that there was an intent to marry while the other denied it. Lawyers and churchmen pressed for rules — that is, for marriage in church with witnesses and a previous examination of the couple by the priest. But they could not deny that a valid marriage could take place without a priest or witnesses. From 1100 onwards a series of Church councils ordered that laymen should not conduct marriages. They still needed to repeat this ban as lately as the middle of the fourteenth century. It showed how marriage had been taken partly, but by no means entirely, out of the secular sphere.

A vow once made could not be unmade, so divorce was impossible. But in practice, to dissolve a marriage was sometimes the only humane course. Church lawyers often found a way to do this by invoking the ban on marriage within the family. It was not hard to find distant family relationships which might be held to invalidate the wedding and so have the marriage declared null — as Henry VIII later tried to do. But the total ban on divorce had long consequences in the history of the churches.

CONFESSION

The custom of confessing sin to other people arose in a strange way. It was part of natural religion, and has been found among native American and African peoples who never before met Europeans. They would confess to a friend or relative or priest that they had committed murder or theft, or broken a sexual prohibition, and would believe this act to be a part of cleansing themselves and becoming reconciled with their gods. Confession is also found in Jainism and Buddhism among monks, as part of the way towards purity of heart. The Jews practised confession; that is how it came to be part of Christianity.

Early Christians had hoped that the convert who was baptized and had all sins washed away would not sin again. To their surprise they found that this was not true. So they needed a rite which marked forgiveness to the soul that sinned after baptism. That pardon could not be given unless the soul was penitent and could be seen by the church to be so.

Before the beginning of the Sunday service the penitent told his sin and his sorrow and asked God for pardon. Soon he or she wore sackcloth and a smear of ashes to show sorrow. At first it was thought that for grave sins like murder, theft, adultery or idolatry this could be done only once: one forgiveness in baptism, a second in public confession, and then no further chance, only expulsion from the Church.

Then pastors felt that this was rigid, and set a human limit to Christ's infinite grace. There were arguments among the clergy. On one side were bishops who thought that to go on forgiving people for grave sins was to make

A confessional box, eighteenth century; by Pietro Longhi.
He liked fashionable Venetian scenes. The first such boxes go
back to the sixteenth century. In the Catholic Church it was
the rule to make confession before communion and at Easter,
hence there could be queues.

it is not by St Jerome, and was made in northern Italy some thirty years after he died. This is the first good calendar of saints, listing the martyrs revered in different cities, and where their graves were to be found or where their memory was kept. Several surviving copies from different places include various scraps of stories about the martyrs' lives or deaths; the original text is lost. Later still we find texts turned into poetry, to make them easier to remember.

These texts do not record anyone called Telemachus; but some of them mention in the entries for 1 January an Almachius, who made a stand against idols and was killed by gladiators at the order of the prefect of Rome. These names must be of the same person. Historians have doubted whether he existed; but something of the kind must have happened, for the Emperor Honorius did ban the games in 404. They continued on a small scale until 681, but we hardly hear of them again.

Because his day was the start of the new year, Telemachus was remembered less often than he deserved.

The Moors of North Africa had the sport of fighting with bulls. When they conquered Spain they brought it with them and held fights in the old half-ruined circuses the Romans had left; and so it became the sport of Spain until the coming of football.

Christians loved the image of the ox and the ass at the manger in Bethlehem. There had long been a feeling that animals were God's creatures and should not need to endure more cruelty than was necessary – for example that a killing of a bullock or lamb or hen for food should be done with as little suffering as possible to the animal. There were those who believed that cruelty by men to animals leads to a habit of mind which encourages cruelty to humans. Because of this feeling, in 1567 Pope Pius v condemned the sport and excommunicated not only those in the ring but also the spectators. No one took any notice. The fans defended it by moral arguments – it was said to be a work of art, or a public moral drama which was a model of courage for the young.

Part of the spectacle was colour, costume, embroidery, procession.

The Spanish bishops condemned it; but the Church could not abolish the pleasures of a people who were resolute to enjoy them. Today bishops condemn the simulated murders that are watched for hour after hour by children sitting in front of a screen; but they cannot expect that anyone will listen to their strictures.

The Church tried to stop duelling. This form of combat reduced deaths in war by allowing armies to fight each other by proxy through champions, for which there was the biblical example of David and Goliath. In the early Middle Ages God came into the argument; his providence, it was claimed, was such that he would bless the right person, so that in a legal dispute the truth could be known by making the two claimants fight. As late as 1077 a council of bishops, which could not agree about whether one or another form of service should be used, settled the disagreement by a duel. Early in the twelfth century a monk in Normandy composed a prayer for use by persons about to fight a duel. Some of the English used a prayer for blessing the duellist's sword and shield as he set out for the contest.

Experience showed that this was a false doctrine, and duels were no longer used as a way of finding the truth. But the duel continued as part of chivalry, and the code of chivalry was favoured by the Church as a way of making war less dreadful. The tournament was partly a game, with horsemen riding each other down with lances. Authorities in both Church and state kept condemning the duel – but not all the moralists, some of whom argued that a person's reputation is part of him and he is as justified in defending it as he would be in defending himself against an attack on his body.

So people went on being killed in duels for centuries to come. As late as 1829 the British prime minister Wellington was accused of dishonesty and fought a duel, though the two foes were careful to miss each other; and in

Engrav'd for Englands Bloody Tribunal.

The Place & manner of Execution of Persons condemn'd by the Inquisition.

A Protestant portrait of an *auto-de-fe* by the Inquisition (not Spanish because it is at Lisbon, probably the Lisbon event of 1682); but hardly a caricature. The scene was consciously made dramatic to remind participants of the day of judgement. Conical mitres on the heads of the guilty, or on the effigies carried aloft (for example of one condemned in absence). Priests provided to minister to the condemned. No carriages are meant to be in the square – but there is one.

1891 an encyclical of Pope Leo XIII, *Pastoralis officii*, excommunicated everyone who took part in a duel, including the witnesses and the doctors. Duelling faded away during the nineteenth century, except in German universities where it was a non-lethal game between students which only scarred faces; astoundingly, German bishops still felt a need to condemn the practice in 1955. Christian morals had an influence in the ending of the duel as they had in the banning of gladiators.

Torture

There was an extraordinary exception to the rule that it was the duty of a Christian society to reduce war, murder and violence against the person. The old Greeks – even Aristotle – and the Romans accepted that torture of a suspect was a necessary part of the hunt for a criminal. The only reliable proof of guilt was a confession, so people must be made to confess. Early Christians realized that torture makes the innocent tell lies. Lawyers insisted that it was necessary but Pope Gregory the

Great was against it. In 1252 the bad Pope Innocent IV sanctioned torturing suspected heretics. Church law did what it could to make it less inhuman by banning clergy from torturing anyone themselves, and trying to set legal conditions for anyone to be tortured: there had at least to be a probability that the suspect was guilty of the crime. Later they tried to insist that before any suspect was tortured he or she must be allowed to state the case for the defence. The common law of England did not allow torture – but of course this went on in the cellars of the police, with official connivance. There was a rack in the Tower of London.

By the eighteenth century Western nations had banned torture; but to abolish something by law is not the same as ending it. It is odd that a society which made efforts to stop war or limit its savagery, and to lessen individual brutality, and to ban spectacles that encouraged violence, felt that in this fallen world, where there must be wars and the best we can do is to limit their horror, there will be crime, and we may have to use immoral methods to cope with it and can only seek to limit the foulness of those methods. It is still odder that such a moral tradition, looking to Jesus at its heart, advised pastors that a man who is ordered by legal authority to torture someone need not feel that he commits sin.

The Inquisition

The Spanish Inquisition is a byword for cruelty, although the Inquisition was not exclusively Spanish, and was of much earlier origin. 'Inquisition' simply means 'inquiry', in this case to make sure error was not taught. St Augustine persuaded himself that the use of limited force against dissenters was right, and his opinion became part of Church law.

No one in the West was burnt for heresy till about 1007. The first special courts to interrogate people were temporary ones set up in France and Germany in the thirteenth century. The Spanish Inquisition was set up in 1478 and became particularly powerful when laws were passed in 1492 and 1502 requiring Jews and Muslims to convert or leave the country. It had the worst repute of any inquisition partly because it was a royal court, and so less inefficient than the others. The pope set up a centralized inquisition for all the Church in 1542, but the decree made little difference except in Italy. The countries least affected were France, Germany and the British Isles.

During the eighteenth century most Catholic countries abandoned what the lawyers had begun to detest.

THE IMITATION OF CHRIST

The early Christians thought they followed Christ, they were his disciples, because they shared in his work. He could not strictly be imitated, because he alone can save humanity. But the idea that his people should try to walk in the way in which he walked while he lived on earth is found in the New Testament. And the more they went on pilgrimages to Palestine, or on crusades, the more they looked at his life on earth and the more they began to think about imitation.

Friars

The word 'friar' is the same as the French *frère* and the Latin *frater*, 'brother'. The word did not appear in English until the founders of the friars had been dead for several decades; 'friary' to mean their dwelling is later still.

Francis of Assisi had a short life, 44 years. Son of a rich merchant of Assisi, he fought when he was twenty in a city war against Assisi's neighbour Perugia, spent a year as a prisoner of war and then was gravely ill. He still had the aim of being a warrior. Then he had a vision of God as the king of a better army. In the almost derelict church of San Damiano he heard a voice that drew him to repair it with his own hands. He settled there, ministering to lepers and renouncing all right

St Francis preaches to the birds. This story comes in the earliest sources and so is not likely to be legend. By Giotto or one of his pupils.

to his inheritance. On the plain below he found the almost ruined church of St Mary-of-the-Angels (the Portiuncula) and repaired that, and there heard the priest read the text of St Matthew where the disciples are to take no money in their purses.

So he became a wandering, penniless preacher. A few disciples collected around him; they called themselves *Minores*, 'the lesser people', later known as Minorites. Their preaching created revival, crowds came and were excited.

Francis wandered through Italy preaching to anyone who would hear. He refused to be a priest.

The founder's way, so personal and so inspired, had to be organized by someone who knew about rules and money and property, all of which were strange to Francis. He wanted to be an anarchic lover of God, he wished the spirit to be free. Yet only twelve years after he started there were 3000 *Minores*, and a century after that there were 30,000. Francis had

St Francis receives the stigmata, the wounds of the crucifixion, on the mountain La Verna; by a pupil of Giotto. The first recorded stigmata but far from the last.

The nuns sing their psalms. They are Poor Clares, the Franciscan nuns. They can all read.

neither the desire nor will to head such an order. He handed it over to Brother Elias of Cortona, who could manage – so far as anyone could run a lot of people who feared that being run would lessen their freedom to follow the vision they saw. Instead of free lay evangelists, they became legally a 'religious order'. Francis had been joined by Clare of Assisi at San Damiano to found an order for women, the Poor Clares. This had to be a 'religious order' because women could not go round begging.

Francis went away to hermitages in the mountains. At Greccio he made the first Christmas crib for the children in church. On Monte La Verna he received the stigmata on his body, bleeding wounds like those of Jesus on the cross. (*Stigma*, plural *stigmata*, is Greek for 'mark', especially a mark on the skin.) This is the first time that these are recorded; but since then the stigmata have been observed on more than three hundred people, often persons of much prayer such as nuns, but sometimes on men or women of a not particularly holy way of life.

Before Francis died, in Assisi, he gave the brothers his famous hymn *The Canticle of the Sun*. Two years after his death the pope declared him a saint and laid the first stone of the church at Assisi for his body, and told one of the brothers, Thomas of Celano, to write his life.

The work gave a rare impetus to religion in the later Middle Ages. It made the imitation of Christ a moral ideal as it had never been before; it made 'holy poverty', as a form of detachment from the world, valued by many ordinary people; and it made begging in the streets of a city a respectable occupation. It held up daily work as to be done for its own sake and not for pennies. It made 'revivalism' in preaching a force among the crowds of the town. And it made a new goal for pilgrimage, the lower church at Assisi.

The Franciscans were known as the Grey Friars because of the colour of their robes (they now wear brown). Other orders of friars appeared, with other goals. The Dominicans, or Black Friars, were founded by Dominic the Spaniard to be preachers; to be good at this they needed study, so they had no use for the disorganized life of some Franciscans. For a time they followed the example of Francis in having no money, but this proved impractical and was given up. The Carmelites, or White Friars, were set up on Mount Carmel in Palestine during the crusades; when Palestine fell to the Muslims they became an order of friars on the model of St Francis. But it was the Franciscans who took care of the sanctuaries in Palestine, as they still do – work which has brought martyrdom to many of them. The fourth order was the Austin Friars, sometimes called the Augustinian Eremites because they started as a group of hermits before they were organized as friars. They modelled themselves on the Dominicans. This was Luther's order.

Some seventy years after Francis' death Giotto or a pupil painted the scenes of his life in the church at Assisi. This series had an aim: to show the life of Francis as an imitation of the life of Jesus. One of these pictures, of Francis preaching to the birds, became the most famous of all pictures of the saint and may have affected human attitudes to animals.

There was confusion about his life story. There were short writings by himself; the official life by Thomas of Celano; several unofficial lives; tales of him and his disciples; and stories collected a century after his death in a book of legends, *The Little Flowers of St Francis*. Trying to find the real man in this mixture of truth, fable and propaganda caused heat among historians.

The Franciscan ideal kept throwing up reforming movements; so there came to be four orders instead of one. The chief difficulty was money: the most numerous order, the Observants, founded in 1368, reckoned they could do without it; the Conventuals took the opposite view. Those who wanted everyone to do as Francis did were called Spirituals or *Fraticelli* ('little brothers') and were condemned as heretics. Reform among Conventuals in 1528 produced the new order of Capuchins, famous because they must grow beards compulsorily.

Few people affected Christian history as much as Francis. Ordinary people lost much of their fondness for monks, preferring friars who went about among them. Fewer people wanted to be monks. This made less difference than it might, because as friars became organized groups of men living in a house, they became more like monks themselves; Luther, who was a friar, called himself a monk. Francis often used phrases from the Bible as he preached, and meditated much on the life of Jesus. He brought Jesus home to the people in a new way, so that they could see the literal following of Christ as a possible way of life. This wave of idealism made for discontent with the churches as they were.

The Protestants thought little of his ideals, and longed to be rid of the beggars who soiled the streets of cities. They accepted that to give alms to the poor is a duty, but that we ought not give them in such a way as to encourage able-bodied men to do nothing but beg. They dismissed the idea of 'holy poverty', preferring to use money for the good of humanity. They accepted the idea of 'work for work's sake, it is God's calling' and built it into what we now call the Protestant work ethic; but they did not attribute it to Francis.

By that time, however, there were countless friars, not all worthy of their founder. For three hundred years after Luther's time Francis was little esteemed in much of Europe; he was seen as a fanatic, harmful to social order. It was not until the French Protestant Paul Sabatier published a life of the saint in 1894 that his reputation was restored.

One effect of Francis's work was that, for the first time, someone tried to write a life of Christ. Before this people took it for granted that his life was recorded in the four Gospels, and any other life was out of place. Ludolf of Saxony, who died in 1378, was a Carthusian at Strasbourg. His *Life of Christ* is a long and beautifully written meditation, with some stories from the early apocryphal gospels, real touches of scenery from Palestine, and an imaginative portrayal of the face, look and manner of Jesus. It was not quite a biography, but was intended to prompt the reader to prayer. Probably it was the most read of lives of Christ. The Carthusians went on reading it at meals till the eighteenth century; Protestants used parts of it; and it converted Ignatius Loyola, who founded the Jesuits.

The words 'the imitation of Christ' are most famous as the title of a book, written about 1424 and published anonymously. *The Imitation of Christ* became the book which, after the Bible, was most read by Christians, to judge by the number of manuscripts and printed editions and translations. It was really four books run together, not all about imitation; the title strictly belongs to the first book.

The author is almost certainly Thomas a Kempis, so named because he came from Kempen near Krefeld in the Rhineland. Thomas was an excessively shy monk who went into the monastery young, was bad at running the house and had no experience of the outside world. Yet this author shows deep knowledge of humanity and the soul. Some said Ludolf must have written it, others said St Bernard, or Gerson the great professor at Paris. But the obscure Thomas must be the author.

Apart from the sensitivity of his understanding of persons, he had an ear for music and his prose has rhythm. He had little use for the schoolmen who dominated the mind of that age: 'Tell me: where now are all those professors who were so well known while they were alive and at their researches? Others sit in their chairs now — and I doubt whether they ever think about them.' Nor did he care for the mystics' assertion that 'everything is God', nor yet for the opposite view that God is so great that any attempt to describe him is meaningless. There are traces of the devotion fostered by his schooling with the Brothers of the Common Life, a group founded by Gerard Groote, a canon of Utrecht, to raise the standards of the clergy and of ordinary people. But Thomas was in no one's school; he was himself, plain, without

The Annunciation by Fra Angelico, for a cell of the Dominican priory of San Marco in Florence; one of the two or three pictures which most helped Protestants, as well as Catholics, to remember St Mary with affection.

artifice, and with clarity. The book is a peerless guide to the vanities of the earth, and to peace of heart in the midst of them.

Fra Angelico was christened Guido di Pietro, but we know nothing else about him until, in 1423, he was mentioned in the records of a Dominican friary at Fiesole outside Florence, already described as a 'painter'. He was called Friar Giovanni; the title 'Angelico' was first given to him about thirty years after his death. It was a Dominican rule that every cell must have a picture. He painted the cells of his convent of San Marco in Florence and a crucifix for the chapter house; then he worked in Rome, where he died.

His painting of the Annunciation, where the angel tells Mary that she is to bear the Saviour, is one of the best known pictures in the world. It was an important influence on posterity, depicting affection, humility and resignation, virtues which cannot normally be seen on walls; the image did more than anything else to keep the memory of Mary sacred among the Protestants when their critics dismissed her cult as superstition. Giorgio Vasari, the historian of Renaissance painting, described Fra Angelico as the painter whose art came out of his religion, who wept while he painted the crucifixion, and always said a prayer when picking up a brush, and used to say that he who illustrates the acts of Christ should be with Christ. His faces have a heavenward look; but the brushwork is too subtle, the colour too delicate, the perspective too profound, to make him guilty of the fault of the pious artist, to paint saints as wimps.

Mystics

The old mystical tradition – Plato, Paul, the Egyptian hermits, Augustine, Dionysius the Areopagite – had a new flowering. Usually it was in the old way: a man of prayer moved out into the woods, where he was disturbed by nothing but hunting horns or nearby monks who resented him as anarchic. He would spend hours in the forest, listening and trying to find what he sought by looking inward for a divine spark; and thence moving outward in

VIRGINIS INTACTE CVM VENERIS ANTE FIGVRAM PRETEREVNDO CAVE NE SILEATVR AVE

A portrayal (1420) of St Paul's conversion, in spurs and
dressed like a late medieval knight with a fashionable
hat, thrown from his horse (which is as astounded as
he); and the Lord saying 'Saul, Saul, why persecutest
thou me? I am Jesus . . .' It was an altar-panel in
St Lambert's church at Hildesheim in north Germany,
removed after the Reformation, now in the Lower
Saxony Museum. Contrast the visions of God
by Augustine on p. 62 and Theresa on p. 223.

affection to the things of creation, because God made them and must be in them. A few disciples would collect to share and to lessen his peace; then pilgrims would arrive to disturb it. Then the censors of thought would discover what he had written and take fright at it, poring over his phrases, doubting words such as 'ecstasy' or his imagined conversations with Jesus. Administrators wrote down long lists of errors in this new kind of writing, objecting to the concept of 'God in darkness', or the 'Cloud of Unknowing', as an unknown English mystic titled his book.

The censors objected and condemned, but they could not stop this influence. One of these mystics, Henry Suso, was forced out of teaching into parish work at Ulm, where he died in 1366. Yet Suso's collection, *The Little Book of the Everlasting Wisdom*, was one of the most used books of prayer in the later Middle Ages. We know Suso's inmost thoughts only because a nun became a devoted disciple. She kept his letters and wrote down what he said.

We are in a new world of educated women, who had their own insights and wanted to share them through books. In Germany there was a charismatic movement of ecstatic nuns, who had mystical visions. We know about this thanks to the schools run by nuns, who produced a new generation of literate women. Hildegard of Bingen, born in 1098, was already a recluse at the age of nine and had visions from an early age. She entered a Benedictine convent of which she eventually became mother superior. She was well read in the Fathers of the Church, and her advice was sought by kings and popes. She wrote down all her visions, which she regarded as revelations from God; some of them were not religious in a narrow sense but advice about medicine and natural science, so that she won a reputation as one of the earliest German scientists. She was fierce against the wickedness of clergy. But for her the Church, despite its suffering and weakness, was the bulwark of God against the darkness of the world.

This was a new weight in the church, not seen since the days of the martyrs (except for some Celtic women such as Brigid, or some queens like Justinian's consort Theodora, who influenced her husband). Now again there was a conscious influence by women. One wrote down her visions in good Latin, another in good poetry, a third was a leader in the care of lepers, a fourth got into trouble because she was so rude about the state of priests and monks in Germany.

These new women writers were not remote from society. The Cistercian Mechtilde of Hackeborn, who died in 1298, not only thought about the heart of Jesus and its place in the devout imagination, but wrote

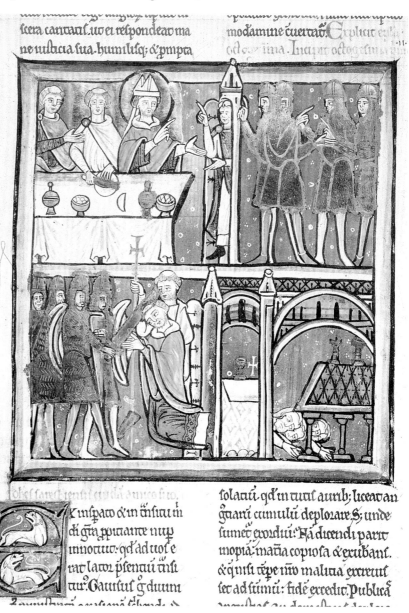

Becket's murder in 1170, in the side-chapel of Canterbury Cathedral, by four knights who thought that this was what King Henry II wished. Notice how bad the writing is compared with the earlier uncials. The text is taken from the work of John of Salisbury who was with Becket when the knights came. Note those praying in the shrine.

about it; and so she founded a new kind of affectionate prayer to Jesus which was to have a large place in later Catholic devotion. For a long time it was a cult of private prayer, and did not come into public Catholic rites until the seventeenth century.

All this was a flowering of the female vision of faith, which dared to use words of love, or of rapture, that men who wrote about prayer before that time hardly dared to think. To the twentieth century the most famous of these women writers was an English hermit who lived in a cell by a church in Norwich, Mother Julian; famous for her total confidence that 'all shall be well', and for her summing up of creation in a hazelnut. But in her own time she was not well known.

THE LAST OF THE MIDDLE AGES

It is hard to say why this apparently Christian society broke in pieces between 1350 and 1550. This was not like what happened to the pagan world during the decline of Rome, a loss of faith in decayed old gods. In 1550 all Europe was just as Christian, to the outward eye, as the Europe of 1350. The Ottoman Turks had conquered the Balkan peninsula and in certain places — south Bulgaria, Albania, Bosnia — made converts to Islam; but in the West, Spain had not only turned the last Islamic power out of Western Europe but, with Portugal, was opening vast new lands for mission in the Americas and the East. The faith of the common man and woman, their churchgoing, their expectation of heaven or hell, their professed desire to do good to their neighbour, were as strong as before; but that very strength was the first cause of the change that was to come. So many people had been filled with ideals — and that meant, so many people were discontented with the society in which they lived.

Nor was it just that the churches split more. Ever since St Paul's day the churches had proved that they were not exempt from the laws of human societies. The churches divided for much the same reasons that political groups divided — because they differed on a principle, or because they disliked a government so much that at last they refused to obey it, or because they thought their leaders had

The cloister of Monreale monastery (Benedictine) above Palermo. The Norman King William of Sicily built it in 1174. Arab and Greek influences make it rare. The capitals flower with beasts, birds and snakes.

A French choir sings a
motet, with only one
copy in large notation for
all to see; about 1500.

behaved immorally. The Roman empire tried to make all the Christians one church, and the result was strong churches outside its borders who would not accept the primacy of the Roman Church or the orders of the patriarch of Constantinople.

Many people were discontented with the clergy; that was not new. But now some laymen had got a good education from the Church and could write. Geoffrey Chaucer's *Canterbury Tales* have little portraits of several clerics, men and women. He was a civil servant, a job which caused him to meet many different specimens. His knight and his 'poor parson of the town' are truly good men. But most of his pilgrims on the road to the shrine of St Thomas Becket at Canterbury are amused by smutty jokes and adultery, or are lovers of money, so that some moderns have wrongly tried to prove him anticlerical and even anti-Christian. Nothing can be said in praise of the morals of his summoner and his pardoner, who sell indulgences to get money for the Church – though it goes into their own pockets. Chaucer could be very funny, and laughed at the hypocrisies of churchmen, but is a still a man of the Middle Ages, not least because his work was held together by a pilgrimage to the tomb and relics of a saint.

The contrast between what men said in the pulpit and what they did on weekdays was now satirized by abler pens and read by many more eyes.

The next warning came from the decline of the reputation of monks. A sign of this was the small number of novices who applied to be monks in the houses of most of the old orders. Large abbeys designed for one or two hundred monks now housed a handful. This was partly because the friars had taken over the best of their idealism and were more revered by the common people. But it was also because the monastery, despite the soup it gave out and its care for the elderly and sick, was seen now as a comfortable place for people who wanted an easy time in a well-endowed establishment, and who liked the single life.

For the first time there began to be a risk

A Romanesque relief, very unusual, of the Ascension; from the monastery at Silos in northern Spain, for which see p. 49.

that states short of cash — and states are always short of cash — would seize money from monasteries, because they could now do it without offending the people or being accused of sacrilege. States were not allowed to tax monasteries directly, but had always managed to squeeze money out of them. In 1312 the king of France forced the end of a whole order because he wanted its money. One of the orders created to fight the Muslims for Jerusalem in the crusades was the Knights Templar, 'the poor knights of Christ and of the Temple of Solomon'. St Bernard had helped them to fame; they fought well to keep Palestine in Christian hands and their bravery brought gifts and wealth — especially in France, for their headquarters were in Paris. They became a power in all Europe and lent money to kings; the Paris Temple was the principal bank of Europe.

In 1307 a nearly bankrupt King Philip IV of France decided to take all their money. He could not do it in the way Lenin took all the money of the Russian Church, simply by decree. The people of France still had to be persuaded that this act was not sacrilege.

Stories had to be put about that the Templars had secret rites in which they spat on the crucifix and worshipped the devil in the shape of a black cat. A deserting Templar was found who accused them of vile conduct. They were all arrested, and preachers denounced their evil ways. They were tortured to give evidence — thirty-six died under torture. In 1312 Pope Clement V, who was a Frenchman, was bullied into issuing a decree suppressing the order and giving its money to the Order of St John of Jerusalem, the Hospitallers. Several Templars, including the last grand master, were burnt as heretics. Naturally the French king, not the Hospitallers, got most of the money.

Never had Christendom seen such an act of tyranny by a Christian ruler. It was ominous because this was not an order in decline, unless it is a fall to turn from being a man of war to being a banker; the Templars still guarded forts that remained in Christian hands. Few outside the Templars denounced the act; society did not mind. The pope had done it, that was still enough to make the people think that it must be right. A protest

The popes' palace at Avignon, then just outside the border of southern France; they lived there from 1309 to 1377 because Rome was not safe. But Avignon needed to be fortified.

Downfall of a pope; the four stones are four gospels; the fall crushes a woman labelled 'hypocrisy'. By Girolamo da Treviso, who painted in Venice, then came to England to be Henry VIII's engineer and was killed with the English army at the siege of Boulogne.

came from Dante in northern Italy: 'The new Pilate, cruel and violent, pushing lawlessly into the Temple'.

There were so many priests that not all of them could be celibate. The bishops accepted that priests who had women might pay a fine for the sin; they could even keep them in their house, but must not marry them. By 1500 things had come to a strange pass. Marriage was honourable, unmarried love was not; but unmarried love was winked at in the lives of many of the persons whom the Church trusted to teach that very doctrine. This could not last.

Although the pope was the Bishop of Rome and bishops were expected to reside in their sees, politics meant that sometimes this was not possible. For a time the popes preferred to be in Italian towns outside Rome, or even at Lyons. Then the little town of Avignon, on the banks of the Rhône, with the most famous bridge in Europe, drew them. In Provence was the small county of Venaissin where a sect of heretics, the Albigensians, had flourished following a form of Christianity influenced by Manichaeism. In suppressing these heretics by the sword, French 'crusaders' occupied the district in the name of the pope. King Philip III of France gave it to the pope and it remained a papal possession till the French Revolution. Avignon was on its border; after a time the pope bought the town to add to the county of Venaissin. The papal palace is still the principal building of the town, and the massive battlements which gird the town were built by the popes.

With Italy in anarchy, popes preferred to live there instead of Rome for nearly seventy years from 1309. Such long absence from his see had the effect of making the pope more of an international figure, more the pastor of Europe than the pastor of his Italians. But international does not mean impartial, and the English, Germans and Spanish feared that a pope living in France and under French influence would be biased in his dealings with nations. Rome was St Peter's, Rome was the place of pilgrimage, no one forgot that this man was the Bishop of Rome. Even contemporaries compared the long absence of the popes to the time when the Israelites of the Old Testament were driven into exile from Jerusalem.

The popes at Avignon were not bad men, and had a perfectly good reason for wanting to live there. But they returned to Rome partly for the reason they had left it – they were not safe. France was in chaos because of the Hundred Years' War with England, and Avignon was threatened by bands of undisciplined soldiers. The only way the popes could hold on to their historic base in Italy was to go back there, however uncomfortable it was likely to be. The Avignon palace still looks more like a fort than a home.

In 1378 Pope Gregory XI returned to Rome but promptly died, and both Avignon and Rome claimed to have elected a successor. The Italian candidate, Urban VI, was bad; the French one, Clement VII, a little better.

Cardinals and the papacy

Cardo is Latin for 'hinge' or 'pivot'. The principal churches in and around Rome became known as *cardo* churches, and the pastors of these churches were called cardinals. The early way of electing bishops was by the clergy and the people; but then the people came to be represented by the king or emperor. In the eleventh century the pope freed himself from control by the emperor; and in 1059 the chief clergy of Rome, the cardinals, were declared to be the sole body with power to elect a new Pope. Some 120 years later Pope Alexander III ruled that election must be by a two-thirds majority of the cardinals, a requirement that has remained in force to this day. This ruling increased the power of the office of cardinal. Occasionally no one could get two-thirds of the votes, so that between 1268 and 1271 there was a vacancy of nearly three years, and the cardinals had to be locked in and threatened with starvation before they agreed. When at last they agreed in despair, they elected a good man.

They did not need to elect one of themselves as pope, and they still do not need to. But the last person to be elected pope though not himself a cardinal was elected in 1378 (and he was a bad choice), so perhaps time has made a rule. Since the office was now international it was absurd that the cardinals should be only the clergy of Rome, and from the end of the twelfth century others began to be chosen as cardinals, though they were then given titles of the *cardo* Roman churches.

Not even this system could prevent rival elections, when the office had grown to such power. In 1046 there were three rival popes; and again in 1409. After the Great Schism of 1378, with two popes anathematizing each other for thirty-seven years, the notion of a Christian society in Western Europe led by the pope could never be the same again.

In the 1370s John Wyclif in Oxford attacked the corruption of the papacy. When the Great Schism began, his attack moved to doctrine – the pope teaches what is not true, the present Church is wicked, the mass is idolatry, saints and relics and pictures encourage superstition. He inspired the first English translation of the Bible. Wyclif had a parish at Lutterworth where he died in his bed; many of his disciples, the Lollards, were far less fortunate.

The failure of the system of papal election was not due to the constitution. Once the disputes had been resolved by a series of councils, the cardinals never divided again in that way. The last rival pope created by a divided election, Felix V, resigned in 1449. No voting system works without pains, but election by cardinals has worked now for some five hundred years without an excess of agony.

The office of the papacy had some compensations. Money pouring in from pilgrims encouraged the supreme artists and architects of the dawning Renaissance.

The Sistine chapel at the Vatican, called so because built by Pope Sixtus IV; the chapel where Popes are elected; Michelangelo's *Last Judgement* is visible on the wall behind the altar, *Creation* above.

The Sistine chapel

Pope Sixtus IV came from poor parents;
educated by the Franciscans, he became a friar
and later the head of the order. Thence he
rose to cardinal, and to pope in 1471. He
ordered the rebuilding of the pope's private
chapel, which is still called the Sistine chapel
after him. A team of artists was hired,
Perugino and Botticelli among them.

Twenty-five years later Michelangelo was
ordered to paint the ceiling. He did not want
to do it and, when forced to, had a fight to get
his way in the design. These frescoes made a
sublime work of Christian art: all the history
of humanity, from the creation and the separation of light from darkness and land from sea;
Adam and Eve driven out of Paradise and
Noah drunk; the old Hebrew prophets and the
pagan Sibyls; the moments in the Old
Testament which were loved as prophecies of
Christ, such as Jonah saved from the great fish
and David knocking down the giant Goliath;
all ornamented by nude figures of cherubs and
angels and watchers.

After another twenty years Michelangelo
was hired again, to paint the *Last Judgement* on
the wall above the altar. He painted a strong
and handsome Christ at the centre, with Mary
just below at his side (not usual at this point in
art), St Peter, Charon the ferryman of souls
(for Michelangelo loved the poet Dante and
his portrait of hell), the damned in despair,
Minos the judge of the underworld – the long
heritage of Christian story and pagan legend
mingled in a huge harmony.

The frescoes of the chapel could not have
been achieved merely by a skilled artist. It
needed a human being with tenderness and a
sense of nobility in character, who understood
men and women, and knew how to bring out
the subtle varieties of humanity through their
faces (not leaving out faces that knew ecstasy
or the contemplation of truth), and loved the
Bible story and the poetry of Dante.

Leonardo's Last Supper

Leonardo da Vinci was hired by the Duke of
Milan as engineer, musician, poet and painter.

Raphael's portrait of Pope Julius II. He
achieved the restoration of the Papal States
to stability and in 1506 laid the foundation
stone for the new St Peter's. But he helped
to cause the coming of the Reformation.

The Dominicans had a friary in Milan, Santa Maria delle Grazie. They asked Leonardo to paint a fresco on the refectory wall. The Dominican prior complained that the painter spent much time apparently doing nothing. After nagging Leonardo for years, he appealed to the duke to tell him to get on with it.

Leonardo gave the duke an answer where it is hard to discern between the attitude of the artist and the quest of the religious man. He said that in creative work people do most when they work least; they conceive ideas which later they will carry out. He said that of the thirteen people at the supper he could not finish two heads: that of Christ, because he could not imagine the beauty of grace; and that of Judas because he was baffled by the idea of a man who could decide to betray the God-man his master. But because the duke

asked, he would stop thinking about Judas and give him the face of the prior who had nagged him. The head of Christ stayed unfinished.

Leonardo did not use the fresco painting technique, which requires quick work; instead he used a new oil-based paint of his own devising. The experiment was not a success; the painting needed to be restored within a few years. Nor were the politics of Europe kind. Napoleon's army used the room as a store; then, in 1943, bombs fell on the refectory and brought down the ceiling. Amazingly, the picture was hardly touched.

Time and restorers have taken their toll of the *Last Supper*, now a ghost of its original self. But it was valued by Protestants as by Catholics; in their devotions when they went to the sacrament the Protestants were encouraged to bring to mind the original meal.

Leonardo da Vinci's *Last Supper*, in a Dominican refectory at Milan, the best-known picture of the scene despite all the damage which it has suffered.

Raphael's *Madonna della Seggiola*; a picture specially valued by Protestants as by Catholics.

Leonardo's portrayal of the supper became the misty background of the commonest 'memory' of the events that evening.

Raphael's Madonnas

Raphael was commissioned to decorate one of the Vatican *stanze*, the pope's own chambers; later he did others. He liked to paint groups, especially family groups. They looked human. If he gave them halos, these were light, almost invisible.

Critics who misinterpreted the gentleness of his work accused him of being a mere illustrator. In some ways it was the Greek world, rather than the Hebrew tradition, in which his New Testament was framed.

Because these paintings – of the child Jesus, or his mother, or John the Baptist – were so evidently real people, they also made a part of the 'memory' of Christians in the centuries that followed. It was like the experience of those who visited Palestine: the figures which were not quite real, because they came in a holy book, were suddenly a piece of a past that could be imagined. Mary and her son came out of the clouds where legend and the supernatural had made them dazzle so that no one could see them as they were. They were personages of history. When Christendom afterwards thought of Mary with her child, it was with a view influenced by the picture we know as the *Madonna della Seggiola*, now in the Pitti Palace in Florence. In older French custom, if you wished to say that a lady had a serene beauty, you said she was like a Raphael Madonna. As with Leonardo's *Supper*, these pictures mattered also to Protestants though they were so often against religious pictures.

These cherubs lean on a balustrade at the feet of the Sistine Madonna from Dresden, by Raphael, and represent at its loveliest how little children enter the kingdom of God.

CHAPTER FIVE

THE NEW WORLD AND REFORM

THE AMERICAS

By the 1490s, with Columbus on the fringes of central America, and Vasco da Gama sailing around the Cape of Good Hope, new worlds were opening. Spain and Portugal each claimed the right to empires and appealed to the Borgia Pope Alexander VI, who at first divided the new lands between them. Spain and Portugal agreed to revise what he decided. The treaty of Tordesillas in 1494 gave Spain all America except Brazil, and the entire Far East to Portugal, except the Philippines and Japan. The Spanish and Portuguese kings were given power over new churches and the duty of converting the natives of any colonies they might establish.

The Spanish had lately won back the southern part of their country from the Moors and were full of the élan of the crusade. They descended on the coasts of America ready to convert the inhabitants by force. The Black Madonna of the Spanish monastery of Montserrat, who had been the patron saint of the war against the Muslims, was the patron of the American conquests. The patron saint of Spain was St James (Sant' Iago) whose relics lay at the shrine of Compostela in north-west Spain and who was thought of as a crusading saint; many places in America including the capital of Chile were called Santiago. When Columbus landed in the Bahamas he did not ask the Indians what the island was called. He simply named it San Salvador, the island of the Saviour.

Some of the conquistadors were irreligious brutes; others were religious brutes; most were ordinary people looking for jobs and a living; a very few were idealists of the best sort.

As for Pizarro, conqueror of Peru, almost nothing can be said in his favour; even his own men joked that he was suckled by a sow. Cortés, who captured Mexico, made his confession with tears, prayed often and preached well, wore a gold chain with a picture of the Virgin on one side and of John the Baptist on the other, never lost his temper, and knew some Latin — a different grade of being from Pizarro; and yet despite the tears Cortés had no conscience about murder, let alone gambling and womanizing. Brutalities were committed not only between conquistadors and Indians but between the conquistadors. The Europeans had discovered

A piece of Protestant propaganda against the Borgia Pope Alexander VI.

ALEX. VI. PONT. MAX

EGO SV̄ PAPA

The Virgin of Guadalupe outside Mexico City, the chief pilgrimage shrine of Latin America; the original vision was in 1531.

a pot of gold that anyone who had the power could seize without fear of retribution; so they killed each other to win it.

The Church faced a task in which it was hindered by the paradox of all crusades: the best fighters are not the best at justice or the gospel of peace. The missionaries had neither the people nor the means to convert the Amerindian peoples. They regarded the Indians as savages and their gods as evil idols. Nearly all the Indians had a natural sense of a creator god. The Europeans treated the high cultures of the Mayas, Aztecs and Incas in the same way as the most primitive tribes they had encountered. They saw human sacrifice and cannibalism, and took it for granted that such devilment was practised by all.

The conditions for the spread of the Christian faith were more unfriendly than in the conversion of the Germanic and Slavic tribes during the earlier Middle Ages or the conversion of so many African peoples in the nineteenth and twentieth centuries; and this although there was so much alike: a people who could read coming on a people that could not, a people with advanced laws, houses and farming encountering a people who wished to learn. We can speak of a Hellenization, or a Germanization, or an Africanization of the Christian faith, as the different peoples took it to their souls; we do not so easily speak of an Amerindianization of the faith — though that would be true in a different way.

Because the voyage and the first settlements were not thought safe for women, this meant half-caste children — mestizos. In time many Spanish families came to the colonies. But the settlements were not possible without the aid of 'civilized' Indians, and without Indian women as wives or mistresses for the white settlers. Because there were so many more males than females, colonial society was tolerant of men begetting children not only by their wives but by other women. We hear of one with thirty concubines, and another with fifty sons he recognized, and it was thought that there were others he did not recognize. It was a help that the children did not suffer in esteem because they were illegitimate, as they would have in Europe. But a European who legally married a non-European did suffer in esteem. Some Indian tribes already practised polygamy and this practice spread to Spaniards. Priests sometimes had to face the problem of what to do when a Spanish parishioner came to church accompanied openly by several wives.

Customs endure: in 1958 the United Nations produced a table of states with the most children born out of wedlock. Latin America held eighteen of the first nineteen places; Panama was at the top with seventy per cent of children. The poor still think of legal weddings as a luxury of the rich.

Most of the early missionaries were members of religious orders, especially Franciscans and Jesuits; about five and a half thousand of them in the Americas by 1600. At first the clergy thought that once the colonies were settled they could turn them into places like Spain, with wayside crucifixes and all the familiar ways of bringing the faith to the minds of those who passed along the roads, and cathedrals in the new towns. They insisted that the Indians sleep on beds and eat off tables and come to church 'properly' dressed and not keep animals in their huts. They tried to make them marry one person, in church. And they did much for them with brotherhoods and charities, hospitals, homes for the old and workhouses for the poor.

By the time the colonial age ended nearly every Latin American male belonged to a brotherhood. To be a member was proof that one was a Christian. The brotherhood used its contributions to pay for welfare and funerals; it decorated altars, built churches and chapels, and supported the cult of its patron saint. There was a class system, in that there would be separate brotherhoods for Spaniards, blacks, Indians and mestizos. Nevertheless they were a way out of oppression for the non-whites.

The Catholic Church was the labourer's social world. It banked his earnings, made loans, settled legal disputes, educated children, married couples, buried the dead, handed out amulets, blessed roads and tried to make them passable, demanded fees. But it was also the labourer's comfort and part of his provision for illness and old age; and it gave him a certain feeling of freedom.

The Spanish and Portuguese studied the Indian languages, making dictionaries and grammars. They wrote catechisms and they translated bits of the Bible; though this was far from welcome to everyone. The translators ran up against the old problem: if you translate the word 'God' as the word the Quechua know, you make them think the Christian God is like the gods of the hills and springs, even the gods of human sacrifice. So they used Spanish words for God and some of the most weighty Christian words: *Dios* for God, *Iglesia* for the Church. The Jesuits, as they were later to do in China, tried to use Indian words for some of these religious ideas. Not only the Jesuits but others used Aztec or Andean music and dance, or built the shrine of a Christian saint over the shrine of one of the older spirits, or allowed people to appear at services in the ritual garments of their older faiths.

This willingness was an invisible force in the conversion of the Amerindian peoples. It created Amerindian versions of the faith which could not be said to be un-Christian, and yet retained a lot of Inca or Aztec religious ideas and practices. In 1653 a priest of the diocese of Oaxaca wrote a letter to his bishop in which he described how his congregation also consulted the priests of their old religion as to lucky and unlucky days, and visited their old statues and performed the rites of the old faith. New Catholics felt no contradiction between the elements of the old faith and those of the new; but they preferred the officers of the new faith not to know what they did, fearing that it would get them into trouble. They gave their old gods the names of saints and turned the shrines into saints' shrines. On the one hand they really did receive the gospel about Jesus; on the other, they carried on much of their old religion under the protection of the Church. The old

ritual dance was now a dance to the glory of God before the altar.

Occasional raids by the authorities produced amazing evidence. Almost a century after Peru was supposed to be Christian, a round-up found 20,893 Indians who were said to engage in 'idolatry', which they were made to give up; 1618 heathen priests, who were arrested; and 1768 large and 7288 small idols and 1365 mummies, which were burnt; while 'the forty worst witches' were shut up in a home to be instructed.

The clergy believed in the grace bestowed

A popular Peruvian statue of St Isidore at a feast to celebrate a good harvest.

by the rite of baptism and so baptized hundreds, even thousands, of Indians without any lessons before the ceremony. They brought the Indians to confession; this was easy to achieve, for many Indian cults had forms of confession in their rites. But an interpreter was needed, and a third pair of ears spoiled the secrecy of the confession. Communion was infrequent in Europe and more so in the Americas; it was more to reward virtue than to help sinners.

There was no heresy, no criticism; everything was done as the clergy wanted: there were colourful processions, church buildings (some very fine), flourishing brotherhoods,

An Inca Madonna, of 1680.

institutions for the administration of charity, such as hospitals and poorhouses; indulgences were sold. The people had the outward signs of being faithful Catholics, though inside they kept many of the old Indian ways of faith. But this was not universal. In remote mountains of Peru or Bolivia the village or tribe carried on as before, except that a priest wandered in every few months to baptize the children, then went away without making any difference to the way of life or thinking.

The Inquisition was imported from Spain to see that there was no dissent. This was organized from about 1569 and was less systematic in Brazil. Officials searched ships in port to see that they landed no banned books. How little dissent there actually was is shown in the small number of people who were burnt in Spanish America, a few hundred against the thousands in Spain. But the court was misused for political ends; for example, in Peru it was used against opponents of the viceroy.

The women who came as nuns in the early days set up schools for children and taught the catechism. The large orders of nuns got leave to found convents in the Americas, both active and contemplative. They usually kept the Indian women as servants and helpers and did not allow them to become full members of the order. But they did a lot of good among local women when they were sick or in trouble with their families. There were a few nunneries of mixed race by the middle of the seventeenth century.

The baroque churches of Latin America were often magnificent, their elaborate façades almost concealed the brutality of the raw new towns. The cathedral of Mexico City, begun in 1573, is the equal of many in Europe. The continent *looked* wonderfully Christian.

It was a world where even bandits thought it prudent to carry rosaries and knelt in the streets at the sound of the angelus and preferred to die with a priest. The belief of the Indians was very near to their pre-Christian sense of the world as full of spirits, and their expectation of miracle. Even more than the

Spanish they were moved by pictures of torment, blood on the cross, the killing of a martyr. Their shrines of Mary are the most visited in the world after that of Lourdes. First of these was the shrine of St Mary of Guadalupe in Mexico, where in 1531 she was said to have appeared to an Indian.

There were not enough people to work the land. The solution was to import Africans, who could cope with the hot climate. By the end of the sixteenth century Spaniards and Portuguese were importing large numbers of Africans to work the fields and the mines, with a large loss of life on the voyage. It was one of the worst crimes in the history of 'Christian' nations.

People who took slavery for granted also took it for granted that it was necessary to the existence of the state, and if it were ended chaos must ensue. Pope Nicholas V, who in Europe was one of the best popes of the fifteenth century but knew nothing about what went on overseas, had already issued a bull in 1452 which allowed the Portuguese to make slaves. Throughout Latin America clergy, monasteries and nunneries were happy to own them. They did try to treat their slaves with justice and humanity, and tried, mostly in vain, to persuade landowners to follow their example. They attacked illegal modes of getting slaves, but seldom the existence of slavery. The spiritual needs of slaves were not forgotten; the Church insisted that Sunday was a day of rest for slaves as it was for anyone else. The governments insisted that owners sent slaves to catechism and church, provided for their marriages, and tried vainly to prevent the splitting up of their families.

Church people divided on whether it was right for men and women to be slaves or to own slaves. This turned into the most important argument that a Christian people ever had with themselves, for it led to the ideal of human rights, which has done at least a little to reduce oppression in the modern world.

When critics deplored the way Indians were treated, some of the whites replied that the Indians were not fully human. More than

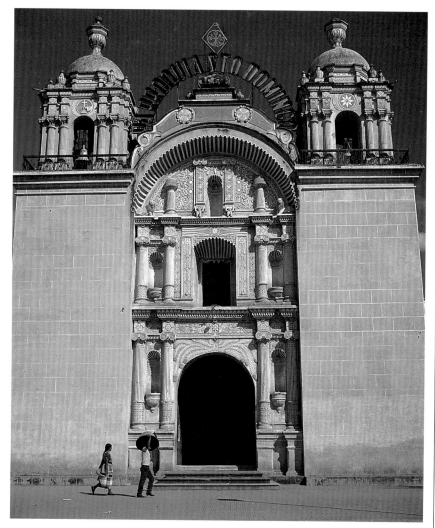

A baroque church from colonial Mexico.

one settler said he could see no difference between the Indians and beasts. The resulting debate raised two questions: what is a common humanity, and what is the Christian belief in this matter?

Almost at once, some priests could not bear the idea of slaves. As early as eighteen years after Columbus landed, a Dominican on the island of Santo Domingo, Antonio de Montesinos, preached a sermon to a congregation of Spanish squires and officers, accusing them of mortal sin because they made slaves of men and women who had done nothing to deserve so cruel a fate, and cared nothing for their welfare or education: 'Are they not human beings? Have they not reasonable souls? Are you not bound to love them as yourselves?' Those who heard were shocked at these words from the pulpit and wrote to

The church of St Francis of Assisi in New Mexico; an early church fortified as a protection against Apache Indians. The Franciscans were the chief missionaries of what is now the south-west United States.

King Ferdinand of Aragon, who told the governor to bring the Dominicans into line or send them back to Spain.

Las Casas sailed on Columbus' third voyage. At first he behaved like everyone else. But he heard Montesinos preach, and began to think about a verse from the Apocrypha: 'Bread is life to the destitute: to take it away is murder.' The experience converted him into a champion of the Indians. He gave up his Indian slaves and became a Dominican. Pope Paul III issued the bull, *Sublimis Deus*, in 1537. This stated that all peoples on the earth are human by their nature; as men and women they have a right to their freedom and their property, and must not be robbed or made slaves; and they are all able to receive the faith and are to be persuaded to it. Emperor Charles V demanded this bull be cancelled, and the Pope weakened. But bulls cannot be taken back, so the original statement stood. It did not relieve the plight of the Indians in the Americas.

Las Casas worked in Spain to get good laws. He helped to draft the 'New Laws of the Indies', issued in 1542, which banned slavery. In the Americas few took any notice, though in Peru there was a small revolt when a new governor tried to enforce them.

The new laws tempted Las Casas back to America as Bishop of Chiapas in Mexico. Here there was a large area still mostly unoccupied.

His belief in the mission of peace as the right way led him to write a book, *On the Only Way to Call People to God*; but no one would let it be printed. Neither the government of Mexico nor the other bishops would give him any support. He told Prince Philip of Spain that the heresies of the Protestants in Germany were not nearly as bad for the Church as what these settlers were doing in the Americas. Eventually his fight for justice brought an armed attack on him. He resigned the see, went back to Spain and worked there for better government in the Americas.

Las Casas had few disciples in his time in the Americas; but he made a big difference. When the Jesuits established their reservations for Indians, they had freedom to act as they saw fit because they had support from home; this was in part due to the efforts of Las Casas.

The new laws slowly made their way in the Americas. Slavery slowly lost its legal status and died out, except in very remote places. But the serfdom of the workers on estates, bound to 'personal service', was slower to end, gradually disappearing in the eighteenth century. It exists to this day on a few estates, and some say that it is growing again.

The Church, which was as deep-rooted in Spain as anywhere else in Europe, was yet not strong enough in its hold on humanity to stop the crimes of pirates and adventurers in remote lands far from the control of a settled government. All it could do was to limit their misdeeds as far as possible, put forward ideals of humanity, preach against corruption and oppression and, where this was allowed, form a separate group of people which lead to a more just form of society.

The plan was to take a big area, keep the colonists out, and let it be run by godly members of religious orders. Thus it became a separate little Indian state into which European temptations did not come; and the Indians, protected from exploitation, could be educated in good schools. The most famous of these reservations were what were called the Jesuit 'reductions' in Paraguay and southern

Brazil. But others were set up, though with less independence, in several parts of the Spanish and Portuguese empires. The first was made by the Franciscans in Guatemala from 1540 onwards; the movement of the peoples into these reservations still influences how and where the people of Guatemala live.

An important feature of the Jesuit reductions in Paraguay was that the Indians were free to leave if they wished; it was not a forced system. Their first motive was purely missionary. You could not convert nomads because they were not with you for long enough; therefore you must give them a good place to live. But their second motive came to dominate: to protect them from oppression and genocide.

To make such a settlement there had to be a law which authorized the priests to run a state within a state, with its own rules. Permission could not be got from the local governor, only from the King of Spain. The first Jesuit reductions were unarmed and were destroyed, with the murder of many of their members and of more than one Jesuit by white bandits, and the murder of three Jesuits by Indians. Father Cristobal de Mendoza was travelling with a group of Christian Indians when they were attacked by heathen Indians while they rested; when Father Cristobal refused to flee because he was ministering to wounded Indians, they tore him limb from limb. One reduction was sacked by white bandits who wrecked the church and turned the high altar into a latrine, and burnt several wounded Indians alive. Some of the reserves were founded by Jesuits setting out across trackless country, not knowing whether the inhabitants would kill them.

The King of Spain had an interest in the safety of the reductions among the Guarani peoples because they protected the frontier of the Spanish empire against the Portuguese in southern Brazil. He allowed them guns for their defence, without which this state within a state could not have survived. Paraguay became the only Latin American state where an Indian tongue is a national language.

In the reductions the Indians were a workforce but, unlike those on the great estates, they were paid. The society was semi-communist, or rather monastic; no one was allowed to own an object, only to use it in trust. A family would be allotted a piece of land to cultivate and would stay there, though they needed to get their trust renewed and they could never sell it at a profit. The Indians were required to work two or three days a week on the land of the community, which provided most of their food and drink and was a source of revenue for paying taxes to the king, alms for widows and children, and the wages of clergy and teachers. The Guarani were good craftsmen and the crafts and arts were fostered – spinning and weaving, cobbling, and metalwork which produced locks, clocks, guns and musical instruments. The Jesuits encouraged Indian music and formed orchestras. They were surprisingly tolerant of Indian polygamy until the moment the husbands or wives became members of the Church. They helped the Guarani by framing their language in writing, but refused to teach them Spanish because they wanted to keep the Indians away from Spaniards. This denial of an international language was to be a loss.

The Indians needed to find their own Christian priests. In the earlier Middle Ages, when Europeans did not worry about uneducated priests, they would have ordained Indians cheerfully. But now the candidate was expected to read texts in languages remote in grammar and structure from Indian languages; not only Spanish or Portuguese, but Latin. Amerindians also had an innate feeling that celibacy was not the best way of life and could not happily accept it. The result was a refusal to ordain Indians or Africans to higher orders, which persisted for nearly two centuries.

There were Indians, especially women, who taught the faith, and some men were readers, catechists or sacristans. There were known cases of an Indian convert going back to his tribe and teaching them, so that they asked for priests to come to make them into a church. In the mid-seventeenth century in Santo Domingo was a black priest said to be the best preacher in the island. But the churches of Latin America had to be European in almost all their higher clergy. And this fostered the notion of a division of society by colour. During the eighteenth century black priests in Brazil became quite numerous; but there was no senior black bishop until the later nineteenth century.

California

The earliest Europeans in the Americas heard of a land which they dubbed California, after a mythical island in an old Spanish romance; it was rumoured to be a paradise. In 1539 a Franciscan father, Marcos de Niza, the first Franciscan to enter Peru, was sent out to find these cities. He viewed, from a discreet distance, one Indian town in what is now New Mexico, planted a cross and called it the Kingdom of St Francis; then he returned and reported that he had found the seven cities. When others sent out later did not find them, they gave up the search. About 1600 Spaniards began to settle in New Mexico and soon founded Santa Fe, 'Holy Faith'. In 1680 there was a massacre of Spaniards by the Indians.

In 1769 Juniper Serra went on a mission to California. He was a Spanish Franciscan who had taken the name Juniper after the simple fool in *The Little Flowers of St Francis*. The friars sent him as a missionary to the Indians in the Mexican mountains; he moved northward into California and set up Indian townships, which in effect were reservations, in places along the coast such as San Francisco and San Diego (named after a Franciscan lay brother who was canonized in 1588). Between 1769 and 1823 twenty-one Indian mission stations were set up; Los Angeles dates from 1781. The friars converted hardly anyone and many of them were killed, but they taught the Indians trades. In 1823 the Mexicans expelled the Franciscans and in 1848 the country was ceded by Mexico to the United States – just before gold was found.

Juniper vanished from history. One of his companions wrote his life and wanted him to be made a saint, but no one read the book. Early in the twentieth century the people of the United States woke up to their Spanish heritage; and then they rediscovered Juniper, and why their two chief cities on the Pacific coast, and the capital of the state of New Mexico, have such pious names.

THE EAST

In the earliest years of Christianity its gospel spread eastward, outside the bounds of the Roman empire into what are now Armenia, Georgia, Iraq and Iran. The Armenians and the Georgians became Christian peoples; elsewhere, communities of Christians developed among peoples of another religion. From Iraq and Iran the Nestorians carried the faith eastward along the old Silk Road, the main east-west trade route; there were bishops in Samarkand and Kashgar. From there these Nestorians passed on into China. Archaeology has shown a flourishing Christian mission in central Asia just at the time that Western Christians were engaged in converting the Germans. It was the first meeting between Christianity and Chinese culture. About 1300 there seems to have been a bishop on the Chinese coast. But these early Chinese churches were for merchants and visitors, and prayers were in Syriac.

Because the eastward journey was easiest by sea down the wind, the most flourishing of these early communities were created by merchants sailing down to the south Indian coasts. Indian Christians attributed the origin of their faith to St Thomas the apostle, though they looked to the archbishop in Iraq as their head and used Syriac in their prayers. They believed that Thomas came to Kerala in the south-west of India, founded seven congregations and was martyred near Madras – visitors are shown still the cave where he last lived and the place of his death. About 540 Cosmas, a merchant from Alexandria, visited Christian congregations along the coasts of India and Ceylon.

Modern Indians tend to suppose that Christianity was brought by the colonial powers. But it is one of the ancient faiths of India, much older there than Islam. In 1500 a Portuguese seaman, Pedro Cabral, landed on the southern coast and was astonished to find a Christian people. The Portuguese were disturbed that these Christians had never heard of the pope. When they set up their Catholic faith in India, with its centre at Goa, they incorporated into their church those of the St Thomas Christians who were willing; the Catholic St Thomas church now makes up about a fifth of the Catholics in India. They did not try hard to make them say their prayers in Latin. Through the centuries there were splits, so that nowadays the old St Thomas church consists of four or five different denominations.

One of these early missionaries, the Jesuit Francis Xavier, won the respect of all Christendom. He was a Basque who spent three years on the south Indian coast baptizing converts, and then moved on to Malacca and the coasts of Indonesia and Japan, where he stayed two and a half years, one of the first Europeans in the country. He died at Shang-chuan, an island off the Chinese coast near Hong Kong from which the Portuguese used to trade (illegally) with China, waiting in vain for a permit to enter the mainland so that he might convert the Chinese. He had excommunicated the governor of Malacca, who had tried by force to stop him sailing to his death.

Xavier was criticized for moving onward so far and fast that he could achieve nothing lasting. He was only ten years in the East and half of that time was spent in voyages and delays in harbour; another quarter of his time was spent not with Indians and Chinese but with ignorant and immoral Portuguese labourers in the ports. He had a faith so powerful that it often lost touch with reality – he wrote home that when he had converted some of China he would return to see the pope in Rome, travelling by Siberia and Russia. But everywhere he went people thought of him as a holy father. He was a big man with so cheerful a face that

The Mogul emperor Jahangir holds a picture of the Madonna, 1620.

when people felt sad they went round to look at him; a special friend of lepers, he would spend the night beside the beds of the dying. His reputation in the East did much to spread the faith along the coasts where the Portuguese ships called. Some of his work did last among the fishermen and coast dwellers of south India and, more than anyone else, he brought Christianity to Japan.

These missionaries were bringing their faith to peoples in India, Burma, Ceylon and China who were Hindus or Buddhists or Confucians; that is, people with deep-rooted faiths of their own. There were those who took the same view of these faiths as the Spaniards in the Americas took of the native faiths which they found there – nothing was good; they must be judged by the worst; you were not able to through Hindu sources which did not give a correct picture. Only towards the end of the nineteenth century was this changed, with the discovery in Nepal and Tibet of Buddhist manuscripts in the Pali language. The first proper Western study of Buddha did not appear till 1878 in London: *Buddhism* by William Rhys Davids. But although the early missionaries knew little, they could not but be aware of the tradition of Buddhist monks and of quiet ascetic life to free the body from its passions, which had parallels with much in the Christian discipline of the soul.

Here was a vast difference from the spread of Christian faith among the Germans of the seventh century or the Amerindians of the sixteenth or the Africans of the nineteenth. In those parts there was no approach to God which could stand for long against the incoming faith, with its mingling of a high religious and moral message with a civilization. Buddhists in China, Tibet, Ceylon or India could be corrupt and superstitious; but so could the Christians. Here was a religion which, like Christianity, could reform a life, and where the best insights agreed with several of those of Christianity; it trusted in a cosmic order shadowed forth on earth in a community with moral laws.

Japanese Buddhists often had open minds, and in the first decades many of them came to accept the new faith. They were discontented with their own moral code, or with the complacent way it was so often breached. Others were unhappy with the obviously superstitious idols of popular cults. They were astonished at the heroism of some of these strangers; for the country was in turmoil and no foreigner was safe unless he was within range of the guns of a Portuguese warship, and such ships called very rarely.

Could the missionaries use the best in what they found? The Buddhists used rosaries, practised meditation, liked processions, had flourishing monasteries (perhaps too flourishing), and there was nothing wrong with their ceremonial robes. The people impressed the incomers by their profound courtesy to them and to each other which, the Europeans felt, must be a sign of true civilization despite the murderous acts of the warlords.

The Jesuits who came after Xavier created quite a big church, partly by converting the local *daimyo* (chiefs) who were then followed by their people. In 1601 they ordained the first Japanese priests.

They were then destroyed in one of the most cruel persecutions ever to afflict the churches. A single *daimyo* was determined to exert supreme authority, which he could achieve only by the destruction of his rivals, including the Christian chiefs. The Christians were also suspected as scouts for an invasion from the West. But their chief crime in Japanese eyes was that they seemed likely to overturn the national culture and religion. By 1630 nearly 2000 Japanese Christians and 71 Europeans had been killed, often after torture. The churches vanished, and the country was closed to Europeans. When it opened again after 1853, incoming Europeans were astounded to be approached by Japanese members of congregations which had been persisting in secret for two hundred years.

REFORM

In 1500 the Western Church could not go on as it was. During the next century and a half it changed radically; almost as radically in Catholic countries as in Protestant, though in different ways.

There were inner contradictions in Western Christianity.

First, the Church held up the Bible as the source of truth. But it taught various doctrines that no one could find in the Bible. This was possible only as long as not many people read the Bible; and not many people did, because few could read, fewer still could read Latin, and even fewer owned a copy. But with the coming of printed books in the 1450s, and a general growth in literacy, this was no longer possible. The contradictions stood clear; the Church must end them.

It could do this in only two ways: either by

a claim that it had the right to teach what was true even if it was not plainly stated in the Bible; or by dropping some of the teaching of non-biblical doctrines. Both ways were painful – the first because it was so deeply ingrained in everyone's mind that the Bible was the source of truth; the second because stripping towards simplicity threatened much that was loved by ordinary people.

The second contradiction was that the Church was rich and powerful; but Jesus had said that it was the poor and the meek who are blessed. The Church was rich because over the centuries pious men and women gave it money or left it estates; because governments favoured it by letting it levy tithes and freeing it from national taxes; and because its work took it out into empty lands which later were settled and became valuable. The ideal of poverty was very much alive, because every monk, nun and friar took a vow to keep it, and friars could be seen begging in the streets.

The Church was rich, but wealth brings duties. The huge cathedrals and churches must be kept from falling down. The parish system which covered all Europe, and which ran schools and hospitals as well as churches and chapels, needed a lot of money. The monks had built large abbeys for many monks; now that monks were less admired, these places were often nearly empty but still had to be maintained. The Church was also pledged to care for the poor, and gave out food and clothing at the monastery door or in the church porch as folk came to services. These handouts were a help but nothing like enough. Idealists thought it would be possible one day to do enough for the poor, not knowing how hard that would be.

So in Western Europe lay wealth – land, houses, rents, woods, farms – which was seen by many not to benefit society as it could. There was a contradiction between the ideals of the Church and the ends for which its earthly means were used – not a sharp contradiction, for everyone saw that priests must be paid, churches repaired, universities and schools staffed, and the sick nursed. Yet there

was feeling that money was being wasted – let us say, on keeping open an abbey which did no good and ought to close, or letting a bishop have a hundred servants.

The third contradiction was that this was a religion of peace. The early Church had not liked its members to fight in armies. When all society was supposed to be Christian, that rule could no longer apply, because someone had to defend society. But the feeling persisted still that bishops and priests ought not to kill, and so should not serve in war. This was made

Pope Clement VII by Sebastiano del Piombo, about 1526; under whom disasters happened to the Papacy – the sack of Rome, the loss of north Germany to the Lutherans, the loss of England under Henry VIII, the loss of Zurich, Basle and Berne to the Swiss reformers. Mostly it was not his fault; he paid for the sins of his predecessors.

197

commanding an army, look quite absurd. Pilgrimages, monks, pedantic theologians and Church dignitaries could never be the same after Erasmus.

Second, he edited and corrected the Greek text of the New Testament and made a new Latin translation; this work, the *Novum instrumentum*, came out in 1516. The editing was hasty work and unworthy of him as a scholar, but was improved in later editions. The union of a new Greek text with a new Latin translation astonished people with its revelation of the contrast between what the Bible said and what the Church did.

Third, he wrote one religious book that stirred Europe: the *Enchiridion militis christiani*. The Greek word *encheiridion* means either a dagger or a handbook, and Erasmus meant

both: 'the weapon of a Christian soldier' or 'a guide showing how to fight for Christ'. It was not a rebel book. It did not attack the big men of the Church; and talked simply of the best kind of religion and religious life.

But its message was strong. Does religion need to engage in dry theological investigation? Do we cheerfully sin and then find arguments to show that what we have done is right? Do we behave sourly and say that we are grave? Do we excuse our harshness by saying it is a just severity? We think we serve God by outward actions – being a monk, or going on a pilgrimage, or touching the image of a saint, or going to church regularly. The true way is deeper than all these. We are being encouraged to make our religion external when it is within the heart. We cannot say, this person must be better because he is a monk and we are not monks. The office of the clergy is one of love; but our clergy make it something to do with power. When we go to prayer we think that we are more pleasing to God the more prayers we say – and this makes prayer another outward act, when it is an attitude in the soul. Rise from the body to the spirit, from the complex to what is simple.

The book was written early in Erasmus' career, in 1503, and no one took much notice because he was not yet well known. But once he was famous, the cry became ever louder in Western Europe that religion is not about what we do but about what we are. Some felt it an inspiration; others resented him – we need these outward things to help us towards what is in the spirit, why should Erasmus tell people that the outward things are not important? For a time there was gossip that the pope would make him a cardinal. But after his death a later pope, Paul IV, could not bear his frankness and banned all his books without drawing any distinction between them. Banning them was a mistake.

Luther

Martin Luther was the professor of divinity at Wittenberg in Saxony, then a new university. Some people have doubted whether the new

An indulgence granted in 1608, long after the reforms that changed them after Luther's attack, to a Florentine brotherhood in Rome, dedicated to the beheading of St John the Baptist, hence the severed head; this printing 1776.

Martin Luther, by
his friend Lucas Cranach
the Elder; one of the
two portraits by which
German posterity would
specially remember the
Reformer.

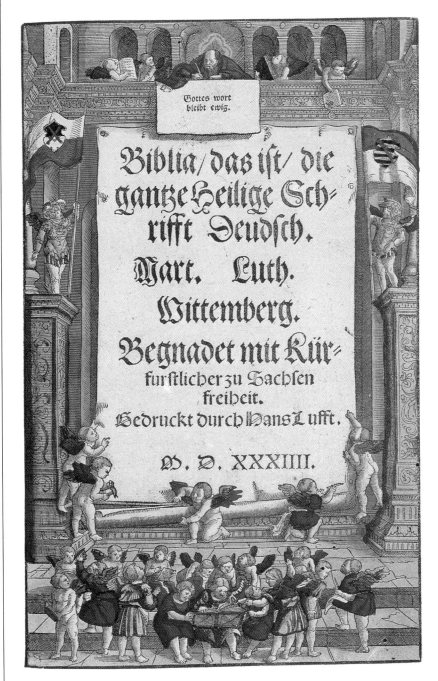

Gottes wort
bleibt ewig.

Biblia/ das ist/ die
gantze Heilige Sch-
rifft Deudsch.

Mart. Luth.

Wittemberg.

Begnadet mit Kür-
furstlicher zu Sachsen
freiheit.

Gedruckt durch Hans Lufft.

M. D. XXXIIII.

The title page of the 1533 edition of Luther's German Bible, which was wonderfully done and affected the German language; the cherubs unroll its pages; it states that it is published with the permission of the Elector of Saxony and by the printer Hans Lufft.

was a part of the truly religious drive towards reform and drastic change, he was never one for academic argument. Sometimes he wrote books all in a whirl, as though when he started he had no idea where his pen would take him. Often his pen took him into bold utterances about which a person with more prudence would have thought twice.

On the last day of October 1517 he issued ninety-five theses against indulgences. They were moderate. But indulgences made a lot of money for good causes and some less good, and they were part of a people's piety; so they were defended. But no one could defend them by saying it is a reasonable act to buy forgiveness, or by claiming that they were taught in the Bible. The only defence possible was that the pope authorized them; therefore Friar Martin was a heretic because he denied the authority of the pope. And Friar Martin of the whirling pen had an easy answer. Buying forgiveness is obviously wrong. If the pope authorizes it, the pope is wrong. It cannot be heresy to say what is true.

He became a European leader because the Emperor Charles V made a serious mistake in 1521: Luther was tried before the Diet of Worms (from late Latin *dieta*, a meeting). There Luther stood alone before all the might of the empire, and stuck to the truth he saw, and so captured the imagination of Christendom. He was declared an outlaw and had to go into hiding.

Germany divided and has stayed divided to this day. Everyone agreed on the need for reform of the Church. Bavaria, Austria and some of the Rhineland decided in the end that reform meant better and celibate clergymen, better schools and universities, and better social care; but Catholic practices of 1600 were much the same as those of 1500. Indulgences were still granted, though the obvious abuses were ended; the mass was little changed and still in Latin; most of the old rituals were carried on; pilgrimages continued; there was still much devotion to Mary and the saints; and there was still the authority of the pope. The north of Germany,

scholarship of the Renaissance, which Erasmus represented, had anything to do with the drive for reform, which Luther and some of the friars represented. There was a saying at the time: 'Erasmus laid the egg and Luther hatched it.' But it was only an epigram, they were amazingly unlike. Erasmus was learned in all the ancient world, Luther was deep in the Bible. Erasmus was clever and subtle and witty, Luther thought those three qualities to be superficial and rather irreligious. Luther

the Netherlands, Scandinavia, Scotland and England decided that the pope's authority was bad for the Church. There was a continuity with the old ways of Bible and sacrament and services; but the rituals were simplified, there were no indulgences and very few days for remembering saints, prayer to Mary and the saints fell away, and services were held in vernacular languages so that the people could know what was said and join in.

At the time, and until the twentieth century when a better understanding came, Luther was hated by Catholics as the friar who split the Church. He could be truculent with them. But the religious side of his work, as distinct from the pamphleteering, was of the first

THE REFORMATION by 1570

Key

- Reformed
- Anglican
- Lutheran
- Roman Catholic
- Roman Catholic and Lutheran
- Roman Catholic, Calvinist and Lutheran
- Roman Catholic, Calvinist, Lutheran and Hussite
- Muslim and Orthodox

NORWAY
SWEDEN
Stockholm
SCOTLAND
Edinburgh
IRELAND
DENMARK
Copenhagen
York
ENGLAND
WALES
Norwich
Oxford Cambridge
London Canterbury
FRIESLAND
SPANISH NETHERLANDS
BRANDENBURG
Antwerp
Brunswick
Cologne
Hildesheim Magdeburg
Wittenberg
POLAND
Rouen
Mainz
Rheims
Paris
Heidelberg
Rakow
Nuremberg
Prague
BOHEMIA
La Rochelle
BAVARIA
Vienna
FRANCE
Zurich
AUSTRIA
Budapest
Bern
Lyons
Geneva
Bordeaux
HUNGARY
Orthez
SAVOY
Venice
Nimes
Milan
Montpellier
Saragossa
Marseilles
SPAIN
OTTOMAN EMPIRE
Toledo
PAPAL STATES
Rome

0   100   200
Miles

Dürer's *Hands in Prayer*; valued and known throughout Christendom as a symbol of prayer.

A Cranach painting of the Last Supper and at each side of the triptych, Lutheran leaders. Left, Melanchthon baptizes; right, Luther. Underneath, a modern altar with CHI-RHO and Alpha and Omega.

lieutenant, Philip Melanchthon, wrote, and presented to the German diet at Augsburg in 1530, the base of Protestant teaching, known as the *Augsburg Confession*. But Luther's Bible, and his catechism, and his hymns, and simply his name, were much the more important in the later history of religion.

Luther's name was always to be linked to a part of St Paul's teaching, justification by faith. If you think you will win heaven by doing things – going to church, taking a vow to be a nun, visiting the sick or putting money into collections – you are mistaken. In this life men and women never cease partly to be sinners. The only way heaven comes is as a gift. In an act of faith you open your soul to your Saviour; and the grace that comes enables you to love your neighbour as you ought.

Dürer and Cranach

Our image of Luther, and of his work, is in part due to two painters, Cranach father and son. The elder Lucas Cranach started as a Catholic painter serving the court at Vienna and then the relic collection of the Elector of Saxony. Like his contemporary Albrecht Dürer he started to make woodcut prints. This technique had been in use in Europe for some three-quarters of a century but was still crude. Cranach's first woodcut was the arms of the Brotherhood of the Sacred Heart, which shows that he was not yet a Protestant; he also painted many Madonnas.

Being in Wittenberg when Luther launched his reforms, Cranach was soon convinced and became a friend and disciple of Luther. He used woodcuts in the propaganda battle between the conservatives and the reformers, making twenty-one woodcut illustrations for Luther's translation of the New Testament; one of which got him into trouble because he showed the whore of Babylon wearing a papal tiara. He painted three portraits of Luther as a monk, one of him as a doctor of the university, and one of him as 'Junker Georg', the lay disguise he had used when hiding in the Wartburg castle after the Diet of Worms. He also painted sacramental pictures for Lutheran

importance to Christianity, in the end even to Catholicism.

He translated the Bible into German. Being graphic, direct, and learned in the two Biblical languages, he was a very good translator. And since one of the chief desires of the reformers was to go back to the Bible, Luther's translation became the anchor of the German Protestant churches.

He also cared for children and for the unlettered. His shorter catechism became the base of teaching in German religion. His chief

Dürer's four horsemen of the
Apocalypse. The first Bibles
to carry illustrations often
restricted them to the Book
of Revelation.

altars, on subjects such as the Last Supper.

Cranach's son, of the same name, was born in Wittenberg in 1515; he was a Protestant from his youth and a devout follower of Luther. The religious subjects he painted were less varied than those of his father; mainly altarpieces on subjects such as the crucifixion. He painted a strong, idealized portrait of Luther; the image by which German posterity was to remember him.

The Protestants and monks

The belief that monks and nuns had chosen a mistaken way of life had been expressed even before the Reformation; but it was the Protestants who closed the monasteries. Many monks could find jobs in a world that was short of educated men. It was a relief for some nuns who had been shut up in a narrow community at an early age by their parents; but on the whole it was much more painful for them. Younger ex-nuns might marry (one married Luther), but older nuns still needed a home, which in Germany they were usually granted.

Schools were improving and more hospitals were built, and there was more need for almoners to care for the poor; all this did provide work for some ex-nuns. But there remained communities of elderly ladies in Protestant Germany, enduring more and more difficulty as they aged.

The effects of reform

The *Augsburg Confession* stated that the Protestants were still Catholic; that differences from conservative Catholicism were small. They taught the Bible, sacraments, prayer, and care for one's neighbour, and the moral authority of the Church. So in Germany many disciples of Luther, and in England some of the Anglicans, were content that services should remain much as they had been, with organs, vestments and rituals, except that the language was now the vernacular rather than Latin. The pastor might lawfully be married if he wished. The Bible and the teaching of its doctrines were more prominent, which increased the importance of the sermon.

Protestant Dutchmen in Brabant, 1568, remove statues and images with the aim of purifying the church from what they took to be idolatry. They always pulled down the rood. Protestant authorities wanted this to happen, but in a more orderly way.

An eighteenth-century Anglican sermon, in a hot summer (see the open fan). The age of wigs; the preacher in a black gown reads his sermon; the clerk is below in the double-decker pulpit to lead responses; an hour-glass on the pulpit; a lady in a low dress; the cluttered altar behind; by the caricaturist John Collett, about 1760.

Zurich, taught the Swiss simplicity; and after the Protestant Swiss all the Presbyterians in Holland, Scotland and New England, the Puritans in England, and the Huguenots or French Protestants, tried to simplify ritual. Hymns were simple metrical versions of the Psalms; they thought elaborate music an intrusion, and usually got rid of the organ. Forms of prayer were simple and still more biblical, and the sermon was even more important. This quest for simplicity applied to pictures and statues, which they threw out, sometimes with violence, and always with a sense of purifying a holy place.

To conservative worshippers these services felt more strange than if they went to a Protestant service in north Germany. But they had clarity, directness and simplicity, with their reassuring reliance on the Bible, and well-known metrical psalms. People came to love them and felt out of harmony if they attended a Lutheran or high Anglican service; they felt repelled by an old-fashioned Roman Catholic service.

The text of the Bible

The first bibles had no chapters. By the time of Jesus various Jewish copies had breaks to make it easier to find the place; some early Christian texts adopted these breaks. It was over a thousand years before the chapter divisions we know were created: about 1200, by Stephen Langton, the future Archbishop of Canterbury who signed the Magna Carta. His arrangement of the Vulgate – the usual Latin text of the Bible – was taken over with little change into later translations.

Reform meant a closer study of the Bible by many more people, so there was a need for a quicker way to find texts. Robert Estienne at Paris had one of the best printing firms in Europe. He was a Huguenot; in 1550 he had to leave Paris and moved to Geneva. There he at once produced a New Testament, and soon afterwards a whole Bible, in which the verses were numbered.

This simple addition made the biggest difference to the study of the Bible since the

There was more singing of hymns. It was easy for congregations in northern Germany, Scandinavia and England to accept reforms which left their familiar services largely intact. They often regarded the new as an improvement on the old, and some welcomed the new prominence of the sermon which increased their understanding; hymns allowed them to join in the praise more fervently. This first type of worship became known as 'Evangelical' in Germany, and 'Lutheran' elsewhere.

The second type was known as 'Reformed'. It was similar in its teaching; the differences were mainly in the ways of prayer and in a less localized idea of the Presence in the Holy Communion, and these were important to ordinary people. In Switzerland Zwingli, a disciple of Erasmus and the chief pastor at

An Anglican minister gives communion.
Note the white cloth on the altar rail. Women
have heads covered, but are kneeling with men
at the altar rail, though they might sit on
different sides of the church. By Francis Wheatley.

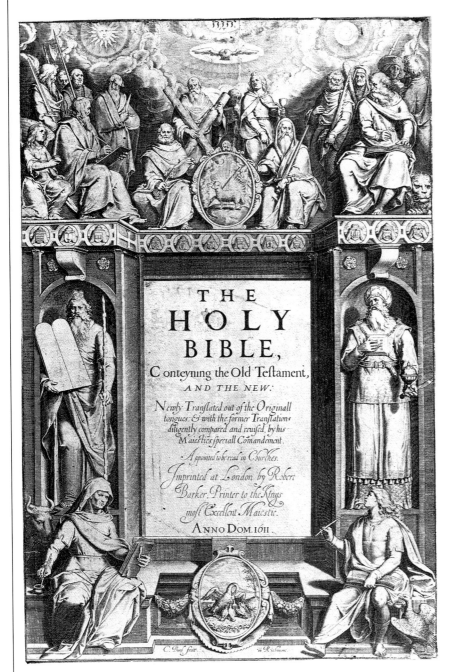

The title page of the King James or Authorized Version of the Bible, 1611; the best English translation till the nineteenth century and perhaps after, with its Shakespearian language and its scholarship, and still beloved by many in the English-speaking world.

importance. In every country of Protestant Europe the translation of the Bible deeply affected both literature and everyday language. A fine English translation of the New Testament and parts of the Old Testament was made during the reign of Henry VIII by William Tyndale, who was obliged to hide on the Continent and was later betrayed and strangled. It was adapted from time to time, and eventually formed the basis of the much loved 'Authorized Version' or 'King James Bible' of 1611.

Hymns

The other big change was the use of hymns. The Greek word *hymnos* is pre-Christian, and means any song of praise. The Jews sang psalms, and when the Christians began to do this they called them hymns. But since most people could not read, the singing was done either by a choir or by a solo cantor. The congregation got to know the refrains – 'Glory to God in the highest', or 'Holy, holy, holy' – and would join in at the end of each verse.

The first known hymn book dates from about 650; it has only the words and no indication of tunes. Many monasteries used plainsong (Gregorian chant) for their prayers and psalms, reading from texts with musical notation; often the monks on each side of the chapel would sing alternate verses. Soon the question came of what it was allowable to sing: psalms only, or words from the New Testament? Poets make verses, may we sing those? Someone, perhaps even St Ambrose of Milan, wrote a great hymn in praise of God as Trinity, the *Te Deum*; could it be sung? A council at Laodicea in Asia Minor said that only what is in the Bible might be sung. But congregations took little notice; private persons used poetry in their prayers; and little by little a body of 'hymnody', distinct from psalms, came into use. Mostly it was sung by choirs, in Latin or Greek.

Select hymns were introduced into the forms of service. At every priest's ordination it became essential to sing *Veni creator spiritus* ('Come Holy Ghost, our souls inspire'), a

invention of books instead of rolls. It was not much liked at first, and some forty years passed before the Protestants adopted it generally. Its danger was that a book of the Bible would no longer be seen as a whole, but as a list of separate sentences. This was outweighed by the ease of finding a particular passage, which was of equal advantage to the preacher, the scholar, and the private person at prayer or study.

These Bibles had a cultural effect of the first

hymn by an unknown author of the ninth century. This and the *Te Deum* were the most beloved hymns of the Middle Ages.

Latin poetry did not rhyme, but rhyme began to be used in the tenth century. People found rhyming hymns easier to remember and sing. This discovery was the start of rhyme in every kind of poetry, not just in holy songs. Towards the end of the Middle Ages the friars used rhymed hymns in the people's language at their mission services.

The reformers of the sixteenth century introduced hymn singing on a much larger scale. Printing enabled them to have copies of a book in church, the drive for education had made more people able to read, and services were now in a language that people understood. There was a new world of hymns: some were translations of the old Latin hymns, others were metrical versions of psalms, and some were entirely new.

The early argument appeared again. Now there were hymns not taken directly from the Bible, was it permissible to sing them? Luther and his followers said yes, and wrote some of the best of hymns, and often took over the tunes of popular songs to make singing enjoyable. The Swiss Reformed movement said no, and restricted themselves to metrical psalms. These became an important part of services not only in Switzerland but in the Netherlands and Scotland, and for a time in England – Anglican hymnals still include many of them.

The radicals

The doctrine of reform was that the Bible is the source of religious truth, and every man or woman can read it and find the truth there unaided.

Radicals appeared in Zurich and south-west Germany, later in the Netherlands and from there into north-west Germany. They refused

The Village Choir, by Thomas Webster, in the gallery at the back of an Anglican village church about 1820; before they were put into surplices and in the chancel. No organ; an orchestra of cello, clarinet, bassoon; women and girls as well as men and boys; still not enough books so singers must share.

An old Dutch peasant woman says grace before her solitary
meal; by Nicolaes Maes. Maes was taught by Rembrandt and
loved the effect of shadows. It would be hard to find such an
act of piety by someone not a nun nor upper class until the
Protestants came, with their care for religion in the home.

to allow the baptism of infants – for every Christian must have faith, and a baby cannot understand enough to have faith. They were known as 'Anabaptists' (the Greek prefix *ana* here meaning 'again').

They studied the Bible in little groups. They held that any use of force is wrong, whether in war or by the courts; they tried to refuse to serve as soldiers, even when their city was besieged. They were persecuted. Each little congregation was hidden and independent, so opinions varied – often, as is the way in a persecution, running to extremism. At first they were concerned about the coming end of the world. Some of their early leaders were educated men, but these were soon killed off and most Anabaptists were working men – more men than women. Their reputation was ruined after 1533, when a group got hold of the city of Münster in north-west Germany and, under siege, advocated violence and polygamy.

In Moravia, now a province of the modern Czech Republic, the Anabaptists were given protection by local squires. There the Hutterites founded communist congregations, 'brother-houses', where all labour was done for the common good, life was communal, and children were brought up by the community. They were soon valued as skilled workers. These communities lasted for some eighty years until they were driven out by war into Russia. Later remnants came to the United States, where they may still be found.

Menno Simons established order and quiet among the Anabaptist groups in north-west Germany. The newly Protestant Netherlands led Europe in being reasonably tolerant to such dissenting groups. Here the Anabaptist vision of Christians as little pacifist house churches, refusing to christen infants, was finally and successfully established. The denomination known as the Mennonites is still respected.

The Netherlands attracted refugees from England who wanted to practise their religion in this way. Some of these were educated. John Smyth was a priest in the Church of

England who led a group of dissenters to Amsterdam and there met the Mennonites. In London in 1612 this group formed the first 'Baptist' congregation in Britain. When the civil war brought greater religious tolerance to England, a number of these congregations were set up across the country.

New England was open to refugees of various kinds from Europe. In 1639 Roger Williams founded a Baptist congregation in Providence, Rhode Island; and thenceforth the Baptist people were always to be one of the main religious denominations in the United States. Through their biblical directness and their flexibility of organization they

George Fox was an itinerant preacher in the English civil war and after, teaching people God is within and true worship is in silence, until the Spirit leads someone to speak. His journal lies on the table; his disciple Whitehead in the 'chair' did most to turn them into a respected denomination, the Society of Friends. Penn, the founder of Pennsylvania, is on the left. The picture (1698) is by an enemy, but he drew the scene faithfully.

made headway among black people in America; to this day, most black churchgoers belong to Baptist churches.

The cause of this departure from the main Christian tradition was not the matter of whether infants should be baptized, but ideas of freedom. This is shown by the rise of the Congregationalists. These, like the Baptists, began as little groups in house churches. But they were often more educated people, they did not accept pacifism as a universal rule, and they baptized babies. Each congregation ran itself as a democracy. They first appeared towards the end of Elizabeth I's reign in England, with groups in Norwich and London. Oliver Cromwell was a sort of

Congregationalist, and under his rule they were respected. In both Britain and New England they became a weighty denomination. Despite their radical beliefs, their standards were such that members of the more traditional denominations did not feel strange in joining in their ways of prayer.

A holy state

When Roman society was gradually becoming Christian, between the reign of Constantine and the end of the fourth century, no one thought that it would be possible to make a society where all men and women were faithful disciples of Christ. On the contrary, it was taken for granted that to be truly faithful you must get out of society, put its temptations beyond your reach, and find quiet in the forests or mountains or desert. This attitude persisted through the next thousand years in both Eastern and Western Europe. There was a brief spell after the foundation of Constantinople when people thought that they could make a truly Christian city; but they soon found that Constantinople was just like other cities. In a monastery or nunnery we may find a community of disciples. Outside its walls we must put up with the original sin of humanity and do what we can to lessen it, but we shall never get rid of it till the last day.

The reformers of the sixteenth century disliked this idea. They thought that the reason society was not as good as it ought to be was that some of the best people left it to seek a cloistered virtue, and therefore monks and nuns were bad for society. To have two standards in morals, the good and the lukewarm, was not what the New Testament taught; so we ought to try to make all society Christian. And since sin is all around, this can only be done by instilling discipline into the minds of ordinary people.

In Geneva John Calvin tried to make this vision real. His attempt failed, but it had an international impact.

Calvin was a French Protestant who left France to escape persecution. By chance he came to Geneva and joined the reformers

Calvin's portrait; underneath, 'he was born at Noyon in Picardy in 1509 and died at Geneva in 1564. France is proud of him as its spiritual leader, and Scotland looks to him as its chief prophet.'

IOANNES CALUINUS THEOLOGUS Geneuensis

Nasc: Novioduni Vero-manduorum A. 1509. 10 Iulij Moritur A. 1564. 27 Martij.

Gallia non alio tantum se Flamine Iactat,
Nec se alio tollit Scotia Vate magis.. O 2.

there. After a while he was expelled, but he was asked back in 1541. For twenty-three years he was chief pastor of the city and exerted such influence that the pattern he and his followers established was seen with admiration. Some found its puritanism oppressive, but Calvin's ideas were followed by many of those who guided the reforming ideas in France, Holland, Scotland, and the Palatinate in the Rhineland, and later in Massachusetts — even for a time in England and Wales.

The plan was 'presbyterian': that is, the church was governed by ministers. These ministers elected other ministers to their number; their choice had to be approved by the representatives of the people. (In some Presbyterian churches today the people elect their minister but the other ministers must approve.) The people elected elders, and the ministers and elders together made up the consistory (in Scotland, the 'kirk session'), the authority for the moral conduct of the city — though it had no civil power and had to persuade the municipal government to impose penalties on those who infringed its laws. There were teams of visitors who had the job of visiting houses and seeing that all was well with the people's morals, and inspecting the children and schools. Deacons and almoners saw that the sick and elderly were cared for.

The Genevan system evoked reverence from visitors from other countries — the happiness and friendliness among the people, the godliness in their attitude to prayer and worship, the affection with which they sang metrical psalms, the care for education, the absence of drunkenness on the streets, the modesty in dress; there was not a beggar to be seen, not a prostitute. The Scottish reformer John Knox visited Geneva and said that he found 'a very perfect school of Christ', and he was not the only one to say so. Visitors did not also see that this could be achieved only by a government that was willing to be harsh; or if they did see this they approved. The need to be harsh with moral failures tended to make such a system shortlived.

The system differed in the various countries

A prayer book (selections from the English Book of Common Prayer) for Mohawk Indians, 1787.

where it was imposed, according to local politics and the links between the church and the state. To achieve such a society there had to be three conditions: the system of discipline had to be properly organized; the people, or a majority of them, had to assent to it; and the government had to agree that it was good for the people and did not intrude into its own right to govern or care for them. Where a ruler believed in it and had the power, it worked — but only until the ruler had a successor who did not believe in it. It could work where government was more or less democratic; but in conditions of war, government needed to be so strong that it only worked in modified forms — as in Holland in its fight for independence, or Scotland in the arguments

Some of the Mayflower pilgrims meet for prayer before setting out from Holland for the New World in 1620; after a painting by Charles West Cope, 1856; a romantic idea of it. The Mayflower finally sailed from Plymouth on 16 September 1620 with 149 aboard, of whom thirty-five were certainly puritan refugees; landfall was by Cape Cod on 9 November.

with the English, or England in its civil war.

Massachusetts was first settled by English Puritans who came from Plymouth on the Mayflower in 1620; ten years later John Winthrop settled Boston. It was natural for such people to set up a little Puritan state: votes were given only to those who passed a religious and moral test, orthodoxy in faith was strict and the moral discipline such as Calvin would have approved. Such high standards could last only while the number of people was small. As immigrants came in the people became more diverse and less easy to bring under a system of discipline, so little by little that system lapsed. Yet it was strong enough to leave traces of an idealism which has lasted in New England to this day.

In England in 1645, when parliamentary forces were winning the civil war, they set up a presbyterian system to make the Church effective and the people more moral. This never worked fully, partly because of the war and partly because it did not have the consent of many of the people. Events showed the difficulty of making a country, as opposed to a town or a small colonial community, godly by law.

John Bunyan

Of all the Calvinists, one Englishman had an influence far beyond the ranks of those who professed themselves disciples of Calvin: John Bunyan. He achieved this by a book, *The Pilgrim's Progress*. Bunyan was a tinker from Elstow, near Bedford. His boyhood was troubled by nightmares, visions of fiends, despair and guilt. He was fourteen when the civil war began, twenty and about to marry when the king's head was cut off; as a soldier he fought in the victorious parliamentary army. Bunyan became exceptionally pious in his prayers and in his behaviour. He kept hearing voices, both from on high and the curses and groans of the damned, and fought mentally with hobgoblins.

He found peace of mind, as preacher to a little congregation in Bedford. As a dissenter he was thrown into prison when Charles II came to the throne, and stayed there for most of twelve years because he would not promise not to preach. Here he mastered the text of the Bible and began to write; first *Grace Abounding to the Chief of Sinners*, which was his religious confession. The printers needed to correct the grammar and the spelling. But he combined a range of religious experiences with a mind steeped in the text of the Bible, and a knowledge of humanity which was that of the worker, not of the ruling class. This made him unique as an author.

After a brief period of freedom he was imprisoned again for six months, and began *The Pilgrim's Progress*, the first part of which was published in 1678. It tells of a pilgrimage through swamps and bogs, menaced by beasts, highwaymen and tempters, comforted by companions on the road and by ministers at an inn. The pilgrim, Christian, is no hero but a weak and worried man, who yet reaches his goal. His weakness and worry was what helped readers who felt the same.

Some readers thought it unfitting that religion should be turned into a child's story of giants and ogres. But many more welcomed it; edition succeeded edition, some with engraved illustrations. The first readers were workers, servants, shopkeepers and tradespeople; the literary world took little notice. But gradually the places that Christian passed on his journey – the Wicket Gate, the Slough of Despond, the House Beautiful, Doubting Castle, Vanity Fair – won a place on the maps of the English-speaking world, and personages such as Mr Worldly Wiseman, Giant Despair and Mr Valiant-for-Truth won their place among the symbols of nations. In New England and the Netherlands the book became a cult; since then it has been translated into more than two hundred languages.

Here was a religious genius who could write a classic though he had no education to speak of, had read few books, and had the outlook of a working artisan. Despite the dedicated Calvinism of the author, thousands of people who knew nothing of Calvinism or were against it felt that the book helped them. Scholars believed that an uneducated man could not have written such a work by himself, and hunted in vain for some older

book that he must have copied. But Bunyan was an original.

The sermon at its height

In the seventeenth century the sermon reached a status and form of art which it had never attained before and was never to attain

The frontispiece of *The Pilgrim's Progress*; Bunyan dreams how the pilgrim, laden with sin, sets out from the City of Destruction to the distant City of God. The City of Destruction is amply supplied with churches.

again. The reforming movements demanded to hear learned but intelligible minds; congregations, where they were educated, were instructed in the Bible, and could follow with close attention; the old system of divinity was still agreed in substance; the new use of vernacular languages for great literature, as in England came Shakespeare and then the Authorised Version of the Bible, enabled the best of preachers to apply their coherence in poetic prose. Naturally these 'best of preachers' were few as the best of poets were few. But it was the only time in Christian history when sermons were part of the supreme literature of two generations.

In England John Donne (died 1631) was dean of St Paul's in London; a former and partly penitent writer of exquisite love poetry and religious poetry. His sermons were as profound religiously as they were evocative as literature. A later generation could hardly understand it but the evidence is that his audiences heard him with rapture. They were not only the 'best sermons', but the language was equal to the best prose of that day. Three decades later in Catholic France Bourdaloue, who began to preach in Paris in 1669, achieved a similar marriage between the use of words and a fervour of religious thinking. He won double admiration, from the religious as a superb teacher and from the literary as the equal of the best writers of that age when French literature flowered. Many of his sermons were taken into school text books to teach the young how to write good French.

Of course there were critics who said that the business of a sermon is not to be beautiful in words, and in both countries this special product of the Reformation faded away.

THE ORATORIO

The word *oratorio* is the Italian for an oratory, or chapel for private prayer. In the 1560s a pastor in Rome, Philip Neri, used his chapel for services which included not only sermons and hymns, but sacred plays performed by his followers, the Congregation of the Oratory.

Italian composers took the form of the sacred play and made it into a musical narrative, with recitative and choruses, to be performed and acted on stage. It was soon clear that the music was more powerful than the acting, which was therefore dropped. But as opera grew in the secular theatre it influenced the oratorio, which became almost a kind of holy opera.

In the seventeenth century the Germans, whose Lutheran faith (in common with Catholicism) valued music as an aid to prayer, took the custom from the Italians and applied it to the story of the Passion. Early in the history of the Church it was the custom in the week before Easter for three priests to sing the story of the crucifixion in the words of one of the gospels; one singer would tell the story, another would sing the word of Christ, the third would portray the crowd. Now all the main parts – the evangelist, Jesus, Mary – were sung by different soloists; a chorus sang as angels, or as the angry mob.

The Germans beautified the narrative with texts from the Old Testament and poetic meditations, and so expressed the feelings of the crowd. Thus a recitation in plainsong by three priests turned into the most glorious form of sacred music ever conceived.

Handel was born in Saxony but moved to London permanently. His *Messiah* was first performed in Dublin in 1742. It was a religious experience as well as a musical one: soon millworkers were singing its choruses on the Pennine moors. Thereafter it never lost its popularity as both a religious and musical event in English-speaking lands. The musicians of that age thought of him as a writer of opera and regarded his oratorios as something of a curiosity. That was not how the people came to think of him. This oratorio was not his most careful work but it was marked by sincerity of feeling and was preserved from his oddities in other pieces because here he kept strictly to the words of the Bible.

Johann Sebastian Bach was born into the leading family of musicians in eastern Germany, earning his first pay as a choirboy.

From the age of eighteen he held various posts as a church organist and in small princely courts. In 1723 he became master of music in St Thomas's church in Leipzig. Here, unappreciated and underpaid, he wrote most of his church music: during the first two years he turned out a cantata every week. He wrote only three oratorios and five passions (some now lost). The evangelist's role became more dramatic; all the soloists had arias of deep feeling; the choruses became moments of both drama and religious meditation. The *St Matthew Passion* of 1729 remains the most beloved passion music of all Christendom. This passion probably brought religion home to many more souls than the words of a thousand curates. At times doctors of music have been nearer than doctors of divinity to God.

CATHOLIC REFORMATION

This is sometimes called the 'Counter-Reformation', but that mixes up the reformation of the Church with the political activities that went on at the same time. Mostly it was not 'counter'. It was an old-fashioned zeal to improve religious life and worship in the old-fashioned way.

Spain, rich with its new empire in America, was the power of the sixteenth century; it dominated Italy, and was mighty in Northern Europe because it ruled the Spanish Netherlands. The Spanish still had the crusading fervour which had come from turning the Muslims out of their land, and this mood infected conservative Europe.

Under pressure from the Emperor Charles V the Council of Trent met to reform the Catholic Church. Its important innovations were a new catechism to educate the young, and an order that those to be made priests should be trained in seminaries – then a new word to mean such colleges. This was the first time that a system of colleges, other than universities, to train clergy was set up in any church. It did not work very well at first because it produced a few excellent institutions and a lot of weak ones.

Pius V, pope for six years from 1566 to 1572, was suited to carrying out reforms of this kind; he was the first pope for 270 years to be made a saint. A Dominican friar, with a duty to teach, he had been an inquisitor with a duty to repress heresy, and wore a hair shirt under his robes. Like Calvin in Geneva, he tried to turn Rome into a holy city, with punishments for swearing, adultery and disturbing the peace on Sunday. He chose good men as cardinals, and tried to ban priests who did not live in their parishes, and fought hard to make them give up their women. He limited the issue of indulgences. His inquisition was severe: Protestantism disappeared from Italy, except in the Alpine valleys where

A sacred concert in the age of Bach, 1732. On the piano, 'everything that hath breath, praise the Lord'.

The Council of Trent, meeting to reform the Catholic Church: legates of the pope presiding; cardinals, bishops, theologians and lay ambassadors of the Catholic states. The picture is much later, about 1800; but not unlike what it must have been.

the Vaudois just managed to hold out. He excommunicated Queen Elizabeth of England and declared her to be deposed; this was the last time any pope did this to a head of state, for it achieved nothing but to hurt badly the remaining English Catholics. This calamity was used as a precedent in arguments much later, for instance whether a pope could excommunicate Hitler. He gathered a fleet to fight the Turks, which won the famous naval battle of Lepanto off the coast of Greece. Friar, crusader, inquisitor, statesman, private ascetic, a man of much prayer, he was the supreme practitioner of reform as the conservative reformation wished to see it.

The new orders

A later (seventeenth-century) portrait of Ignatius Loyola who founded the Jesuits; earlier in life he was a soldier.

The Jesuits and the Capuchins were indispensable to these reforms. Both became so powerful that their names became terms of abuse: 'jesuitical' was soon used to mean deceitful or hair-splitting, and a 'capucinade' was a sermon which was a waterfall of words but taught nothing except platitudes. Abusive or not, these words were a sign that the new orders mattered.

The Capuchins were a reformed order of Franciscans founded in 1528, and distinguished by their beards and pointed cowls (Italian *cappuccio*, 'hood'). Their object at first was the simple care of simple people – the sick and aged, orphans, prisoners, alcoholics. But soon they were the people's preachers in cities, addressing large crowds. Like St Francis himself, or the early Methodists, or the best American evangelists, they made an epoch in popular evangelism. The missions in East Europe and the Americas, Africa and the Far East could not have got on without them. By 1764 they numbered more than 34,000.

The Jesuits were founded by the Spanish ex-soldier Ignatius Loyola. Their object, as

The Escorial, near
Madrid; built as
monastery, palace and
mausoleum by Philip II
of Spain, powerful and
devout to fanaticism.
The union of grandeur
with austerity expressed
the man and made for
dullness. He felt a
mission to keep Europe
Catholic by force; yet
failed in England through
the Armada, and in
Holland through Dutch
dykes. The monastery
was Hieronymite, a
fourteenth-century
pastoral order,
suppressed in Spain
in 1835.

SCENOGRAPHIA FABRICÆ

S. LAVRENTII IN ESCVRIALI

In the mountains,
In the lonely wooded valleys,
In the islands flung across the sea,
In the roar of the river,
In the breath of the caressing wind,
Thou, my Beloved, art there.

Two sides of this unusual mind were exceptional. First, the Carmelites looked back to their origin on Mount Carmel in Palestine. John imagined the life of the soul as an ascent of Mount Carmel. As it climbs it meets darkness, 'the dark night of the soul', where it is passive; and yet it comes to a hymn of the spirit and feels within itself a living flame of love. In this pure praise of the heart it attains union with the divine. Second, the metaphor for this union is unashamedly taken from sexual love. In this Spaniard the Old Testament attained its Christian climax in the boldest use of the Song of Songs; originally an erotic poem, but taken by the Jews as an allegory of divine love. John of the Cross used it as never before:

O happy night which was my guide,
Night brighter than the noonday,
Night which to the lover
Brought his bride,
And then didst make them one.
He stayed. He let me rest
My cheek upon his breast.
All things did end; and there
I let fall all my care
Forget them all
Among the lilies.

Theresa's metaphor was that of a castle with wall after wall, as she wrote in *The Interior Castle*, in Spanish *Las Moradas*, used to mean 'the mansions of the soul'. This is a progress from the sense of God as present (mansions 1 to 3 – but the courtyard has reptiles crawling in it); through the 'prayer of quiet', in which God comes and makes the soul free while the mind can think of nothing else (mansion 4); 'the prayer of union', in which the soul is sure of its unity with God like the silkworm in its cocoon (mansion 5); then, through darkness and ecstasies, to the betrothal of the soul with God (mansion 6); and to the soul in the immediate presence of God and the marriage to him (mansion 7).

After John of the Cross and Theresa of Ávila the mystical strand in Christendom seemed to have attained its apogee, with nothing left to say that was worth saying.

WARS OF RELIGION

Religious differences start wars. Why, when the religious ideal is one of peace? The Saracens seized Jerusalem. They had no right to it, it was aggression, a war to take it back would be just; so there were crusades. But would the crusaders have gone all the way from France to Palestine to rescue Jerusalem if Jerusalem had not been the city where Jesus died? It was the name of the place, it was a religious affection for it, that set them off to free a distant city. As in any war, they were joined by thugs who were only out for loot. The crusaders won a hard war and had a kingdom of Jerusalem for nearly a hundred years – 1099 to 1187. Then they were driven out; after a time it was considered not sensible, nor even moral, to go back and fight more.

The Reformation divided Europe into Catholics and Protestants. At first it did not make a difference to wars: Catholic Frenchmen were more likely to invade Catholic Italy than were Protestant Swiss or Germans. The emperor's army that sacked Rome in 1527 and forced the pope to flee to safety had Protestant and Catholic soldiers, but both of these were in Rome for loot and religion had nothing to do with it.

In France there were 'wars of religion' – civil wars which continued sporadically from 1562 to 1598. The main cause of these wars was not religious: the sudden death of King Henry II in an accident in 1559 left a headless country and a struggle for power among the barons. But it kept on in good part because of religion. Henry II had conceived the mad policy of killing Huguenots – and since there were now hundreds of thousands of them, this forced Huguenots to arm for their own protection, and provoked a 'just rebellion'. On the other side, when Huguenots became a majority in a town, as in Lyons, Rouen, Nîmes or Montpellier, they took over the Catholic churches. This was illegal, and the government was justified in using force to stop it. Deaths led to a call to arms.

The French wars ended when the Edict of Nantes gave toleration to Protestants and allowed both religions to exist legally; a landmark in the history of toleration. But another reason was that at last France again had a capable person as king, Henry IV – who had been a Protestant but became a Catholic to get peace in the country.

In Germany the Thirty Years' War raged from 1618 to 1648. Most of one side was Protestant and most of the other side was Catholic, so this also is sometimes regarded as a war of religion; but it was not. The Czechs wanted independence from Austria. A rash German prince, the Elector Frederick of the Palatinate, who was a Protestant, allowed himself to be made king in Prague. Austria smashed the Czech revolution easily and found itself so mighty that it could extend its power over other German Protestant states – who then were afraid and defended themselves. The war ceased to be a 'war of religion' when the Catholic French entered it on the 'Protestant' side.

Today Cyprus is divided between Greeks and Turks – one side Christian Orthodox, the other Muslim. Is the religious difference, then, nothing to do with the halving of the island? No one would claim that.

Religion is one of the ways in which a people is conscious of its identity. For example, when the Russians, who were mostly Orthodox, occupied the Polish capital, Warsaw, in 1813, and ruled it for 104 years, they soon built an Orthodox cathedral in the great square. When the Poles, who were mostly Roman Catholics, won their independence at the end of the First World War they soon pulled the building down.

Religion is part of the conflict between Northern Ireland where the majority is Protestant, and those who claim to fight for an Irish republic where the majority is Catholic. It is ingrained in the conflicts in former Yugoslavia, where Bosnia has a lot of Muslims, the Croats are Catholic and the Serbs Orthodox. Yet the war in Yugoslavia was not started for religious reasons, except in so far as religion helped to identify the various parts of the old state.

THE BAROQUE

With the coming of reform, whether Protestant or Catholic, came a new mood in art and architecture which a later age would

A baroque pulpit in the form of a ship with the miraculous draught of fishes from Traunkirchen, Austria.

The ceiling of the church
of S Ignazio in Rome,
1685 onwards; up and up
and up towards heaven;
by Andrea Pozzo. He was
asked to build a dome
but the Dominicans
nearby said it would
darken their library so
he built a pretend-dome,
one of the most beautiful
of baroque feats.

call 'baroque'. The word first meant 'misshapen' — an insult for a church or a painting which was fussy, over-elaborate, extravagant, even corrupt. Not till the end of Queen Victoria's reign was the word used as a compliment to a religious endeavour which had its own kind of excellence; its splendour was not mere show but spoke of glory, with its own delicacy and strength.

A supreme example of seventeenth-century baroque was Gianlorenzo Bernini's design for the circular colonnade in front of St Peter's in Rome, built from 1656 onwards. He had already covered the altar of St Peter's, built over the saint's tomb with a *baldacchino* or canopy which, with its barley-sugar columns, is the very essence of baroque; later he applied the same style to the altar and papal throne in the apse. But his square was unique;

colonnades reaching out to coax the worshippers towards the porch of the basilica, and enclosing a piazza where crowds could stand for services in the open air. It was the most attractive frontispiece ever built for a church.

Once the Catholics had an open space, they gave it colour and shape. Stucco made possible intricate mouldings and writhing statues. Some of the Austrian monasteries, such as Melk, had a sumptuousness which belied their purpose. Inside a church the altar might rise for storey after storey until even the most Protestant visitor stood in awe. But the effect did not depend only on size. The pilgrimage church of Wies in the woods of the Alpine foothills is small, dazzling in colour, so warm in its impact as almost to embrace the people — one of the loveliest churches ever built.

Protestants were even more in need of a

St Peter's, Rome, built 1506–1626; Bernini designed the arcades as if to draw people towards the porch; the jumble of housing in front was cleared away by Mussolini to make a vista from the river Tiber; the hill at the back right was soon built over. The obelisk in the square was brought to Rome by Caligula. A photograph taken in 1928.

The baroque *baldacchino* over the altar of St Peter's, Rome, by Bernini.

The west front of St Paul's cathedral, London; the fourth cathedral on the site, one of the oldest religious sites in England; first a wooden church, burnt; then one of stone, destroyed by Vikings; then the big cathedral, ended in the Great Fire; and then Wren's masterpiece. The statue in front is of Queen Anne, in whose reign it was finished.

Rubens' *The Descent from the Cross*,
for an altar in Antwerp cathedral;
movement and struggle without loss of
serenity, light from the right brilliantly
reflected in the shroud and the body.

space where many people could listen. It was a problem for them because they wanted simplicity; but a big, bare space would look like a barn. Among the Lutherans and the Anglicans the need for space created noble monuments in a baroque style only slightly less exuberant than that of the Catholics. The Frauenkirche in Dresden was a magnificent example; destroyed by bombs in 1945, it is now to be rebuilt.

The chief Protestant example is St Paul's Cathedral in London. Like the builders of St Sophia, Christopher Wren was not a builder by training, but a scientist who combined expertise in mathematics with delicacy in drawing. His chance came when the City of London was burnt down in 1666. The old St Paul's was already falling down before the fire; afterwards they tried to prop it up but more fell down as they worked. Wren had begun to design the first of fifty-two new parish churches, to make London full of little places of prayer where preaching was easy. Now he began to plan the purest baroque cathedral built in Europe. It took forty-one years to complete. He was content with small fees, and the evidence shows that he was a man of simple faith and gentle personality, with a sense of building for God. He cared about religion and beauty as much as he cared about accurate engineering.

But we are much more likely to find ornate baroque in Catholic churches than in Protestant. Contrast two nearly contemporary painters, Rubens and Rembrandt; for their work shows what the church public now wanted – though both were geniuses and rose far above mere satisfaction of popular demand. Both lived in the old Netherlands, one in the Catholic part, which was to be Belgium, one in Holland, which was now Protestant. Rubens, born in 1577, was the painter of the baroque at its most dynamic. In Fra Angelico's painting of the Annunciation a slim, beautiful angel brings the news to a slim, beautiful and composed Mary. In Rubens' version of the same subject a strongly built angel in a flowing robe makes a dramatic

announcement to a stalwart Mary, who recoils in astonishment and a swirl of rich fabric. His cherubs were bouncing and rubicund; never before did the messengers of God come with such gusto. Yet the result can be religiously moving, as in *The Descent from the Cross*, where a group struggles to bring down the body, yet there is no confusion in the movement, all is harmony, with a brilliant white light on the shroud coming from the right.

Rubens' style was as far as it could be from the bloodless saints, who made goodness look pallid. God's world pulsated with exuberance, where humanity was sensual and yet the sensual was innocent and lifting towards the divine. He loved what can only be described as drapery, garments that flow and curl and engulf bodies in movement. These religious paintings were at their best when their subjects were taken from the New Testament – the three wise men, the descent from the cross, the transfiguration, or the massacre of the innocents, where the mothers fight tooth and nail to defend their young. As a Catholic he was able to do what the Protestants rejected: to paint legends into churches, such as the upside-down crucifixion of St Peter, whose manner of death is not known. He could ornament scenes from the New Testament with persons the gospels did not mention; in his vast *Adoration* in Madrid (he loved size in painting), the wise men have armoured warriors, richly dressed chamberlains, slaves and camels in their retinue.

Rembrandt worked mostly at Amsterdam in a Reformed society. His religious paintings are simpler, smaller and less exuberant than those of Rubens; but many think his religious paintings all the more powerful because of their natural quality. Here the figures of the Bible are real human beings, yet his genius makes them evocative of another world. Some of the New Testament scenes were never equalled – Jesus as the gardener meeting Mary Magdalene, the woman taken in adultery, the two pilgrims walking to Emmaus, Christ before Pilate. He loved his wife Saskia and his son Titus, and expressed this feeling in his

pictures of the Holy Family, shown as a carpenter's family in their humble shop. Saskia was often his model for women of the Old Testament, such as Bathsheba or Delilah. After her death his colours grew more sombre, the sufferers more helpless, the subjects grimmer, as when Joseph is accused of attempted rape by Potiphar's wife; but his mastery remained total.

BAYLE AND VOLTAIRE

A new world of Christian attitudes began with two Frenchmen.

The first was Pierre Bayle. He was a professor of philosophy at a Protestant college in Sedan; when this was closed he fled to Rotterdam, where he wrote most of his religious and philosophical works. He died there in 1706 at the age of 59, at a moment when the French Protestants were under threat from Louis XIV; it is not surprising that his writings were against Catholics. But his way of criticising them was so unusual that it changed the arguments not only about the Catholic way, but about the religious way as a whole. If someone is an atheist, is he or she always immoral? That was taken for granted in Europe in 1700. Christianity was able to rely on the wide agreement that a society is only tolerable, can only exist as a society and not as a band of brigands, if most people are moral in their lives, and they will not be moral unless they are also religious. Therefore religion is as necessary to a society as food and dress.

Bayle denied this: it might be so, but it need not be. If faith says yes to certain ideas, but does not transform the will, its influence on human behaviour is small. Bayle separated what hitherto had been regarded as inseparable: religion and moral behaviour. People might be bad though they were religious, or good though they were irreligious.

His main work was an encyclopaedia, the *Dictionnaire historique et critique*, which was translated into many languages. The best encyclopaedia at that time, he wrote every word himself, and nothing he wrote was dull.

He was an able historian, with insight into whether a source is telling the truth or is lying, or is a forgery. He was one of the first to apply serious historical method to the study of the Bible and its documents. He had no use for the idea that every word of the Bible is dictated by God. In the first edition of the encyclopaedia his article on King David so shocked readers that it had to be removed for the second edition. Till then David was thought to be the author of the Psalms, the boy slayer of Goliath, the hero and sweet singer of Israel. Bayle described him as a leader of bandits. With no use for allegory as a way out of difficulty, he described for the first time the barbarity of the portrait of God in early parts of the Old Testament. He showed that an act by the patriarch Abraham was immoral, then quoted sermons praising it.

After Bayle no intellectual could treat the Old Testament in the traditional way. There had to be a sense of growth, of gaining insight into the truth. Yet Bayle had a low opinion of our reason, seeing it as certain to lead us astray. What reason tells us is one thing, what God reveals is another kind of knowledge. He was devoted to the idea of toleration; faith can never be forced. These ideas, stated powerfully, helped to create the age of ideas we know as the Enlightenment; though that word is not found until the end of the eighteenth century, when some people in Europe were suddenly proud of being reasonable beings.

Voltaire was fifteen when Bayle died. He made his name as a poet and writer of tragedies. Sometimes he was famous and welcome in France; he was made the historiographer royal, and elected to the French Academy. At other times he was notorious. He was twice imprisoned in the Bastille, spent three years an exile in England, two years in Lorraine, several months in Belgium and nearly two years in Prussia; in the last years of his life he lived on the Swiss frontier, though he died in Paris.

He was mischievous and quarrelsome and never quite said what he believed; but he certainly had faith in God and thought Jesus a

A Reformed sermon in the Old Church
at Delft in Holland; by Storck and Streeck,
about 1700. Notice that it was usual for men to
keep hats on during sermons, for warmth;
they doffed them for the prayers; dogs were
allowed in and children walked about.

man like the rest of us. He was exceptionally clever and at times exceptionally superficial, partly because of the speed with which he wrote. Many in Europe regarded him as the arch-enemy of Christianity. He was famous for saying that it was a duty to *écraser l'infâme*, 'destroy the infamous thing', which was generally taken to mean the Church. Church people misinterpreted *infâme* to mean not the Church, nor Catholicism, nor Christianity, but Christ himself. In fact what he considered infamous was the 'persecuting orthodoxy in whatever form and shape' which tries to kill freedom of thought. He was passionate in fighting against censors.

Humour and satire kept breaking in, but no one who looks closely at Voltaire can fail to see the religion in him. On his estate at Ferney near Geneva he built a church, acquired a relic for it from the pope, and inscribed on the wall: 'Voltaire built this for God.' From Ferney he defended oppressed people all over Europe, usually those who were in trouble because of their opinions. Some of his books were unkind about religion or religious people, for example *La Pucelle*, about Joan of Arc. His novella *Candide* was a brilliant attack not on religion, but on those who think that to be religious is to suppose that all is for the best in this world, even when appalling disasters happen – he was writing just after Lisbon was destroyed by an earthquake. The Old Testament does present extraordinary stories, and Voltaire loved to make fun of them, treating them as Bayle had done but with more satire and mockery. He wrote articles for the French *Encylopédie*, and later collected these in his own *Dictionnaire philosophique*, in which the anti-Church strand in him was at its most powerful. People thought him only a mocker, that everything was on the surface and nothing deep, that he had nothing to say that could help humanity, he was a knocker down and not a builder up, a clever man but not a thinker.

But he did make a difference to Christian history. The churches, carrying their message of hope for humanity, were encumbered with

an increasing load. The Inquisition was a symbol of its attempt to control by force opinions that its leaders found unacceptable. Almost as burdensome was the conviction that every word of the Bible must be true. People were more educated and realized that the doctrine of God in parts of the Old Testament was impossible. It became ridiculous to contend that in order to believe in God Almighty it was necessary also to suppose that he made the world in seven days, or drowned everyone but eight people in a universal flood, or told

Voltaire. The Latin reads 'later he will be beloved by posterity, at the moment he is loved by his friends'.

King David to count his people and then killed seventy thousand of them for no good reason.

Voltaire may have hurt the churches with his pen; but he started them on a necessary revision of their teachings. Attitudes to persecution, fanaticism, superstition, could never be the same. Voltaire, jesting to the last, ordered that his tomb at Ferney should be half in the church and half outside it. His jests usually carried truth. He was spiritually half outside because he could never be comfortable with the Church as he found it; and half inside because he was aware of influencing the churches for the better.

There were aspects of morals as then taught which he assailed, and by doing so began to change them. He wrote an encyclopaedia article called 'Why?'. Why do half the girls in Europe say their prayers in Latin which they do not understand? Is it right that divorce should be impossible to get in half Europe and difficult to get in the other half, and does this make for moral behaviour if we wish to make adultery less common? As for adultery, if the woman commits it she is pilloried and penalized, if the man commits it no one minds; is this just? He did not agree with Bayle in thinking reason a useless way to find the truth. And, though Bayle was more obviously a Christian than he, Voltaire did not share his view that morals could be separated from religion without danger to society.

CHANGES IN CHRISTIAN IDEAS

There began to be adjustments in Christian doctrines, and for the better. Partly this was a discarding of old myths, though few noticed that they were being discarded. Examples are the myth of Antichrist, and the nature of hell and of Christ's descent into it.

Antichrist
The word 'antichrist' is found three times in the New Testament, in the letters of St John; but as a general word for an opponent of Christ, not as an incarnation of evil. He was a person who teaches untruths about Christ;

especially that he was not the Messiah and that he had no human body. The idea of a supernatural opponent of Christ was a borrowing from pre-Christian myths, of battles between good and evil powers in heaven. By AD 200 Christians began to pen books about Antichrist, as a king who sends out his messengers, and the chief enemy of God. St Augustine used the language of the Book of Revelation to describe him bringing in a reign of a thousand years in which he torments the disciples.

By 950 Antichrist had a biography. He was born of human parents, but was soon possessed by the devil and endowed with the desire to make himself into a god. He was born in Babylon, educated at Bethsaida and trained by magicians. His aim was to make a kingdom of the devil on earth. He was held in check by the Church and its bishops and kings, but in the end he would win for a while and have a world empire with its capital in Jerusalem – until Christ and the archangel Michael destroyed him on the Mount of Olives. He was no longer a literary myth; the people in the pews knew about him. And as he became real he could be applied to any power that was thought wicked, even a 'wicked' emperor such as the German-Sicilian Frederick II; while dissenters against the papacy used his name to abuse the pope.

Martin Luther was slow to take up the idea when he revolted against the pope; but he did believe that the pope stood for the opposite of what was true; and so Antichrist came into Protestant thought, no longer as a person with a biography, but as a living institution, the Curia of Rome. This usage lasted in Northern Europe for nearly a century and a half. It then vanished except among eccentrics. The idea of Antichrist yielded to the less mythical one of an anti-Christian. But he remained in some forms of literature; in the late nineteenth century he was central to the thinking of Nietzsche and his notions of the superman.

The history of Antichrist shows how a myth could be taken up, expanded and used – and then, suddenly, within only two or three decades, seen to be nothing to do with faith.

Hell

Martin Luther disliked the idea of purgatory. Hell was in the Bible, but not with crude pictures, and Luther did not lay much stress on it. What mattered was heaven; he wanted to be rid of medieval pictures of torment.

In the seventeenth century there were teachers who said that because God is love, hell cannot be eternal; but we should not say this aloud, for it would make the people worse. By 1700 a few voices began to question whether hell was as sharp a spur to good life as had been thought. No one believed they had done anything worthy of such a fate; they were all sure that, however vile, what they had done would be forgiven.

There began to be a long Protestant doubt about hell. For many, the future pain ceased to be physical and became mental, and was caused by the free will of the subject and not by God. Some suggested that the wicked cease to be; there is no hell, only extinction, which is the natural fate of humanity, while heaven is for those who have a kinship with God. There were those who said that God would in the end bring all humanity to himself. If it were said that society needs the restraint of hell, the reply now might be that Christianity is not there to police society but to lead to God.

After 1700 there was far more liberty and variety of belief among the churches. But the power of hell and the conviction of its reality, however mental or spiritual that reality might be, were shown much later, in the early twentieth century.

John Henry Newman was a liberal-minded English Roman Catholic who had been an Anglican and the leader of the high church movement known as the Oxford Movement. In 1865 he wrote a poem, *The Dream of Gerontius*. This is the agony of a man near death who knows that the devils are at him and hell looms; and the poem tells how with the help of angels he comes through to faith and a conviction of safety. The public at first took little notice of it. But thirty-five years later it became a public profession of the fear of hell, when the composer Edward Elgar made the poem into an oratorio, his master-piece. It was performed again and again, not only in Britain. In theory people could listen to the music without paying the least attention to death or hell. But oratorios have a strange power to drive words into the listener's mind. Newman's poem achieved a far wider influence than the words by themselves could have won. Despite the doubters of the eighteenth century, it did not seem that hell had died — perhaps not even purgatory.

Christ's descent into hell

The early Christians thought of Christ as going into Hades, the realm of departed spirits, to show them the Gospel; and so the saving grace of God was not to be denied to those who lived before Christ. Sometimes they saw him as fulfilling for our sakes the worst fate of humanity, submitting himself to the rulers of hell. In their forms of worship the sense was of victory, over all the powers of darkness.

The words 'he descended into hell' were added to the creed in 359 by a council at Sirmium (in modern Serbia). In the later Middle Ages the story had a big part in mystery plays. One of the earliest plays to be written in the English language, at the beginning of the fourteenth century, was *The Harrowing of Hell*. People felt the subject important because it answered a puzzle about God's pity: did he condemn everyone who lived before Christ? The Eastern Church used the idea much in paintings: Christ stands over the gate of hell and pulls up his forerunners such as King David, King Solomon or John the Baptist. In the West they were often drawn out of the jaws of a wild beast.

In the Reformation some thought that in the creed the word 'hell' meant only the grave. But Dürer and Tintoretto still drew the scene. Then the West lost interest in it. With the decline of the moral importance of hell as a place of punishment, people stopped making pictures of the descent into hell. The phrase in the creed became a relic, a poetic assertion of the solidarity of Jesus with all the dead, no longer needed as proof of the justice of God.

CHAPTER SIX

THE MODERN AGE

THE FRENCH REVOLUTION

In 1789 France had the most flourishing Catholic church in the world. Then an anti-Catholic government murdered priests and nuns and drove many more of them out of the country, shut churches and tried to destroy religion. What had happened to the religion, supposed to be of meekness and quiet, that it could arouse such hate?

The first reason is one of mob psychology. Compare the Spanish civil war of 1936: Spain was a very Catholic country, yet Spanish republicans and anarchists all over the country murdered priests and nuns who had done them no wrong. They were the symbols (though only in part the reality) of conservatism. But a more important reason is that they did good, and in a desperate fight you must pass the point of no return by doing something unforgiveable; to shoot nuns who minister to the sick is the most unforgiveable of acts.

The French revolutionaries did not start with murder in mind. At first they did no more than Protestants had done centuries before. They seized the property of the Church to rescue France from bankruptcy. They abolished monks as useless and cathedral chapters as unnecessary, lessened the pope's power over bishops, and let bishops and clergy be elected by the people in an effort to make the Church more democratic. Pope Pius VI naturally condemned these changes, but they had a chance of working – until the new leaders of the state moved away from religion altogether.

Then was the religion of Europe less deeply rooted than anyone thought? Did everyone go to church because the king did, and the upper classes, and the village needed to conform? If you cut off the king's head and exiled the ruling class, would prayer no longer be found in ordinary men and women?

It looked alarmingly as if, when the murders were over and France returned to sanity, nothing could restore the status religion had before the old state broke down. After Napoleon put down the radicals and restored a bourgeois France, he again made the Catholic church an accepted organ of the state. But when he invaded Russia and thousands of his soldiers lay wounded in Moscow hospitals, the chaplains who ministered to the wounded found little in their heads but ignorance of religion, and hardly any wish for its consolation in their pain. That was something new in Europe.

INDUSTRY AND THE CHURCHES

The new industries did good to churches. First, they made wealth. That made it possible for churches to build many more places of worship in the new towns to which the people were moving. Never before was there such an age of church and chapel building as now in the nineteenth century. The styles were various; Gothic, classical, or Greek/Russian Orthodox, with soaring vaults, splendid domes or corrugated iron roofs. But the favourite was Gothic. People valued the old churches, which were mostly from the high Middle Ages, and thought that modern churches should look like them.

New industry needed many more educated people. New wealth enabled the making of a national system of education. The number of people who could read and write rose rapidly.

The new towns needed new ways of collecting congregations. The chief of these started in Britain: the Methodists. But their first inspiration came from among the German Lutherans.

In Germany reform kept throwing up idealists discontented with the church system. The most important were the Pietists, founded – as far as any one person was responsible – by Philip Spener, a pastor in Frankfurt from 1666. He set a new standard of piety by adding to the church services meetings in the home where laity led as easily as pastors; they studied the Bible, practised prayer and fostered charity, and the stress was on the inner life more than on any ritual.

The movement enriched evangelical devotion in Germany, and Pietist hymns added to the range of hymnody.

From among the Pietists Moravians brought a form of German evangelical Pietism into Britain. If the Lutheran church in Germany needed inwardness, so did the Church of England. John Wesley was touched by the Moravians, and created his Methodists as quiet groups of godly, Bible-reading people, standing by the Church and not separated from it. From this movement also came a rich heritage of hymnody.

Methodism was a response to the coming of the machines and the new industrial slums where there were no churches. If the official churches were slow to help them, then let an unofficial church send people out to show them the true message. Touring the country and addressing meetings of as many as 30,000 people, he travelled more miles on horseback than any previous evangelist. The separatist trend of all Pietist groups finally made the Methodist churches part from the parent Church of England even before John Wesley died in 1791.

THE MODERN HYMN

The hymn as we know its use in modern days could only flower when the people were literate; that is, when education reached nearly everyone, which it began to do after 1800. During the eighteenth century, English evangelical writers, Methodists and others, wrote

hymns of all kinds; two of the best were Anglicans – Charles Wesley, John's brother who wrote 'Hark, the herald angels sing', and the troubled William Cowper, who wrote 'O for a closer walk with God'. Their heirs produced a flood of beautiful hymnody (and a good deal of doggerel) in which leading poets took their share. Newman's 'Lead, kindly light', a portrait of a soul walking in darkness and unsure of the way but coming through to faith, suited the mood of many in the nineteenth century, who hesitated in their belief and yet longed to come through the gloom to make an act of faith.

This modern flowering of the hymn changed the feel of Christian worship. During the nineteenth century the clergy even began

John Wesley in 1766; the best-known portrait of him, by Nathanael Hone; in the normal dress of an Anglican preacher of the age, and at a time when Methodists had not yet formed a denomination, though plainly that was coming.

to allow the singing of carols in church services. The people used their lungs in praise and prayer as they had never used them before. It did not do to examine the words too closely: Good King Wenceslas really existed, a pious king of Bohemia who was murdered; he was not known to have looked out over the snow on the feast of St Stephen.

Critics were not sure at the way things were going; they thought that if you bellow 'Praise, my soul, the king of heaven' at the top of your voice you are unlikely to consider what the words mean. But this was not the common opinion. Certain groups, such as some (but not all) of the Quakers, rejected hymn singing, maintaining that we are aware of God's presence through silence, and so all prayer and praise should arise out of silence.

THE 'END' OF SLAVERY

Not long after the French revolution, the churches made a big different to the ending of slavery.

People disagreed as to whether it was possible or right to abolish it. In the eighteenth century Samuel Johnson, a devout Anglican, was passionately against slavery; his biographer James Boswell records that 'Upon one occasion, when in company with some very grave men at Oxford, his toast was, "Here's to the next insurrection of the negroes in the West Indies."' Johnson said that moral right was being forced to give way to political convenience: 'No man is by nature the property of another.' Boswell, a Scottish Presbyterian by upbringing, protested (though not to Johnson's face) that it saved many Africans from a worse fate.

The two attitudes lasted long. During most of the Middle Ages the work of freeing slaves by ransom was regarded as a good work; and orders of monks, such as the Mercedarians, were founded to win liberty for slaves. Yet when the great campaign began in the late eleventh century to stop the clergy from having wives, it was ruled that such wives, as illegal persons, might be sold into slavery.

The opening of the Americas, and the desperate need for the good labour without which the American colonies could not exist, made the moving of slaves across the Atlantic the most profitable trade in the world. Slavery was not only an American phenomenon. When Francis Xavier, to whom none can deny the title of saint, heard that the college at Goa was in debt, he suggested that a way out was to buy some slaves.

Morality has no force to stop the most profitable of trades when there is no physical means of stopping it. Until the coming of steam-powered warships in the late nineteenth century it was hard to patrol the seas and intercept slave ships. Between 1750 and 1865 it took a huge effort by European sea powers to stop the slave trade; and in the United States it took a civil war.

The leaders in the campaign against slavery were of five kinds: the intellectuals of the Enlightenment; the more humane of the American and French revolutionaries; Catholic missionaries in the Americas (the Jesuits never allowed slaves in their settlements); some radical Christians, such as the Quakers (William Penn would not allow slaves in 'his' colony of Pennsylvania), and devout English evangelicals led by the parliamentarian William Wilberforce. This last was of importance because Britain had much to lose, in money and property, through ending slavery. It abolished the slave trade in 1807, and used its warships to enforce those laws; this had a great effect on other nations. But Britain did not finally abolish slavery itself until 1833.

This was an influence of the churches on a moral stain which could be abolished only at the cost of many people's prosperity.

The abolitions went on, slowly. Russia abolished serfdom in 1861; there were still half a million slaves in Cuba as late as 1875; Brazil did not abolish slavery till 1888; it persisted for even longer in some Arab countries. But it was a doctrine of the ancient Greeks that slavery cannot be got rid of however hard you try, and it often continued in secret.

There has been some evidence in the 1990s of a revival of slavery, perhaps in Brazil and elsewhere in Latin America, perhaps in North Africa, perhaps in the Middle East.

Spirituals

The slaves in the southern United States created a rare form of worship. As the frontier of the States moved westward, it was always ahead of the builders of churches. Services often took the form of 'revivalist meetings', with large crowds but no priest or pastor, just someone who led the singing of hymns. These hymns were not of the usual kind, but often had the character of folk songs. Others were versions of hymns sung at early Methodist camp meetings. Their unusual feature originated in an old habit started in the sixteenth century when pastors taught their people, still largely illiterate, to sing. It was called 'lining out': the pastor sang a line or two of a metrical psalm and then the congregation sang the words after him. On the American frontier the leader would sing a line and then the crowd sang a refrain or chorus. In these conditions the leader could vary or ornament the tune a little, and members of the crowd could add interjections of 'Glory' or 'Alleluia' or sing a descant. It was no longer formal singing, but free. Following a custom that had existed since the early Middle Ages, the higher male voices carried the tune.

The southern blacks of the United States applied their African genius for music to these camp hymns and created what became known as 'spirituals'. The oppressed on earth sang of their longing for heaven, of faith in the coming glory, of the rout of Satan, of forgiveness, of healing, of freedom from the chains of the world, of the brightness of the light to come. Sometimes the melody was accompanied by free descants and rhythmical swaying, or clapping, or nodding the head. They were sung not only at meetings, but as work songs to ease any repetitive task, such as unloading at the docks or paddling up the river. They were very biblical: there were more references to the angels Michael and Gabriel than to the saints; there were Martha, Mary and Lazarus, and Moses passing through the Red Sea, Jacob wrestling all night at the ford, and his ladder running from earth to heaven, and Daniel safe in the lions' den.

> *Leader*: De talles' tree in Paradise
> De Christian call de tree of life.
> *Chorus*: And I hope dat trump might blow
>   me home
> To de new Jerusalem.
> Blow your trumpet, Gabriel, blow
> Louder, louder,
> And I hope dat trump might blow me home
> To de new Jerusalem.
> *Leader*: Paul and Silas, bound in jail
> Sing God's praise both night and day.
> *Chorus*: And I hope . . .

The spirituals were far from the metrical psalms which made the tradition of modern hymnody. They were unique in Christendom, stemming partly from the African love of song and partly from the social conditions. After the American civil war and the freeing of the slaves, the music was taken up into a wider context and once more influenced by historic European hymnody. Conversely the spiritual affected the form of white folk songs, of which the most famous was:

> John Brown's body lies a-mould'ring in
>   the grave,
> But his soul goes marching on.
> *Chorus*: Glory, glory, alleluia . . .

Except for the form and the simplicity, this was very unlike the spiritual in feeling. The magic of the spiritual was its peace of heaven; John Brown was a fanatic who killed to free slaves, and this was a war song.

THE SHRINKING WORLD

The postal service became cheap and rapid. This started the Christmas card; the first one was sent in Britain in 1843, only thirteen years after the opening of the first passenger

Millais' *Christ in the House of his Parents*; painted 1850, a landmark in the history of the realist painting of the Holy Family; bitterly attacked at the time for its realism.

railway. The custom grew rapidly, and not only in Britain; it spread to non-Christians. By the time Queen Victoria died, everyone was affectionately familiar with the biblical scenes such as the nativity – the manger, the ox and the ass, the shepherds, the three wise men. The Christmas card helped the popularity of the carol, and vice versa.

The railway made pilgrimage possible as never before. Rome and Jerusalem became well known to Westerners, Greeks and Russians alike. The experience was less spiritually transforming than before: pilgrims no longer arrived after months of plodding through country infested with brigands, but in Pullman cars and charabancs. But in an age when the world was growing more secular, the shrines evoked a new fervour and new crowds, sometimes numbering millions.

The engraving had been known since before the Reformation, but now reproduction of pictures was cheaper. Working-class homes started to have religious pictures on the walls.

One of these images had a special place in the English speaking-lands. Holman Hunt was a member of the 'Pre-Raphaelites', a group resolved to promote a truthful style in painting. In 1854, when he was a young man and not specially devout, he painted Christ as *The Light of the World*. In it Jesus stands bearded and barefoot, with a crown of thorns on his head, in a long priestly robe and carrying a lantern. His white halo is bright against the darkness behind. With his right hand he knocks on an old door, long unopened, for up it grow weeds and creepers. Hunt intended the picture as a symbol of Christ asking to be let into the minds that are shut so obstinately. In painting it he found his own conversion, and spent several years in Palestine painting scenes from the New Testament.

At first the picture was poorly reviewed by the art experts, but within thirty years there would be a print hanging on the walls of many poor people as well as of the children of the well-to-do. The subject was taken up by poets and made the matter of sermons. In Britain, among the British overseas and in America it became a picture as well known, and as important in religion, as a Madonna by Raphael or Leonardo's *Last Supper*. Popular affection for it lasted right up until the Second World War.

Other sacred pictures were popular but did not reach quite such an enormous public. One enchanting work by Hunt was *The Triumph of the Innocents*. Mary and her child ride to Egypt to escape from Herod's massacre; on the road they are escorted by a little host of friendly children or cherubs, the spirits of the babies who were killed.

SOCIALISM

In Europe in the 1830s there were for the first time idealists who offered to make a Christian society although they could not themselves profess Christian faith in any known form. Would it be possible by state action to make a society where there are no poor people; where all people are educated and no longer brutes in their morals? Get rid of poverty, not by handouts or unemployment pay, but by changing the structure of society. Society can be made better, not by better morals instilled by religion, but by changing the laws so that no one will need to steal. Burglary will not be necessary, and capitalist exploitation will not be possible, because all property will belong to the state.

Some of the theorists held that private property is theft. They applied to all the world the doctrine of the monks, that no one owns anything but everyone is allowed to use what belongs to the monastery. Most church people disliked this doctrine on the grounds that to own things is an essence of human freedom and that the right of a human to be human depends on a measure of possession.

Second, the proposed redistribution of goods could not be done without revolution, since those who 'owned' the goods would not let them go without a battle. There was talk of a class war – the poor against the rich – to achieve the rights of the poor. The churches certainly could not accept a doctrine which

John Keble, poet and pastor, one of the best of Victorian clergy in England; by George Richmond.

recommended members of a community or a nation to kill other members, even to achieve equality among the survivors. They believed in God and the individual, and they feared a doctrine which seemed to say that certain persons had no rights in the community.

But as they thought about the schemes of this sort that were offered, some of them saw that the theory might be married to Christian ideals. The Hebrew prophets from Amos onward were full of the cry for social justice, the hatred of oppression, the wickedness of 'grinding the faces' of the poor. The Virgin Mary's hymn, the Magnificat, was quoted: 'He hath put down the mighty from their seat: and hath exalted the humble and meek.' They looked in the Acts of the Apostles and found that the earliest community at Jerusalem had 'all things common'. And though they did not much consider the sixteenth century, they could have appealed to some of the thinkers in the early Reformation, who argued for cities doing with their money and for their poor

Holman Hunt's *The Light of the World*, 1854; much used in modern devotion.

something like what the new socialists now wanted.

The name 'Christian Socialist' was thought a contradiction in terms when it was first heard in 1848, a time of fear of a Chartist revolution in Britain. During a huge demonstration on Kennington Common, a group of three — one being the professor of divinity at King's College, London, Frederick Denison Maurice — adopted this name. They were not very socialist except that they had vague ideals for the workers, but the name they took was destined to a long history in the churches of Britain, Germany, Italy and the United States. In 1849 Paris saw a banquet of 33 'socialist priests' who drank a toast to 'Jesus Christ, the father of socialism'.

In 1864 Pope Pius IX formally condemned socialism. Kaiser Wilhelm II of Germany said that Christian Socialism was a nonsense and a contradiction. An occasional German Lutheran pastor took a socialist line, but would usually be expected to resign his position. It was a long time before the Lutheran Church would tolerate socialists as pastors. The German socialist parties were more anti-Christian than the Labour Party in England ever was; for many of the British socialists were trained in their young years as pious members of dissenting chapels, many others were Irish labourers who looked to their English Cardinal Manning to present their radical needs, and members of the middle class looked back with respect to the theologian Maurice who first invented the idea of Christian Socialism.

Leo XIII published the encyclical *Rerum novarum* in 1891. This still condemned socialism. But *Rerum novarum* went so far in accepting what socialism stood for that afterwards it was looked back on as the key that allowed priests to work with socialists in the reform of society. It spoke of the dignity of the worker and his or her rights as a human being; of the right of the state to act in creating conditions of social justice; of the right of workers to form unions to protect themselves; of their right to a decent wage and a share of the profits. In the long view this encyclical made possible the Catholic social democratic parties of the twentieth century in Italy, Germany and Belgium and at moments in France.

The German Karl Marx provided a theory of the reconstruction of society for the benefit of the worker. He called religion 'the opium of the people', a way to keep them happy in illusions until society is made just, after which they would not need religion, so it would vanish. He was not overtly hostile to religion: although it was part of the society that needed overthrowing, it still helped the people. He did not want states to persecute it, because he expected it to disappear of itself. But disciples of Marx, such as Engels and Lenin, took a grimmer view: this thing called religion hurts the people by turning their eyes skyward, away from what matters — food and material well-being.

By an accident of history — Russia's war-weakened state in 1917 — Lenin came to power. He was dedicated to hard forms of the theories of Marx; in the civil war that followed his coup, in which many churchmen were against his Bolsheviks, his forces destroyed churches, shot their priests and bishops, and seized their properties. The Russian Orthodox Church survived, but it was regarded by the leaders of society as a bad influence on the state and the people, which must be discouraged so that children did not grow up to follow their parents. No Christian could now be given any responsible office in the civil service or in teaching, no Christian books might be published, and many churches were closed and turned over to other uses.

Yet the worst time for the Church and especially for the clergy was not under Lenin but under his successor Stalin, in the later thirties; for when Stalin started a murderous repression of the middle classes (including leading communists), he killed many priests and exiled many others to Siberia.

It was only when the Nazis invaded Russia in 1941 and the Russian armies suffered calamities that the mood changed. Stalin still held the same crude opinion about the Church. But he realized that he needed the backing of every Russian if Russia was not to be conquered by Hitler, so he allowed it limited freedom. Khrushchev, when he came to power in 1955, renewed the persecution to some extent, locking up dissidents, shutting churches, and having compliant stooges appointed bishops and abbots; but Russia never went back to the fearful days of the thirties under Stalin. When at last liberty came again with Gorbachev, the Church had an organization in being to train clergy, foster congregations and revive monasteries. It was an astonishing survival: an all-powerful government had tried for seventy years to destroy the Orthodox Church, but it was still near the heart of the true Russia.

The cathedral and the atheists

In 1812, to celebrate his victory over Napoleon, Tsar Alexander I commanded a cathedral to be built. Vast sums were spent, but not a stone was laid, and the architect was sent off to exile. Tsar Nicholas I chose a new architect and a site next to the Kremlin wall, where he pulled down a church, a convent and some other buildings to make room. The building was designed to have space for 10,000 people. Round the ambulatory were paintings of the history of the war with Napoleon. It had five domes, and the top cross was 320 feet high. It took more than fifty years to build, but at last the Cathedral of our Saviour was consecrated in 1883, an occasion for which Tchaikovsky composed his *1812 Overture*.

After the revolution the dean was taken away to prison and never came back; the archpriest was executed; so was his successor. The city council decided that the building was useless. They needed a new palace of the soviets, so they blew up the cathedral; the top dome came down with a tremendous crash. But the palace of soviets was as slow in building as the cathedral, and was still unfinished in 1941

A rare early photograph of the cathedral of Saint Saviour, Moscow, built 1830-85 to remember victory over Napoleon, destroyed by Stalin.

The church of St Mary of Smolensk in Moscow, built by the Tsar Basil early in the sixteenth century to celebrate the capture of Smolensk from the Poles; in 1680 it was given a superb iconostasis which marks the start of Russian baroque; and the bell tower (to the left) a few years later.

when Russia faced a new invader. Work stopped. The result, after four Tsars and two dictators had spent vast piles of state money, was a space which was used as the site of a public swimming pool; even this fell into disuse. In 1994 there was a proposal to rebuild the cathedral – not that there was any money to do so, just as a gesture of defiance towards the memory of Stalin.

This history has a lesson. The defence against Napoleon's aggression was a just war, fought against heavy odds. Victory called for an act of thanksgiving; and the traditional way for a state to show gratitude was to build a church. When a Tsar built a church it had to be impressive; it was a matter of his reputation, his respect among the people. It was like Justinian and St Sophia, or Henry VI and the chapel of King's College, Cambridge, or Julius II and the new St Peter's. Such a building was hard even for a rich state to pay for, took many years to finish, and then had to be expensively maintained. But the building was an assertion of national pride, a people's thanks for rescue from conquest. When the religion, not of the people but of the managers of the state, changed in 1918, they tried to substitute their own form of church, a palace of the soviets. That failed, not because it was harder to pay for, but because the new religion of the state was feeble in comparison to the old religion of Holy Russia.

La Sainte-Chapelle

An atheist state was not alone in doing odd things to churches. The Sainte-Chapelle in Paris is a reliquary, a casket to house sacred relics. It was built to honour the crown of thorns that the soldiers put upon Jesus' head before his crucifixion. We first hear of this crown during the fifth century, when it was kept reverently in a church at Jerusalem. About the time of the Norman conquest of England, the Muslims in Palestine turned against Christian pilgrims; so for safety the crown was moved to Constantinople, where it became one of the prized possessions of the Byzantine. When the fourth crusade sacked

Constantinople, the invaders installed an emperor who was a Frenchman and a Roman Catholic. These new Latin emperors of Constantinople were always short of money. One of them, Baldwin II, sold the crown of thorns, with part of the lance said to have pierced Jesus' side, for a large sum to the very religious French King Louis IX (afterwards St Louis).

Louis determined to build a home worthy of so sacred an object. The Sainte-Chapelle is a superb example of the Gothic style at its peak, with audaciously slim walls framing huge windows showing the passion of Jesus, stories from the Old Testament, and St Louis with his relic. Later he bought and added fragments of the true cross. His royal successors used to show the crown to the people on Good Fridays; when the English briefly ruled Paris during the Hundred Years' War their commander displayed the relic as proxy for his king, Henry VI.

Just before the French revolution the French government, as short of cash as Baldwin had been, closed the chapel. The revolution brought anti-religious riots; the chapel was polluted; most of the relics were evacuated to Notre-Dame, where they still are (the lance went to the national library, where it was lost). The chapel became a clubroom, then a warehouse, and then an archive for lawyers, full of dusty files.

It was fifty years before the government felt shame that this supreme example of Gothic art should be full of junk. It was opened for services, and romantic architects with middling taste restored it. Then the anti-clericalism which was a bitter legacy of the revolution was provoked by the Dreyfus scandal; in 1905 Church and state separated, and the chapel was emptied.

So the Sainte-Chapelle stands now — crowded with sightseers, as cold and elegant as ever, but without heart. How odd is Christendom! The very crown of thorns that was said to have circled Jesus' head, and for a thousand years and more was instinct with the recollection of his suffering and given all that

devotion could do to surround it with beauty was sold by a bankrupt pseudo-emperor, rescued from an atheist mob only to be forgotten in a cathedral treasury; and left behind it the art that once surrounded it, beauty frozen into a box of ice by the contempt of the twentieth century; enthralling to the student of medieval art, painful to the lover of God.

National Socialism

Hitler was a lapsed Austrian Catholic who hated Catholics and despised Protestants. When he was made chancellor in 1933 he said that his government saw Christianity as the unshakeable basis of the moral life of the German people. He had a clear idea of how to get the backing of those who distrusted him. But he also had a dogma of his own which was vague but powerful — that providence was in him. He did not feel a man of God, but a man of destiny. This quasi-religious conviction did him nothing but good in the first months of his rule, when he won the trust of most of the German people.

In retrospect it was hard to understand how so many church people, both Catholic and Protestant, could back such a person who, for all his fair words, was already beginning to destroy what they stood for. Christianity was international and stood for peace and harmony between peoples; the new German leaders hated anything international and thought that peace in Europe was a plot to keep Germany in chains. To the outside world the ideals of Christianity and the ideals of the Nazis were opposite.

That was not how it looked to people inside Germany. For the ten years before Hitler they had had inflation on an unimaginable scale, massive unemployment, poverty. The new leaders called for moral qualities in the nation: self-sacrifice, hard work, honour, courage. Lucky to have gained power when the economy was recovering (which they ascribed to their own skill), they appealed to the nation to work together as one people under one leader to save Germany and restore it to its rightful place in the world. When Hitler gained

The Sainte-Chapelle, Paris,
built by St Louis to house the
crown of thorns, now with the
religious shrine empty at the
apse and with no religious
services.

power, only about a third of the people voted for him. By the end of the year he had about two-thirds in his favour, so powerful was his call to the nation. And among them were many devout Catholics and Protestants.

The next year, 1934, saw the start of a change in opinion. The Nazis decreed that no Jew could be a minister in a Christian church, and that Jews ought not to be in the same congregation as Germans. Some churchmen, led by Martin Niemöller, pastor of Berlin-Dahlem, found this intolerable. Around this main issue gathered other doubts about Nazi interference with the churches. At the end of May 1934 a protesting synod met at Barmen in Westphalia and created the Confessing Church, a loose group of all those who would not accept the exclusion of the Jews and reasserted the need of faithfulness to the truths of the Bible. The fight was partly about doctrine (because of the Jews) and partly about the freedom of the churches from the state. They were much influenced by the Biblical theology of the Swiss Karl Barth, who in June 1935 was forced out of his professorship at Bonn and moved to Basle. From Switzerland he continued to be one of the leaders of the Confessing Church, though his works were banned in Germany.

The German leaders of the Confessing Church were continually liable to bans on preaching, heckling in their church services, seizure of papers, house searches and imprisonment. In March 1935 some five hundred of the Confessing pastors spent a short time in prison. Niemöller was arrested in July 1937, effectively acquitted by a court in March 1938, and at once rearrested by the Gestapo; he was to remain in concentration camps till the end of the Second World War. His rearrest caused a wave of international condemnation and made the Confessing Church leaders heroes to the outside world.

While this restored the honour of Christianity in Germany, the result was schism among the various German Protestant churches, which weakened their ability to stand together against the state.

Those who were ready to hope for the best from Hitler joined what was called the 'German Christian' movement. This aimed to increase the weight of the churches in society by uniting all the Protestants into a single organization under an archbishop called the *Reichsbischof*; by accepting that Jews could not take part but should have their separate congregations; and by redrafting theology to make it less remote and archaic, so that it spoke more directly to working people – this included discarding the 'Jewish' Old Testament. The most effective of these groups was in Thuringia where two evangelists – Nazis in social thought and radical Lutheran in dogma, using jazz and nationalistic songs as well as hymns – enthused crowds.

As Europe edged towards war the repression of the churches worsened. Almost all religious education stopped, many more pastors went to prison, where a few were murdered, the last surviving parish magazines were closed. It became clear that if Germany won the war the Nazis would try to destroy

Dietrich Bonhoeffer, aged 29, Christian resister to Nazi philosophy, and a martyr.

the churches. One of their last victims was a courageous and thinking younger member of the Confessing Church, Dietrich Bonhoeffer, who had a small part in the plot to kill Hitler which failed in July 1944.

The Catholic Church in Germany suffered as badly or worse under the Nazis, though it was less divided. In July 1933 Pope Pius XI shocked the democratic world by signing a concordat with Hitler, which was very favourable to the rights of the Catholic churches in the German states. The Nazis had no intention of keeping this agreement, and gradually moved towards outright repression; they staged prosecutions of monks for homosexuality, with the maximum of publicity. In 1937 Pius issued an encyclical, *Mit brennender Sorge* ('With burning anxiety'), in which he listed all the breaches of the concordat committed by the Germans. The encyclical was smuggled into Germany and read from pulpits on Palm Sunday. It made the repression far worse; but it too was necessary to Christian honour.

When the Second World War began and the Germans conquered the Catholic country of Poland, the Nazis shot many Polish priests and a few bishops. Perhaps this was more because these clergy were leaders of the people than because they were ministers of religion. Yet the religious element was there, and many Poles were true martyrs: six bishops, 1926 priests, 580 monks, 289 nuns and many more went into concentration camps. Only Stalin committed a worse persecution of a Christian community. It would be known in history as the Martyrdom of Poland if it were not overshadowed by a worse crime.

An Anglican priest in a Stepney parish, east London, early in the Second World War.

The Nazi onslaught, combined almost at the same time with Stalin's murders of church people, caused a revival of respect for religion in the West – for a decade or two. If these massacres happened when Europe started to repudiate Christianity, the answer must, at least in part, be to return to all that was best in the moral traditions of Christendom. An attack on human rights could be condemned only if human rights had a place in the scheme of the universe; that is, only if there existed a religious apprehension of humanity and its place in the world.

The Holocaust

The killing of Jews was made possible by total war on the eastern front, which began in June 1941. But it was made easier to carry out by the hatred of Jews poured out by Nazi orators during the previous years. It was the worst stain yet on an allegedly Christian Europe. The horror raised two questions that troubled the Churches to their depths.

First, how could it have happened? How could fanatical, irrational antisemitism grip educated men and women? At the end of the war there began a long enquiry into the causes. Even the old Romans had looked down on Jews because they did not conform. Was that all it was, nothing to do with religion, merely that a majority in a society disliked a minority which rejected its customs? Was it a case of better weapons to kill?

This cannot be the sole explanation for anyone who studies the nature of antisemitic fanaticism.

Or – and this was what was so troubling – was it anything to do with Christianity? Christianity was a religion which sprang from the Jews. Was blame – blame is too weak a word – cast on a whole people and religion because centuries earlier a few of the Jews had pressed a Roman governor to crucify Jesus?

The second question that troubled them was their own record. Did religious folk let the killing happen by keeping silent out of fear for themselves? In 1960 the Israelis kidnapped Adolf Eichmann, who had organized trains to carry the victims to their deaths, and tried him in Jerusalem. This brought the debate on the Holocaust to the centre of thought among the churches and made for a new attitude to Judaism, which was helped by a more sympathetic attitude among Jews to Christianity. Every weighty meeting, Catholic or Protestant, had a resolution to condemn antisemitism or any talk that the Jews should be blamed for the death of Jesus. In April 1986 Pope John Paul II represented this turn in everyone by joining in prayers at the synagogue in Rome, the first Pope ever to do so.

CONSCIENCE AND WAR

The early Christians recognized that there had to be wars at times, because that is the nature of the fallen human race. St Augustine said that the idea that war is always wrong is a heresy. His idea of a just war included advance into another's land if that land was in a state of anarchy – he would regard as a just war an invasion of Bosnia or Rwanda by United Nations armies to stop murder and lawlessness. Everyone agreed that the aim of a war must be to gain peace. A war is good if it stops evil being done.

Does the duty to obey the state mean that a man must serve in an army which he thinks is engaged in a bad cause? Yet the soldier must obey. The medieval schoolmen were agreed that no one ought to obey an order he knows to be immoral. According to this doctrine it is no excuse, say, for an SS man in Poland who kills a Jew to claim that he was ordered to shoot and had to obey. But the schoolmen allowed the plea of ignorance. Often soldiers have no idea whether what they are told to do is moral or not; and if so they have a duty to obey.

So there arose the idea of just and unjust war. When is it right to go to war? And what is it right to do when one is at war – what weapons may one use, how should one treat prisoners? In the earlier centuries the first question was much the more pressing; in the last two centuries the second became the more urgent. The second question was first raised formally in 1139 at the second Council of the Lateran when it condemned the newly introduced crossbow as an immoral weapon not to be used in a Christian fight, but as allowable in a war with Saracens if the other side used bows. As with all later condemnations of types of weapons up to hydrogen bombs and bacteria, the generals took no notice and the crossbowmen became the most important corps in several armies.

These debates influenced the treatment of prisoners of war, forbidding their murder; and of non-combatants. Their judgements would certainly have condemned the area bombings in which all sides engaged during the Second World War because the chief sufferers were (and sometimes were intended to be) non-combatants, innocent townsfolk.

The rise of large sovereign national states cast a doubt on the idea of the just war. For the eighteenth-century war was part of a political game between states, an instrument of policy, an extension of diplomacy. The idea that war could be moral was rejected because it led to 'holy wars', 'crusades', when people went to fight through passion rather than reason. Even when the great powers founded the League of Nations in 1920, with the aim of ending all wars, they did not build in the idea of just and unjust war, because henceforth no war could be just.

But modern societies found that they could not do without the idea of the just war. Christian opinion continually condemned the use, and usually the holding, of atomic weapons on the ground that their only use must be to kill innocent persons. The opinion was not unanimous; for there were those who held that if the destruction of many non-combatants ended a war it would save more innocent lives than it destroyed, and so could be held to be justifiable. On this plea some defended the atomic bomb dropped on Hiroshima in Japan in 1945 because it brought the Second World War to an end and stopped a wider killing. But the first meeting of the World Council of Churches at Amsterdam in 1948 passed the resolution that in the age of modern inventions the idea of the just war is no longer sustainable, and we must regard the idea as of great value in the past as a step towards ethical standards.

In the 'theology of revolution' since the Second World War, the idea of the just war was central; but now it was a just revolution against oppressors.

Pacifism

Meanwhile the old strand in Christianity – that it is always wrong for a Christian to be a soldier – which was kept alive in the Reformation by the Anabaptists and then by the Quakers, was given new force in the modern age; partly by the savagery of modern war but even more by Napoleon's invention of conscription whereby all men, and later women, could be called on by the state to fight. Wars were no longer deadly games between princes but wars of peoples. When the law obliged everyone to serve there came into existence the modern 'conscientious objector', who usually objected to military service on religious grounds, though some refused on general grounds of morality.

A few moralists rejected the argument that the conscience has a right to refuse to fight. Mercenary armies, they said, are a chief source of atrocities in a war. A citizen army, which is what conscription brings, preserves war from its worst excesses; and therefore everyone has the moral duty to serve and no one ought to be exempted for reasons of conscience.

With the wars of the twentieth century the pacifist movement grew in strength. It had leading thinkers on its side for the first time since the early centuries. But no one put the right to refuse military service on grounds of conscience into the list of human rights ruled to be binding on all states. It was agreed that where the citizen was allowed to refuse to be a soldier on grounds of conscience, he or she had to offer other service to the state in its crisis. The Nazis decreed the death penalty for anyone who refused to serve as a soldier.

The war memorial

A soldier usually died in a far country and was buried there. Christendom had no early tradition of remembering him by a tablet or memorial. The first such tablets appeared in churches during the fourteenth century. In one German town a plaque was put up in the church with sixty names of people who died in a battle nearby; but this was exceptional. The first war memorials as we know them date from the beginning of the nineteenth century.

At first only the more illustrious were remembered – the officers. Then people began to list all the dead. This was due to the change from an army of mercenary soldiers to an army of conscript citizens. The mercenary wanted the war to continue, the conscript wanted peace and to get back home. The mercenary needed only the motive of pay and loot, the conscript had a new motive – being ready to die for one's country.

So the first war memorials had Christian images and inscriptions. Michael the archangel, who fought a war in heaven, became a more familiar saint in the West; he was already well known in the East. Medals to reward bravery were made in the shape of crosses. The names on the war memorial were treated as a much earlier Church treated the names of martyrs; both gave their lives in a just cause. There was sufficient difference to make some war memorials less religious in their design, especially if the memorial stood on the village green rather than in the church. The war memorial was slowly made secular – it went into the street instead of being near the altar. After the First World War a Tomb of the Unknown Soldier was placed in Westminster Abbey, but the main celebration of the memory of the dead was at the Cenotaph in the middle of Whitehall.

THE COLD WAR

Because Russia won the eastern side of the Second World War, Stalin could install communist governments from East Berlin to

Vladivostok, and from Estonia to Bulgaria. These puppet governments were required to imitate their masters in attacking religion.

The result varied from one country to another. It was a general rule that education must be atheistic in its slant and that no pious persons might be employed as teachers; that no professed Christians might be in the civil service, which now meant all really responsible jobs in the state; that other, secular forms should be provided for sacraments, so that, for example, there was no need to go to church to get married; that no religious books could be sold in the state bookshops, which meant all bookshops except the odd stall at the back of a church or mosque; and that no religious broadcasts could be made.

A village war memorial, at Harefield, Middlesex; special to Australian and New Zealand memory because of a hospital for their troops here during the Second World War; hence the flags on Armistice Day.

257

The fiercest attack on religion was in Albania, where the people had three religions, Catholic, Orthodox and Muslim. The dictator Enver Hoxha thought that the only way forward for his backward state was to get rid of the lot, and murderously repressed every outward sign of religion, announcing Albania to be the first atheist state in the world's history. The least troubled were Poland and Romania. In each country religion was tangled with the freedom of the nation. The Poles had asserted their rights against the Russians by being Catholic rather than Orthodox in faith. The Romanians had asserted their rights against the Ottoman Turks by being Orthodox in faith. Therefore no government in Poland or Romania could want to be accused of being against the faith of the majority of the country. For example, though all religious education was forbidden in state schools, it was impossible to ban classes held at home by priests – these would have been illegal in most other communist countries.

But even in these two countries control of religion by an irreligious government could be oppressive and at times murderous. The Polish murder of most consequence, because it made a national martyr and weakened the government irretrievably, was that of Jerzy Popieluszko, a worker priest with the union Solidarity. Even in the countries where religion had strength, all the Catholic leaders spent time in gaol: Cardinal Wyszynski in Poland; Cardinal Mindszenty in Hungary, who also spent years sheltering in the American embassy; Archbishop Beran in Czechoslovakia; Cardinal Stepinac in Croatia, where a show trial was staged to brand him a war criminal.

East Germany was the one country under communist rule where the majority of religious persons were Protestant. The government was equally hostile to religion. It introduced the *Jugendweihe* ('youth consecration'), a secular form of confirmation for young people, who had to make an oath to the state; conscientious religious people felt that they could not do this, and were branded as disloyal. But in its later years it was the only communist government to allow radio or television time, however limited, for religion, and the only one to keep state pay for professors of theology in the universities.

Upholders of the Christian Socialist tradition tried to reconcile themselves with Eastern European communist governments. Justinian, the Patriarch of Romania, was an able man with a background in Christian Socialism; he cooperated sensibly, though his critics thought too readily, with the dictatorship. In Prague an eminent European theologian, the Protestant Josef Hromadka, held that the churches could cooperate in this communist regime which put forward ideals of social justice – until he was utterly disheartened by the Soviet invasion of Czechoslovakia in 1968. Such people tried to set up debate with Marxist thinkers who ruled the universities. It did not work; communist professors did not like to give respectability to religious people by being seen to be willing to debate with them.

All this collapsed with the fall of the Berlin wall in 1989 and the subsequent fall of one communist regime after another, including that of the Soviet Union itself. In Hungary, Romania, Czechoslovakia and East Germany, and especially in Poland, the religious convictions of the people helped to precipitate that breakdown.

CHINA

Russia had a long common frontier with China, and socialist doctrine as practised in Russia made headway in China as early as the 1920s. Under Mao the Communist Party profited by the collapse of order during the long civil war to impose the dictatorship of the proletariat in 1949. But this was socialism interpreted by a vehement nationalism which resented Western influence and wanted to assert the historic values of China – at least those that were not religious.

The churches that Mao found were of two main types. Protestant missionaries had begun work in China at the start of the nineteenth

A Protestant missionary in nineteenth-century China.

century. The first translation of the Bible into Chinese was made by the Scot Robert Morrison in 1823. The missionaries were allowed in under treaties with Western powers, some of which had been forcibly imposed. But they had only slow success among the Chinese people. Many missionaries were simple people, dedicated to the Bible. But a lot of others were like Matteo Ricci – that is, they wanted to teach the Chinese the truth about God, but also to help them to the higher education and science that the West was acquiring. There were more Chinese Catholics than Protestants – about five million Catholics to about one and a half million Protestants; Rome made six Chinese bishops for the first time in 1926. But more of the educated Chinese Christians were Protestants, and some of the Protestant schools and colleges in China did much to bring China into the modern world. Because of these two different origins, the simple, direct biblical and

the intellectual, the churches of China were of both kinds; there were many Bible-reading and intensely religious Chinese, and a body of Christians with a strongly moral religion in which the inheritance of Confucius still spoke.

Mao did not at first try to destroy religion; but he expelled missionaries because they were Western, and left the Chinese churches to stand on their own feet. He demanded their unconditional support for the new Chinese state. This caused problems of conscience both for the biblical Christians and for Catholics who were told that they could not obey the pope because he was a Westerner.

The Christian Socialist influences among Catholics and Protestants were willing to support Mao on the ground that it was right to back the reconstruction of society for the sake of justice. Most Protestant congregations accepted this – they were under severe pressure to do so. A Catholic Church was formed without the pope; Rome refused to recognize

**A Mogul painting of the
Last Supper.**

its bishops. The powerful tradition of social morality, partly inherited by the Christians from the Confucian ideals, made it easier to think the state right. But the state was against religion, and the congregations were pushed into little house churches.

Then in 1966 came the madness of Mao's Cultural Revolution. Gangs of teenagers were encouraged to smash temples and churches alike, and to turn their intellectual seniors into farm labourers. This was no longer Marxism, but a new religion, a salvation by permanent revolution. For a time it had an extraordinary influence on young people in the West, and even in some Western churches; temporarily the Chinese churches disappeared. But when the storms passed and China returned to something like sanity, the churches were found to be still doing their work.

That work was not easy: they were still under a committee of the Communist Party called the 'Patriotic Church', and there were still pastors and priests in gaol for refusing to break links with the churches abroad. In 1995 there was still a way to go before the now accepted human right to practise religion was allowed fully.

INDIA

The fate of the churches in India made an extraordinary contrast with their fate in China. But then India was the most religious country in the world.

In the European expansion of the nineteenth century the churches made progress all over India. In the south, mass movements into the churches continued into the twentieth century. The Bible was translated into many Indian languages. Missionaries started schools, which sometimes grew into colleges and then into universities, which were not specially missionary in character, but just tried to educate well. Doctors brought in European medicine; some of the best of them also acted as missionaries, linking Christ's message with healing, but they always remembered the doctor's moral duty to heal all regardless of their faith. Missions started farms to spread more modern methods of agriculture, and set up printing presses and publishing houses.

Observers have seen the chief work of Christian missions in India as the making of communities, which persuaded some but also influenced the religion of Hindus who remained Hindus, among them Mahatma Gandhi. Others saw the importance of the missions as a selfless means of propagating the best of modern education, science and medicine; in the process creating a large number of educated Indians who made it right and necessary that India should be free and independent and that Indian churches should have Indians at their heads.

The missionaries had problems with the deep-rooted customs of the country. The most obvious was the caste system, which condemned those of low caste or no caste to remain at the bottom of society; many of these outsiders took part in mass movements into the churches. Most of these mass movements were in the south, but they also happened among the Telugu people north of Madras, and various tribes around Chota Nagpur and in other places such as the hills of Assam. These conversions enormously increased the number of Christians in India, but also embarrassed the churches, which had problems of education and morals with such numbers of converts. They had nothing like enough people to cope with the demand for teaching and pastoral care.

There came to be an Indianization of the Christian faith. Deep in the Indian people was a mystical sense of God's presence, a quietness, patience and simplicity of life, and a

A nineteenth-century missionary in an Indian village.

Mother Teresa; Albanian by origin, trained as a nun, dedicated herself to the care of the poor in Calcutta.

desire for an ascetic ideal which was like the way of Christian monks. The Hindus had the *ashram*, a place of retreat and contemplation not unlike an early monastery. Some of the best Christian institutions in India were and are ashrams, where groups of people live simply and quietly, praying in silence and serving their neighbours.

When India became independent in 1947 and was split into two, the Christians had a high moment of vocation, for while Hindus murdered Muslims and Muslims murdered Hindus, they were trusted by both sides to provide places of safety and hiding.

Christians were numerous but not many in relation to the whole. In India, which proclaimed itself a secular republic where all religions were free, they made up slightly more than three per cent of the people. In Pakistan they were fewer, less than two per cent; in 1956 the country proclaimed itself an Islamic republic and numbers fell. These figures were not spread evenly: Christians were much more numerous in the south, and much fewer in some other regions such as Kashmir.

With the flow of Asian immigrants into Europe and America in the years after 1950, the higher aspects of Buddhism and Hinduism began to attract religious people in the West as never before. The Buddhist sense of peace and the Hindu feeling for simplicity reinforced the quiet strands of Christian feeling.

THE DECLINE OF FAITH IN EUROPE

The pope was still the centre of the Catholic Church; after the fall of Fascism in 1945 he had a friendly Italy at his back, for the first time since the eighteenth century. His authority in the West was still great, both in doctrine and in morals. Nevertheless, after Europe had tried to commit suicide in two world wars, he was as dependent on the United States as on Italy. The Curia in Rome became less and less Italian as the Catholics of Latin America and Africa far outstripped Europeans in number. During the Cold War the pope's influence was reduced in the lands of Eastern Europe where there were large Catholic populations – especially Poland, but also Lithuania, Slovakia, Croatia, Hungary and Transylvania. The election of a Pole as Pope John Paul II in 1978 was a sign that the papacy had become more international and less Italian.

Catholics still revered the pope but took less notice of what he said. Popes held to the old morals of marriage and family in a time when the habits of industrial societies changed moral needs. He outlawed divorce even in cases where natural justice would find it the only course; artificial contraception was forbidden, though there were far too many people in the world and though women found liberty of life with its aid. He opposed the priesthood of women at a time when many Catholics in America, Canada and the Netherlands believed that now women had a chance to be as educated as men it was right that their pastoral abilities should be brought into the priesthood, partly because it would help the pastoral work of the churches, and partly because it would show the churches' commitment to a world that was trying to give an equal chance to the female sex.

The Reformation left the Protestants with no single leader; there was a Lutheran body with its heart in Germany and Scandinavia; a Reformed body with its heart in Switzerland, Edinburgh, Holland and New England; an Anglican body centred on Canterbury and a Methodist body deriving from it which was weighty in the United States and Canada; a Baptist body with its main weight in the United States.

If in 1914 it had been asked where was the centre of gravity in the Protestant churches, the answer would still have been the same as during the Reformation: in the German universities and their faculties of theology, where Martin Luther had taught. The leadership persisted there until first the Nazis and then the communists destroyed it. After 1945 the Lutherans in the United States were as important to the Lutheran churches as those in Germany and Scandinavia.

The British and American churches aimed to rectify the imbalance of leadership with a World Council of Churches. The formation of the council took from 1910 to 1948, when its first meeting was held at Amsterdam. But it was a world council only in name, for the Catholics and many Orthodox Christians refused to take part. The pope condemned the plan in an encyclical of 1928, and the Russian Orthodox patriarch denounced it at a synod in Moscow in 1948.

But it met a need. The organizers persisted. The Orthodox took part at the meeting in New Delhi in 1961. The Catholics never became full members, but they sent official representatives. The council was important to churches in India, Africa and Latin America as it was the only world body through which they could make their needs felt effectively.

Was it necessary to attend church to be a Christian? Many Jews decided that it was not necessary to attend synagogues to be a faithful Jew; could the same be true of Christians, although their tradition since the time of the apostles rested on the coming together in prayer and praise? If most people did not attend church (except for baptism, marriage or funeral), did it follow that they no longer had faith in God as their Maker, or that they no longer accepted the revelation of love as the moral key to humanity? The new social scientists spent much time guessing at the answer to this riddle.

The statistics were only reliable where a state still taxed the people for the benefit of churches; for where such taxes survived, there was always a clause allowing citizens to say that they did not want to pay it; and so it became possible to see how many people in the state refused to support churches. Those who supposed that Europe was growing un-Christian found these numbers surprisingly small. But little by little they began to disturb the churches. In the Netherlands the official number of 'non-religious persons' grew from 92,960 in 1909 to 1,114,943 out of a population of 6,841,000 in 1930 — just under a sixth of the people. Another survey which was carried out midway between these dates, 1920, estimated the number of Protestants at 2.8 million and Roman Catholics at 2.4 million.

Catholics' attendance at weekly mass fell from 77 per cent in 1948 to 46 per cent in 1970, and 31 per cent in 1976. That does not mean that the number of Catholics in Holland declined as sharply during those years. But the fall in attendance was paralleled elsewhere in Western Europe, and led critics to ask whether Europe was ceasing to be a Christian continent. Meanwhile immigrants from the East and Africa poured into Europe.

LIBERATION IN LATIN AMERICA

When Napoleon occupied Spain, the Spanish colonies in America, from Mexico to the Argentine, soon declared their independence. That meant a long quest for a government that worked. Nothing worked for long. Most of the time there would be a dictatorship or oligarchy, sometimes led by a general who had seized power in a coup, sometimes by a self-proclaimed 'emperor'; rarely, there might be a sort of democracy. The nations were divided by race, and by the gap between the great landowners and the Amerindians or half-caste serfs, and the state was usually bankrupt or nearly so.

In the struggles between rich and poor, between generals, and between gangs, the Church was at risk from all sides. It was usually assumed to be on the side of the ruling class, though in the peasant revolutions parish priests were always among the leaders. The liberal bourgeois class was usually anti-Catholic, and liable to make laws banning monks, or expelling Jesuits, or confiscating Church property. The peasants were very Catholic in an Amerindian way – that is, they still used pre-Christian rites, which the middle class despised as superstitious. There were occasional persecutions of the Church, and occasional risings of guerrilla peasant bands. Most of the time the states and their churches rubbed along together, none too cordially.

Let us take the three states whose troubles made a sharp impact on the world at large: Mexico, Cuba and Nicaragua.

Mexico

After decades of civil war or near war, in 1884 Porfirio Diaz made himself a stable dictator; he held on to power for thirty-five years. This was done with the aid of the Church; he kept the existing stiff laws against it but did not enforce them. The country was prosperous, the rich grew richer, the poor grew poorer. During his time the Church reorganized itself, made better parishes, worked for pastoral care in the rural areas, and restarted a movement to reform society for the benefit of poor factory workers and the Indians. When Diaz was forced to resign by a revolution, he left no proper political structure – only army commanders, bandits

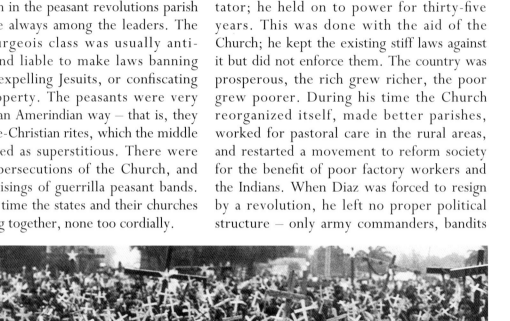

Young people on pilgrimage to the votive Temple of Maipu, Chile.

and, for a moment, a National Catholic Party.

After years of local wars an ex-journalist and poet, Calles, gained power. He also decided to destroy the Catholic faith. The anticlericals thought that they were civilizing Mexico by freeing it from an old and backward culture. They thought that Catholicism was what kept Mexico backward, and that it wanted to keep the people ignorant; it was a sore in the state which must be abolished. The governor of Tabasco province, Garrido, was a fanatical teetotaller and a fanatical anti-Catholic. Private houses were searched for their little statues, priests could only exist if they married and were over forty and had studied 'anti-religion', gravestones were forbidden and the dead were marked only by a number, there was a ban on phrases such as *vaya con Dios* ('goodbye'; literally, 'go with God'), women were marshalled to bring statues from churches to a vast bonfire.

The result was the worst guerrilla war in Latin American history. When his officers tried to close churches the people resisted them by force. Calles retaliated by ordering hideous desecration of churches, intended to show the Indians that God would not defend the Church: there were parodies of services, nuns were raped, and any priest captured in the countryside was shot – though mostly his men did not hunt down priests hiding in the towns.

At first the peasants were routed; they had only sticks and stones against guns. But soon they began to destroy battalions sent against them and seize their guns. They called themselves the Cristeros to demonstrate their defence of the Church, and were devoted to the Virgin of Guadalupe.

Only two in every five of the Cristeros had ever been to a primary school. The women organized administration, espionage and the supply of ammunition, which they carried in their clothes; they made explosives.

The Cristeros tried to make a pure and good society. They tried to organize schools in the villages, severely limited alcohol, forced men with concubines to marry or separate,

banned prostitutes, harvested as well as fought. Everybody said the rosary. They usually had no priests, celebrating 'white masses', led by a layman with the reserved sacrament. Where priests bravely stayed with them (many lost their lives as a result) they were troubled. A few priests became commanders of guerrilla bands, but their colleagues told them they ought not to be in this violence.

The Cristeros had astonishing success: by mid-1929 they controlled western Mexico. Calles gave way. Peace was agreed, and the government allowed the churches to reopen. Masses were celebrated again; in December 1931 the 400th anniversary of the Virgin at Guadalupe was a feast with more than half a million worshippers; but even in those years some 5000 Cristeros were murdered. The devout Catholics hated bishops who had compromised with the atheist state. In 1933 there were fewer than 200 priests in all Mexico; in 1810 there had been 7341. There was a second guerrilla war in 1935, but it had far less popular hold and the government behaved more sensibly. A successor deported both Calles and Garrido. In 1940 even the President, Camacho, dared to say, 'I am a believer'.

This persecution became the most famous in modern history because of the novelist Graham Greene. He went to Mexico for a mere six weeks in 1937, during part of which time he suffered from dysentery. He met an exiled bishop, and priests secretly at work. He came out loathing Mexico – the food, the insects, the sanitation, the police, the shuttered churches. He went to Tabasco because it was one of the last two states where religion was still banned, and endured a terrible journey by mule. Out of the loathing and pain came a book which was a masterpiece, one of the rare Christian novels to change the attitude of an epoch.

His book *The Power and the Glory* is the story of a bad priest – a drunken adulterer – who, at great risk to his life, refuses to desert his province of Tabasco where he is the last priest, even though many people in the villages where he arrives in disguise do not want him because they will be shot if they give him shelter. In the end he is captured and executed. This lamentable and yet heroic priest is contrasted with a police officer, moral and puritan, hunting and killing priests for the most ethical reasons, to save the people from superstition. The intention of the novel at its simplest was to illustrate the old doctrine that 'the unworthiness of the priest hindereth not the effect of the sacrament'; but it was a bigger novel than that alone, for it told, in a rare way, how God used such utterly inadequate tools as humans are to help his people.

Cuba

The Cuban revolution of 1959 was not due to poverty; the island was among the more prosperous Latin American republics.

In 1961 Fidel Castro became a disciple of Lenin and declared himself an atheist. The Church leaders said that Christianity and communism were not compatible, and condemned the atheism which went with the communism. Archbishop Perez said, 'The Church is on the side of the poor but never on the side of communism,' and that the Marxist doctrine of man is not Christian because it denies human rights, abolishes property and uses terror. Castro replied that bishops were on the side of the rich and some of the clergy were fascists. He deported the archbishop and some 150 Spanish priests, and started to discriminate against Catholics in education and public life. The governing Communist Party refused to accept Christians as members.

There was no Cristero rebellion – there could not be, because the popular backing was not there; before Castro only seventeen per cent of the people attended any sort of church. And it was not a fierce persecution like that of Calles in Mexico; no priests were shot. In 1957 there were 700 priests and 2400 nuns in Cuba; twenty-three years later there were 230 priests and some 200 nuns, so the Catholic church could still do its work though on a much reduced scale.

Castro was against churches, but talked of Jesus as the great revolutionary. Pope John XXIII sent a nuncio, who accepted the revolution and spoke of finding Christian virtues in it. In 1969 Pope Paul VI allowed the appointment of a new archbishop of Havana, who talked of the Christian struggle for freedom – which disturbed Cuban exiles in the United States. Castro was moved when he saw what happened in Nicaragua, when church people whom he thought of as likely to be reactionary led the revolution there.

But the flight of 300,000 exiles, mostly middle class, was bad for Cuba and worse for the Cuban churches. For Christendom it was more important in its effect outside Cuba.

In 1985 a Brazilian friar, Frei Betto, who was both a priest and a Marxist, and had served four years in a Brazilian gaol as a political prisoner, persuaded Castro (the least silent of men) to hold conversations with him about religion. Betto printed these conversations as *Fidel and Religion*. The book became a world bestseller and was translated into several languages. In it Castro remembered that his mother was very religious and lit candles to the saints every day, though when he was a child there was no church in her village. She had christened her son after St Fidelis, a German Capuchin executed as a spy in 1622 when he went into the Swiss Alps to try to convert the mountain people. Castro recalled how he loved the three wise men because on their day of Epiphany the children got presents, and how as a boy he kept saying *Kyrie eleison* without any idea what it meant, and how he was first excited by war through reading the Old Testament. It was his study at the university that made him a communist.

Nicaragua

In the Spanish empire Nicaragua was a backwater, and remained one for many years afterwards. It achieved world fame in the 1970s because the Christians were not only on the side of revolution but among the chief makers of revolution.

Three men of the Somoza family ruled Nicaragua as dictators from 1934. It was a tyranny. A secret opposition was founded in 1961, the Sandinistas. In their origins they were not Christian; but the justice of their cause began to attract Christians.

Ernesto Cárdenal was a Trappist monk who felt the need of a new kind of monastery to serve the poor. He went to live among the Indians at Solentiname, a group of little islands in Lake Nicaragua. The monastery's way was original: it admitted both sexes and children; prayers were very simple and there were dialogues during the services; there were no vestments and the 'habit' was jeans and a peasant blouse; and, strangely, there was a library which became the best in all Nicaragua. The monastery was always in debt. Its members had an extraordinary sense of being reborn.

Cárdenal at first held the view that the Christian way was never to use violence, that Gandhi and Martin Luther King were right in the way they had changed the world, and that as a priest he could never take up arms. But as he and his people prayed and studied the Bible – and the speeches of Castro and Mao – they discarded the doctrine of Gandhi, and came to believe that there was nothing wrong in a Christian being a revolutionary and that an alliance with Marxists was possible. The altar of Mary had a picture titled *Mary, Mother and Proletarian*.

Marxists began by thinking Christians a squadron of the enemy. But in these conditions of a fight against tyranny, they found that the doctrine of the equality of humanity was strong; that the ethic of love of one's neighbour was not compatible with oppression; that Christians aimed at humility and generosity; that they valued poverty and therefore the poor; and that they looked for the kingdom of God even if their vision was directed towards another world.

The monastery of Solentiname gradually became an odd sort of secret army camp; with the result that in 1977 government troops burned it and destroyed the library.

Ernesto Cárdenal was far from being the only priest in this struggle. In that same year the Nicaraguan bishops, led by Archbishop

Ernesto Cárdenal, radical Christian leader in Nicaragua, Central America.

Obando y Bravo, denounced dictatorship and allowed the people's right to struggle for freedom. In July 1979 the Sandinistas won the war. Their new government included four priests, among them Ernesto Cárdenal as the minister of culture, and his brother Fernando as minister of education. It also had several Marxists. The Sandinistas took over a devastated country, with half a million homeless, most of the people illiterate, and an unimaginable rate of inflation. The ex-government forces formed a guerrilla opposition known as the Contras, aided by the United States. It was easier for Christians to be revolutionaries than to be united in a government faced with insoluble problems. Pope John Paul II disapproved of ex-monks being cabinet ministers. Archbishop Obando led the opposition to the more radical acts of the new government. What followed the Sandinista victory was no holy state but constant friction.

Liberation theology
These battles brought the idea of 'liberation' to the front of thinking.

The poor, it was said, are taught to suffer poverty passively; the servants of Christ are allies of unjust regimes, and help people to accept them. In some cities – São Paulo in Brazil the chief – Marxist ideas were strong in the university, and theologians thought that they could ally with them.

Pope John Paul II preaches in Nicaragua.

In Colombia the priest Camilo Torres took the step to active collaboration with the communists. He argued that property is in the hands of a minority and the Church is part of that minority; it is absurd to expect the minority to change the situation, so it must be fought. If the clergy do not struggle to help their brothers, the priesthood is superficial ritual; so a priest must engage in the struggle in order to show love of his neighbour. Torres joined the guerrilla war as a fighter and was shot dead.

'Revolution' is an idea that fits all sorts of different circumstances. A theological base for it needs to be vague.

In 1971 a Peruvian priest, Gustavo Gutierrez, made all this famous in a book, *The Theology of Liberation*. He argued that we should not go in for guerrilla war like Torres or the Cubans; but we should have open minds and be prepared to work with the Marxists. We need a faith that touches the oppressed – that is, true faith always has a bias towards the poor.

The Vatican suspected that these 'liberation priests' were corrupting Christianity into politics; if people were to think like this, they should be laymen and not priests. All over Latin America, but especially in Brazil, little groups of lay people known as 'base groups' met to study the Bible and what could be done for a better society.

In the Argentine a bishop was murdered; in San Salvador Archbishop Oscar Romero was shot down while he was saying mass. If the Church was suspected of blessing revolution, there were damaging consequences.

There was surprise when in 1986 Pope John Paul II praised the liberation movement in a letter to the bishops of Brazil: 'The theology of liberation is not only opportune but necessary.'

An uncomfortable Latin American reminder of the complex relation between churches and states; the parade on the day of Our Lady of Peace, at Cochabamba, Bolivia.

Archbishop Oscar
Romero in San Salvador,
soon to be murdered,
celebrates mass.

The Pentecostalists and charismatics

These were people who felt the power of the Holy Spirit in their lives. At services they might stand up and prophesy, as the apostles had at the feast of Pentecost – hence the name 'Pentecostalist'. They were also called 'charismatics', because the gift of tongues was an aspect of *charisma*, divine grace. These groups grew up among the Protestants of the United States during the earlier twentieth century. After the Second World War some Catholics started to feel the same power and show the same effects. In the modern age they have become numerous in Latin America.

There were three reasons for this. First, the churches of the United States, where charismatics were strong, always felt responsibility towards the Americas to the south of them; now that their missionaries had been ejected from China and Vietnam, they had men and money to spare. Second, many South Americans were of African descent, and one of the aspects of Christianity which drew Africans towards conversion was the sense of this free power of the spirit in the soul. Third,

the political predicaments of the Latin American states created anxiety among the people, many of whom found peace in these charismatic communities. The rapid spread of such ways of worship led many in Latin America, hitherto an entirely Catholic continent, to become Protestants.

The movement had unpredicted effects among the young. On a Sunday in June 1994 ten million people over the world took part in a 'March for Jesus', with rock music, cries of praise, and sincere passion. The largest marches were in the United States, London, Berlin and Brazil. In Moscow the march ran into trouble with the police and representatives of the Orthodox Church, but was allowed to go forward. No march was allowed in any Islamic country.

FUNDAMENTALISM

In the United States religion was important to the structure of society, for many immigrants had escaped from persecutions in Europe so that they might be free to practise their faith in a new land. As the frontier moved westwards it carried with it a tradition of evangelical mission from the time of John Wesley and before. Early in the eighteenth century was the 'Great Awakening', a series of revival missions.

The loose structure of the country made for many groups or sects, especially in the frontier states. The evangelical mission became a constant part of the religious scene; it helped to make the United States a country where more people went to church or chapel on a Sunday than in any other European-occupied land of modern times.

It was not an accident that the movement for civil equality was led not by a politician but by a black clergyman with profound religious idealism, Martin Luther King Jr. Black congregations expected that their pastors would voice their political as well as their religious concerns.

During the 1970s and 1980s an unprecedented form of association between Christianity and politics appeared in North America. Though the name was not accurate, it was usually called 'fundamentalism'.

The fundamentalists first appeared in the United States about 1900. They were Protestant evangelicals, biblical and conservative in religion. They held the view that had been losing ground through the nineteenth century: that the entire Bible is written by God and every word is true: Adam and Eve were the first two humans; the earth was covered by a flood; heaven and hell are real places to which souls will go; the devil is at work; people must be saved if they are to go to heaven; the old virtues are as valid as before in the new society. They fought the new liberalism in their own denominations, and the right of state schools to teach the theory of evolution to their pupils. The old faith was powerful; the fundamentalists made converts. This did not happen only in the United States; but because of the evangelical tradition here it had a force not found in most other countries.

The fundamentalists thought more of another world than this, and usually kept away from politics. Billy Graham, the most respected of evangelists, kept telling them that they must never make a political programme into a religious cause. But they thought it wrong that the constitution of the United States, so predominantly a Christian country, should forbid children in a state school to be taught about the Bible or be shown the way of worship. In 1963 the Supreme Court ruled all prayers in state schools to be against the constitution. There arose a campaign to change this judgement.

As society developed after the Second World War – especially with the two new inventions, safe methods of birth control and nationwide television – the fundamentalists' concern about ethics, and the laws that affected them, grew rapidly. Was it right that

A fine United States parish church from former colonial days; Christ Church, Shrewsbury, New Jersey.

abortion should be on demand, or that homosexual unions should be treated like married unions, or that some drugs should be made legal, or that pornography should be freely sold? On all these matters the fundamentalists aligned themselves with the conservative forces in American life.

They were not the only Americans who shared these concerns. But they were more outspoken than most others. The evangelist Jerry Falwell coined the phrase 'The Moral Majority' to describe the political weight they could wield. The phrase was misleading: those who claimed it were not a majority and were far from being the only group with ethical ideals. Almost all the leaders in the Moral Majority were Baptists. Their organization was unpopular, but their defence of the old moralities was far more popular than their movement or methods.

Television had two effects in promoting their cause. The screen brought home to millions of firesides, as never before, the ethical chaos of humanity. And it made possible huge

Christian meetings: Billy Graham preached to a congregation of a million in Korea, Pope John Paul II celebrated mass for a congregation of three million in the Philippines. Within the United States the missionary became a 'televangelist' and for the first time gave his followers a sense of their voting power, with rallies and the chance of electing a candidate who cared about morals as they saw them.

In the south in 1985 the fundamentalists captured the leadership of the most numerous of the American Protestant denominations, the Southern Baptist Convention, comprising some twelve million people with others affiliated. They achieved this by a campaign against the milk-and-water religion which, they thought, liberal compromise engendered. They saw the congregations of the mainstream churches, Roman Catholic, Episcopalian, Methodist or Presbyterian, in decline and were resolute that this should not happen to them. Their quality of Sunday-school teaching was the best in all America, and their missionary work among the most effective.

A modern missionary rally. Billy Graham preaches; a Baptist minister who from 1950 became the most respected of English-speaking evangelists.

Liberal pastors and laity could hardly understand what was happening; that in an age of science and modern knowledge educated people could still believe in the truth of every word in the Bible – for surveys showed that many of the fundamentalists were not ignorant, and that such opinions were often found among engineers and technocrats. President Carter was a Southern Baptist. He was trained in science; and he knew some theology.

The fundamentalists' doctrines were more flexible than many of their opponents supposed. They thought much of guidance from God and so had the mentality of seekers and pilgrims, not the fixed mind of those whose wish is to get back to the past they once knew or imagined to exist.

The television screen and the 'megachurch' had a disadvantage in that they promoted cults of personality – a televangelist under the spotlights had more difficulty in looking like a saint than, say, a hermit alone in a Saharan oasis would have done.

In 1994 the movement was associated with the victory of the Republican Party in the Congressional elections; as though conservatives in religion and morals were leaders in the political swing of the American people towards the right. That was an illusion, caused by such catchphrases as 'The Moral Majority'. The swing to the right had social and political causes which were not religious. But the continuing spread of fundamentalist opinions within the old churches, and the formation of new denominations which accepted their opinions, were warnings to the churches as they adapted themselves to modern science and history. The leaders of the historic communities had to ask themselves whether in their adjustments to the age they were not so much seeking truth as compromising with axioms that were hardly Christian and that weakened the force of their message to the world.

By a curious process the word 'fundamentalism' was taken out of America and applied to ultra-conservative forces in both Judaism and Islam. This had a sinister side, because

those Muslims who were terrorists identified their crude nationalism with religious literalism in their understanding of the Koran – or rather misunderstanding, for nowhere does the Koran counsel such behaviour. But the true fundamentalists of Islam were seldom nationalists longing for holy war.

The violent side of Islamic extremism was alien to American fundamentalism, for the Americans knew the Bible well and studied it hard for light (usually in the Authorized or King James version of 1611). The result of this transfer of the name was to make American evangelicals repudiate the old word 'fundamentalist', which now made them look like backwoods folk, or even the sort of

An unusual example of contemporary church architecture: the Crystal cathedral, Los Angeles.

273

savages who shoot doctors at abortion clinics.

Fundamentalism, in so many different shapes across the world, could nevertheless show certain vague resemblances. In Islam many groups wanted to drive women into the home, even back behind the veil, in an effort to preserve the family. This could be entangled with everything that was nasty in a mixture of religious and political fanaticism; as when a law of 1989 in Iran ordered 74 lashes and prison for any woman not 'properly' veiled, and her family to pay for her upkeep while in prison. The American evangelicals were as far as possible from such harking back to a barbaric age. They were committed to the rights of women. But because they cared so deeply about the home and family, of which the mother had always been queen, some of them questioned whether the cause of women's equality was being over-pressed; and on biblical grounds some of them tried to exclude women from becoming pastors.

What the Jews, the Muslims, the evangelicals and the pope had in common was an antipathy to some aspects of the liberal European culture pervading the world, and a determination to resist it by appealing to the founding documents of their faiths.

AFRICA

The transforming change in Christian history in the twentieth century was the conversion of large parts of Africa south of the Sahara. So many new Christians appeared here that by 2010 there will be many more Christians in the world than there were a hundred years earlier.

The conquests of Islam reduced the Christian peoples of North Africa to a remnant, of which much the largest was the Coptic Church of Egypt, and with the special exception that Ethiopia remained throughout the centuries a Christian country, almost inaccessible to the advances of Islam.

When the Atlantic and Indian oceans were opened, that also opened the coasts of Africa to Portuguese missionaries. As late as 1800,

outside Egypt and Ethiopia, Christian Africa was confined almost entirely to whites and their African dependants. The main part of black Africa was untouched.

A great change in European attitudes came with the desire to stop the slave trade from Africa to the Americas. The slave trade could be diminished by making it illegal and sending out warships to arrest slavers. But everyone saw that African chiefs sold slaves because they had no other way of preventing their people from starving; and therefore that to stop the slave trade could not be done without finding a way to help black Africa towards a reasonable standard of life.

The first idea was to create settlements of freed slaves in Africa – by the British at Sierra Leone, then next to Sierra Leone by the Americans in Liberia (bad Latin for 'the state of the free'). These communities had a fair number of Christians. In South Africa, where the whites were many, there were soon strong missions probing northward among the Bantu peoples. The Scot David Livingstone dedicated his life to opening Central Africa, as much as an explorer as a missionary. Every one of the main European denominations took a part in building up the churches in southern black Africa. Once there was a powerful Christian presence in Southern and Western and Eastern Africa among black people, no longer restricted to the dependants of whites, the spread of the faith took off without the necessity for European help.

Black missionaries came over from the Americas, where they had had the chance of education and growth in a strong black community. The first black African bishop outside Ethiopia was Samuel Crowther, a Yoruba (from what was later Nigeria) born in 1809 and sold into slavery at the age of ten. A British warship rescued the slaves and put them ashore in Sierra Leone. There he was educated; he became an Anglican missionary on the Niger and was made a bishop in 1864. His work was controversial, but he was successful in spreading Christianity among the Yoruba.

The 'partition' of Africa between the powers moved the Europeans at home to vast efforts in encouraging education and Christian work among the peoples of the continent. It was not only among the powers with colonies, for Americans, Swedes, Norwegians and Danes worked as hard as the rest.

Among the Catholics the most effective religious orders were the White Fathers and White Sisters, founded by the French priest Charles Lavigerie in 1868 and 1869. Their way was like that of the more radical Protestant missionaries in that they encouraged black culture and the use of native languages, and aimed at the ordination of African priests and bishops. It was slow work, partly by design because they wanted to build on foundations that were stable; the first black priest was ordained in 1909, the first bishop made in 1939 (in Uganda), the first cardinal in 1960 (in Tanzania). Africans who became clergy found it hard to accept the Catholic requirement of celibacy.

The progress of Christianity in this new world, despite the active presence of Islam in East and North Africa, led to an absurd optimism; so that the missionary conference at Edinburgh in 1910, with members of the new churches represented, talked foolishly about 'the conversion of the world to Christianity in this generation'. Four years later the First World War destroyed almost all German missionary work in Africa – the Germans were doing some of the best work in education and medical mission – and shattered African respect for the moral idealism of the Europeans. But it did not for an instant interrupt their wish to find faith for themselves. On the contrary, it made them depend less upon their white helpers, and organize their

A rare quatrefoil font for baptisms, from sixth-century North Africa.

An Ethiopian Nativity and flight into Egypt; unlike either Eastern or
Western. In their version a handmaid went with Joseph and Mary to Egypt,
and she carries the picnic on her head. The language above is Ge'ez, no
longer spoken but the language of services. The Ethiopian Church went
back to the fourth century and, isolated in its mountains, kept primitive
customs like circumcision and the keeping of the sabbath.

congregations. One effect of the war was that most religious services in Africa were led by lay people.

This also meant that many African churches were not in union with the historic churches, Catholic or Protestant. A wandering black missionary would begin to teach, people would gather; but they had no idea that they were Methodists or Catholics or Lutherans. This freedom, or anarchy, was powerful in its impact. Something like half of Christian Africa is to be found in churches separate from the traditional churches of Europe. They were closely based on the Bible; some of them laid much stress on healing; their worship was often glowing, charismatic, emotional; they loved hymns; their morals were puritanical though they often accepted the custom of polygamy; some held to the teachers of the historic churches while others venerated their own prophets; and many were willing to absorb into their faith a sense of divine presence that had existed in the cults of animism and superstition out of which they had grown, not excluding the feeling of an immediate link with the dead. In these conditions, experiences of conversion were powerful.

At times the experience could be so powerful as to be dangerous. The old tribes were full of witch doctors and witchcraft. Many of these witch doctors did good or at least no harm, and might still be consulted by Christians. But the new converts repudiated witches, and in places turned against them with a ferocity reminiscent of the old witch-hunting crazes of Europe and New England.

Some of these 'churches' were little groups made by an inspired leader, and when he went they disappeared; many of those groups which survived remained very small. But several established themselves as big denominations.

The chief single church of this free kind was in Zaire, the church of Simon Kimbangu. At first a Baptist, he saw a vision and gathered a congregation; and after his death in prison in 1951 this grew to a church of two million people at least. His followers expected his return and thought of him as a second Messiah; and yet the church of Kimbangu was not wild but a sort of 'Protestant' radical church which in time became a member of the World Council of Churches. These Pentecostal churches were helped to stability by the presence of the traditional churches with their ordered education and teaching. The more stable of the bigger groups started schools and developed ways of training pastors.

In Africa, without systematic attempts to stop the old cults, an absorption helped to make the passage into Christianity comfortable. But then, more than in the Americas, the converts felt a conscious breach with their past. They burnt fetishes as symbols of their repudiation of an old world. They wanted a break with what they had known. This was partly why the evangelical experience of sudden conversion like that of St Paul on the Damascus road was more common among Africans. This applied as much to Catholics as to denominations commonly called evangelical.

Desmond Tutu, (Anglican) Archbishop of Cape Town from 1986.

The front page of
The Missionary News in
1866; above, worship
from all nations; below,
on the Congo.

Religious experiences made places of pilgrimage. Healings took place, as wonderful as those at Lourdes or Medjugorje in Europe, and then the shrine became a focus for people for miles around who came to say their prayers or bring their sick. A shrine was often the place where the founder of the group died and was buried; often it had rooms for prayer in retreat, or wards for the ill to lie. Travelling catechists as they went about might be asked to lay on healing hands, or expel evil spirits. The world of demons was still close, and the evangelist was valued as one who could rule over the powers of darkness.

With the freeing of the colonies in the 1960s the churches of Africa received African heads (with rare exceptions, as when the diocese of Masasi in Tanzania kept Trevor Huddleston as bishop because they knew this Englishman as a champion of Africans). The climax of this was the election of Desmond Tutu as Anglican Archbishop of Cape Town in 1986, for here was the strongest church in Africa, with many white members.

A majority of priests still came from Europe or the United States, which mattered more in Africa because most of these people were white. Although the bishops were now nearly all black, African schools were not yet turning out enough people who went on to higher education and then to the ministry. Thus most services in Africa were still led by a lay person, usually a catechist or the local teacher.

There were many African languages, some spoken by only a few people. The task of translating and writing religious literature was heavy. The effect of translating the Bible into African languages was the same as its effect earlier in Europe: the biblical language affected the literary language of those communities.

In some places Africans preferred to use English or French in their worship because the language did not separate them from their neighbours of a different dialect. One of these European languages was also the official one in states where there were several peoples speaking different languages. Naturally it tended to be used for prayer, and gained a

status a little like Latin in the Middle Ages: familiar but not really understood by most people.

Africans loved freedom but they also liked rituals. Their sense of reverence wanted the pastor to be clad in a seemly if not an elaborate way in church so that God should be honoured. African Protestants remained Protestants, but they liked more ceremony than European Protestants would approve. The Methodists, who started in England as men and women with a very plain way of worship, in Africa often became communities with vestmented bishops; one church even had a pope and cardinals. But this sense of hierarchy and order, which Europe had found to be a safeguard for truth but a hindrance to the spontaneity of prayer, was found compatible among Africans with freedoms in worship – dancing, drums – that were hardly found in Europe.

Part of African society was and is polygamous. The Christian missions would not tolerate it; and since they converted many women who were in a plural marriage, and some men with several wives, they all had a 'catechumenate' of members who were really full members of the church but could not come to the sacraments.

The debate was less easy than it looked from Europe. What happens to a second (or third) wife if a husband puts her away to come into the church? The insistence on putting away plural wives cast defenceless women into the streets. Yet the arguments for moving towards a society where one husband had one wife (and vice versa) were very clear.

After decades of Anglican defence of a rigid rule, the Lambeth Conference of 1988 voted a resolution that monogamy is God's plan but that a polygamist may be baptized into the church, without putting away any of his wives, provided that he promises not to marry again (unless all his wives are dead) and that his baptism has the consent of the Anglican community in which he lives. This was one sign of the way in which the new African power among the churches of the world made

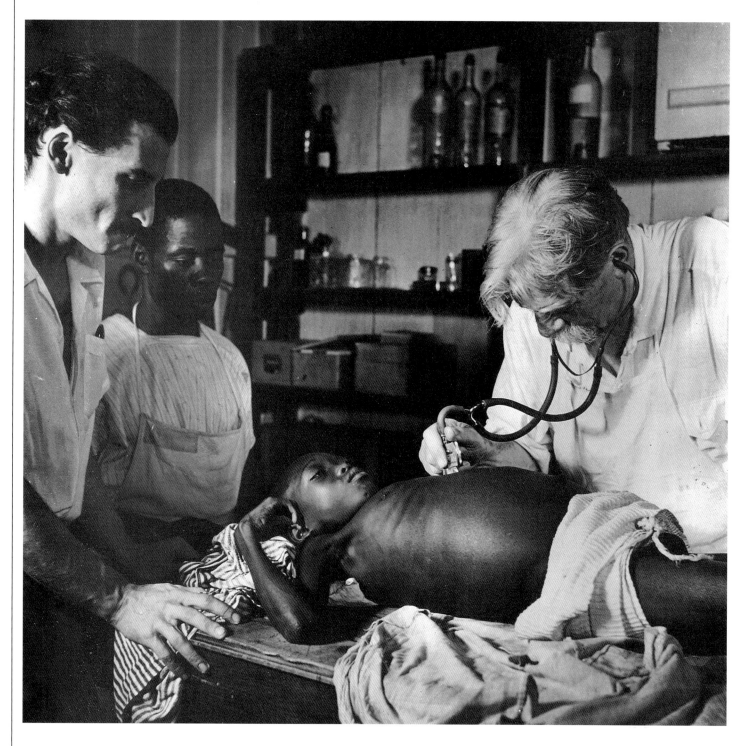

Albert Schweitzer, theologian,
musician and finally, from 1913,
for many years missionary
doctor at Lambarene, French
Equatorial Africa.

for a more flexible attitude. Certain other African groups argued that the custom is not wrong by Christian standards, that it is an integral part of African social tradition, that it is approved in the Old Testament, and that Christians should be allowed to take more than one wife if they wish. This viewpoint remained that of a small minority. Yet it has been reckoned that in certain countries about one in every five African Christians is not a full member of his or her church because he or she lives in a polygamous marriage.

Christianity flowered in Africa with a speed and potency that had no parallel elsewhere in the world. The speed brought problems, which were made far worse by the bloody civil wars that convulsed several African states. But it was an event of Christian history as important as the conversion of Germans after the fall of Rome.

African leaders soon became aware that though Christianity can unite and reconcile, different sects can divide a people. Just as part of the civil war in Bosnia or a small part of the guerrilla war in Ireland was caused by a difference in religion, so the confrontation between Islam and Christianity helped to cause civil war in the Sudan and in Biafra; and differences between Catholics and Protestants contributed to civil war in Uganda. Dictators such as Amin in Uganda and Mobutu in Zaire tried to keep their states united and obedient by suppressing not Christianity itself, but various denominations of it, and ordering everyone to be reconciled, so that there came to be a state umbrella for a very few main churches; they also banned all forms of church newspapers because these were likely to criticize the government. This rough way of dealing with the churches did nothing to keep states united.

A modern Nigerian crucifix.

NEXT?

People who do not study history think that the purpose of knowing history is to guess the future. It is not so. History shows how events often turn in a way that no sane person could have predicted. Let us nevertheless guess.

281

Since about 1900 in many countries women have been as well educated as men (not that all men are educated). The increasing number of educated women will mean more churches accepting women as pastors, priests and bishops. That will ease the difficulty of finding pastors in countries where there are not enough for the needs of the churches, for example, parts of Western Europe, parts of Africa, and nearly all of Latin America.

If there are qualities special to the sex, such as a compassion or an affection more committed than can be detected in many males, that should help churches to be more Christlike. But it will not make much difference to pastoral care, because for centuries women have been effective ministers in the churches — though not called so formally unless they were deaconesses or abbesses or prioresses.

Churches run by clergy forget that most of their valuable pastoral work is done by lay people, even though clergy or ministers are indispensable to the work of the churches.

To use women fully will provoke division because it is a big change, and any big change divides.

Scientists have proved that Genesis is not a true story of the way the universe began. For a hundred years, about 1845 to about 1945, it was accepted that there was a conflict between science and religion. Science, it was claimed, disproved miracles; might it disprove God? But then it came to be seen that science had no claim to 'disprove God'. The old conflict faded into the past; religious people valued truth if it were proven even if it was uncomfortable, while scientists were aware of their limitations in deciding what is right or wrong

An Anglican woman priest celebrates her first sacrament of Holy Communion, Bristol, England, March 1994.

in the way men and women act. But this conflict left an inheritance to the Church, in two ways.

First, humanity looks for a natural explanation of mystery and knows this is necessary. Since many unaccountable and inexplicable things still happen, we prefer not to call them 'miracles'. Instead we call them 'wonderful' or 'unpredictable'. If we use the word 'miracle', we use it to describe events which are natural and yet marvellous, like the coming of a baby into the world, or the unearthly quality of art or music, or anything at all that trails clouds of glory whether or not we think of it as 'natural'.

Second, the churches are still rooted in the Bible and could never be otherwise. But their base in the Bible has shifted its emphasis. The Old Testament has become less important, and so less well known – except for certain beloved stories such as David and Goliath, Jonah and the whale, or Daniel in the lions' den, while African spirituals tell of how Jacob wrestled all night at the ford. Christianity is still the heir of the Jewish faith – the Jews expected a Messiah and the Messiah came – but its churches moved a little away from the Jewish inheritance. The two faiths still share a common allegiance to a moral law, summed up in the ten commandments. But as the

The sick waiting at Lourdes in south-west France; there have been healings there since 1858 when the girl Bernadette had visions of the Virgin.

A meeting at Taizé in Burgundy; a community originally founded by the Swiss Roger Schutz in 1940 to help Jewish refugees from the Nazis, it then turned into a Protestant/Catholic place of prayer and religious life, cutting across denominations.

churches moved away from the Old Testament, they needed to take care that the overriding Christian law, that you should love your neighbour as yourself, is still backed by absolute rules of right and wrong. The hardest of these moral laws to keep used to be 'Thou shalt not covet . . .'. That is still the hardest; but almost as hard, in the age of the contraceptive, is 'Thou shalt not commit adultery.'

Television and the computer moved life away from the factory and the office, into the home. Television brought prayers to the bedridden in hospital or in their bedrooms, one of the blessings of modern invention. There were fit people, too, who felt they could join in more heartfelt prayer by their fireside, where they could switch off if they wanted to, than by going out to a church where they risked being bored. From the time of the apostles onwards the home has been as intimately linked with faith as the church building. The effect was likely to be the

expression of faith in more house churches and quiet, smaller groups.

But these could never replace the full life of music and congregation and sacrament. If the churches went in this direction, there was a danger of imitating the hermits of the Egyptian desert or the Anabaptists of the Reformation – the world is so awful we had better keep away and sit it out in silence.

Nevertheless, withdrawal has always been in Christianity – quiet; waiting in silence; contemplation; the ashram; the monk and the nun, whether or not they are called by those old names; the shrine, whether Catholic like Lourdes, Orthodox like Patmos, Protestant like Iona, or, indeed, ecumenical like Taizé in Burgundy. Withdrawal has been part of the memory of a life and death, and linked with the supper, communion, mass or eucharist that daily or weekly presents that life and death; the sense of eternity; the conviction of an ultimate order and purpose in the universe.

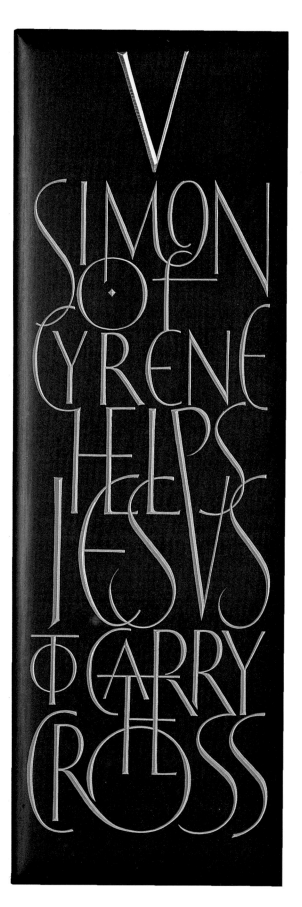

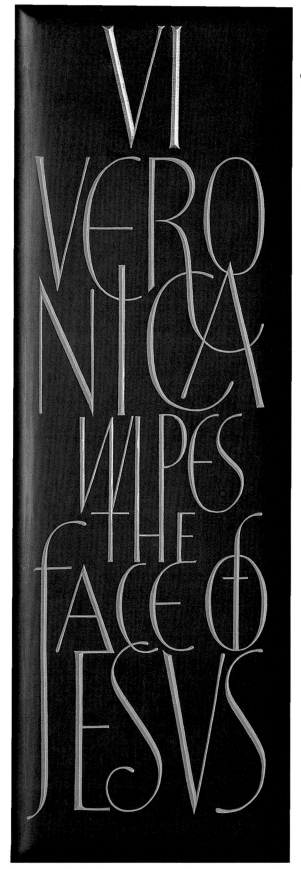

Contemporary stations of the Cross; the two of Veronica and Simon of Cyrene; by David Kindersley for the Oratory School, London.

Chronology

c. 4 BC
Birth of Jesus. At this time the Roman empire ran from the English Channel to Egypt and Palestine, with good communications by sea (though ships tended to stay in port in winter) and overland on the straight Roman roads. Roman provinces often had satellite kings, such as Herod the Great in Judaea, founder of the last Jewish royal family. He brutally crushed any resistance to Rome and had all possible rivals murdered, but otherwise was not too bad a king. When he died in this same year, the Emperor Augustus divided Palestine between his three sons, one of whom was Herod Antipas. One by one these provinces were put under direct Roman rule.

c. AD 28
(If St Luke is right) Baptism of Jesus by John the Baptist, later beheaded by Herod Antipas.

c. 30
(In the spring, but year uncertain) Crucifixion of Jesus.

c. 35
Conversion of St Paul.

43–4
Persecution by Herod Agrippa I (Herod the Great's grandson), killing of James the Lord's brother.

45–64
Paul's missionary journeys to Cyprus, Asia Minor, northern Greece, Athens and Corinth. He appeared before Herod Agrippa II (son of Agrippa I) in Caesarea, appealed to Caesar, and went to Rome for the hearing.

60–100
Writing of the four gospels.

64
Nero's persecution of Christians in Rome; Peter and Paul probably died here.

66–70
Jews revolted against Rome; Jerusalem was destroyed in 70. Jewish Christians were much weakened.

c. 100
Paul's letters collected into a little book.

c. 107
Ignatius, Bishop of Antioch, wrote seven letters on his way to martyrdom at Rome, among other things urging that the Church should be governed by bishops; he was the first person to use the phrase 'the Catholic Church'.

111–13
Letters between the Emperor Trajan and Pliny the Younger, governor of Bithynia, on how to treat Christians. Trajan ordered that they should not be hunted; anonymous letters should be ignored; if accused and obstinate in their faith they should be punished; if they said they were sorry they should go free.

c. 120
The schools of 'gnostic Christians', including those of Basilides in Alexandria and Valentinus in Egypt.

c. 140
Christians began to write 'apologies' to clear away untruths about them and to persuade heathens.

140–200
Slow agreement on the canon – which books are to make up the New Testament and which should be kept out.

c. 144
Marcion excluded from the church in Rome because he wanted to be rid of the Old Testament and the Jewish origins of Christianity, claiming that Paul was the only apostle to understand the teaching of Jesus. Marcion founded a quite successful church with congregations from southern Gaul to Syria.

c. 150
Christians began to collect accounts of the court cases of their martyrs – the Acts of the Martyrs.

155
Martyrdom of Polycarp, Bishop of Smyrna; first sign of a 'cult of the martyrs'.

*c.*165
Martyrdom of Justin Martyr, the apologist, in Rome.

161–80
Reign of Emperor Marcus Aurelius, a Stoic philosopher.

c. 170
Montanist prophets active in Asia Minor: they thought that the New Jerusalem would shortly come to earth.

178
Irenaeus became Bishop of Lyons in Gaul (he wrote in Greek).

c. 180
First version of the apostles' creed (not called by that name till about 390) drafted in Rome for use at baptisms.

c. 180
Compilation of lists of bishops in the largest sees, going back to the first choice by the apostles, and so proving the continuity of religious truth from that time.

*c.*197
First apology to be written not in Greek but in Latin, by Tertullian in North Africa. Tertullian later became a Montanist. He was the first Christian since St Paul whose personality was so knobbly that we feel we can know him as a human being.

c. 200
Latin began to be used in some church services instead of Greek; but the chief Christian strength was still in the Greek East.

c. 200
Foundation of the Christian school of Alexandria under first Clement, then Origen.

235
Hippolytus, able theologian in Rome (writing in Greek), exiled to Sardinia.

250
Beginning of systematic state persecution by the Emperor Decius. Origen died in Syria after torture. Fabian, Bishop of Rome, killed. The priest Novatian in Rome founded a separate church, because he thought that any Christian who had become an apostate ought not to be let back into the Church. He was the first theologian to write in Latin.

258
Cyprian, Bishop of Carthage, martyred. Letters and tracts survive and are important evidence.

268
Paul of Samosata, Bishop of Antioch, deposed.

c. 271
Antony became the first hermit in Egypt.

c. 280
Communities of hermits and monks began to grow in Egypt and Syria.

284–305
Reign of Emperor Diocletian, who began the last of the great state persecutions, 303–11: pulling down of churches, burning of scriptures, forcing all Christians to sacrifice to the emperor. Large number of martyrs, and of apostates. By 305 the persecution was over in the West; in the East under Galerius, whom Diocletian chose, it was worst 305–11.

c. 310
Various martyrs who later became famous: George, perhaps Cecilia.

311
Donatist schism in Africa; they refused the new Bishop of Carthage because he was made bishop by a bishop who had sacrificed in the persecution. Galerius forced into edict of toleration by threat from Constantine in the West. Galerius' successor, Maximin, renewed the persecution but died in 313.

312
Constantine had a vision of a flaming cross before the battle of the Milvian Bridge.

313
Constantine and the Eastern Emperor Licinius issued the Edict of Milan, formally giving toleration to Christians.

314–35
Reign of Pope Silvester I. Later legend said, falsely, that he converted Constantine.

c. 320
Building of the first church of St Peter's in Rome.

324
Constantine won control of all the Roman empire.

325
Council of Nicaea (called later the first Ecumenical Council). First draft of the Nicene creed.

325–81
The Arian controversy. Arius, priest of Alexandria, taught that Christ, though unique Son of God and Logos, was not 'like' his Father in everything; so he tended to turn the Trinity into three Gods; which the churches with their strong monotheism from the Jews could never accept. Most of the controversy was not about this but about what language you could rightly use to show that it was wrong.

328–30
Constantine made the old town of Byzantium on the Bosporus his new capital under the name Constantinople (also called New Rome).

328–73
Athanasius bishop of Alexandria. A stout defender of the Nicene creed.

337
Constantine accepted baptism before he died.

337–61
Constantius, son of Constantine, chief and then sole emperor.

339
Death of Eusebius of Caesarea in Palestine, who wrote the first history of the Church, an indispensable book for the first three Christian centuries.

341–83
Ulfilas bishop of the Goths in the Balkans. He was the first to convert the Germans on a large scale; he translated the Bible into Gothic. His creed differed a little from the Nicene but among such peoples that meant little.

361–3
Julian, cousin of Constantius, reigned as the last non-Christian emperor.

364
Valentinian became emperor in the West (d. 375); Valens, his brother, became emperor in the East.

370–9
Basil bishop of Caesarea in Asia Minor; a chief guide for Eastern monks thereafter.

374–97
Ambrose bishop of Milan, then the Western imperial capital; he had much influence on successive Western emperors.

378
Valens died in the battle of Adrianople against the Goths, a terrible Roman defeat opening the way to the empire's military decline.

379–95
Reign of Emperor Theodosius I, appointed during the crisis because he was an able general. Already devout, he was baptized in 380. He was the first truly pious and orthodox emperor. After his death the two parts of the empire steadily grew apart politically.

381
Council of Constantinople, later called the second Ecumenical Council; it settled the Nicene creed and the Arian controversy.

381
John Chrysostom ('golden mouth', a name given later) began preaching in Antioch. His famous sermons survive and are the chief examples of early Christian preaching in the East, though most modern scholars prefer the Latin sermons of Augustine.

386–7
Augustine, born in North Africa, was converted in Milan.

386
Jerome, from near Venice, settled at Bethlehem as a scholarly hermit and devoted himself mainly to translating the Bible into Latin, the first version of what was later called the Vulgate, the most influential of all Bible translations.

392
An imperial decree banned heathen worship, but it was not put fully into force.

395–430
First flourishing of monks in the West – first at Nola, not far from Naples (including the poet Paulinus of Nola) and around Marseilles (the island of Lérins, and John Cassian who came from Egypt to found two houses in Marseilles).

396–430
Augustine bishop of Hippo in North Africa. His writings dominated Western thought for a thousand years.

398–404
John Chrysostom patriarch (bishop) of Constantinople.

406–7
Invading Germans smashed the Roman frontier on the Rhine.

408–50
Reign of Emperor Theodosius II, grandson of Theodosius I.

410
Roman troops withdrawn from Britain, which was now wide open to invasion from Germany and Scandinavia. The Goths under Alaric sacked Rome. Augustine wrote *The City of God* as a meditation on the calamity.

416–25
Spain lost to the Visigoths.

429–30
North Africa lost to the Vandals.

430–61
Pope Leo I, the first pope to exercise wide authority in the West outside Italy. This was partly due to the fall of Roman power and the churches' need for help in the new German kingdoms.

431
Council of Ephesus (later called the third Ecumenical Council) accepted the title 'Mother of God' for St Mary. It also deposed Nestorius, patriarch of Constantinople; his followers, the Nestorian churches, were to make an important Christian presence eastward from Syria as far as China.

431
Bishop Palladius was sent to convert Ireland. But it was Patrick, about the same time, whom Ireland and the whole Church was to remember as the bringer of its faith.

438
The Theodosian code, the first Christian codification of law – so called because it was drawn up in the reign of Theodosius II.

451
Council of Chalcedon (the fourth Ecumenical Council) tried to settle the arguments over Christian doctrine, but did not fully succeed. The argument: God and man are united in his Son; is the union rightly called one person in one nature (*Monos physis*, so Monophysites), or one person in two natures (Chalcedon and Orthodoxy)? The Monophysites refused Chalcedon and became a big group of churches to this day, including Armenians, Copts, Ethiopians, and some in Syria and Kurdistan and in Malabar in South India.

476
The last Roman emperor of the West, Romulus Augustulus, deposed.

488–553
Ostrogothic kingdom in Italy. Its founder Theodoric was a friend of Gelasius, pope 492–6, who drafted the theory of two powers that govern the world, the state for bodies and the Church for souls; the latter being more important.

498
Clovis, King of the Franks, who created a Frankish kingdom from Belgium to the Pyrenees, baptized with 3000 of his men on Christmas Day at Rheims; the most important conversion in the acceptance of Christianity by the German tribes.

c. **520**
Dionysius Exiguus created the system of dating by BC and AD.

527–65
Reign of Justinian I, Eastern emperor; he won back, for a time, most of Italy and North Africa.

529
The code of Justinian; revision and improvement of the Theodosian code of law and earlier codes; the basis of the bodies of law of Christian Europe.

532–8
Building of the cathedral of St Sophia in Constantinople.

c. **543**
Death of Benedict, the founder of the abbey of Monte Cassino north of Naples and the author of the Benedictine rule, the most influential of all documents (except the Psalms and gospels) in monastic history.

590–604
Pope Gregory I, 'the Great'; a statesman of the first rank, and first pope to have been a monk.

596
Gregory sent Augustine to convert England and be the first archbishop of the English.

597
Death of Columba on the island of Iona off the Scottish west coast.

638–56
The Arabs conquered Palestine, Iraq, Syria and Egypt.

711–16
The Arabs conquered Spain.

726–843
The iconoclastic controversy in the East; many pictures and icons destroyed.

732
The Arabs driven back from France by Charles Martel.

735
Death of the Venerable Bede, ablest historian of the early Middle Ages, at the monastery of Jarrow in Northumberland.

800–40
(year unknown) The Donation of Constantine, giving wide secular powers to the pope, was forged in France.

771–814
Charlemagne reigned as King of the Franks.

800
On Christmas Day, in Rome, Pope Leo III crowned Charlemagne as Roman Emperor; 'restoration' of the empire in the West.

816–17
All monasteries in the empire told to follow the rule of St Benedict, by order of Benedict of Aniane.

829
Anskar went to try to convert the Scandinavians, without lasting success.

858–67
Pope Nicholas I, the only powerful pope for two centuries.

858
Photius, then the most learned person in Europe, became Patriarch of Constantinople.

860–87
Collapse of Charlemagne's empire under his grandchildren.

863
Cyril and Methodius, Orthodox missionaries from Salonica, worked in Moravia (modern Czech Republic and Slovakia). They began the use of Church Slavonic, which became the language of liturgy in the Slav world.

871–901
Reign of Alfred King of England; he fought long against the heathen Danes, and his partial success helped to Christianize the Danish settlers in England.

910
Founding of the abbey of Cluny in Burgundy, from which much reform of monasteries came.

929
Murder of King Wenceslas in Bohemia.

962
Otto the Great, Duke of Saxony, restored the Holy Roman Empire – now covering Germany and most of Italy, but not France. He based public order on rule by bishops, and so started the later 'prince-bishoprics' of German history.

966
The Poles under King Mieczyslav I were converted.

987
Vladimir, Prince of Kiev, baptized; the growth of the Russian Church.

995
Norway converted to Christianity, partly by force.

997–1038
King Stephen made Hungary Christian.

1000
The Icelandic Thing (Parliament) legalized Christianity.

1012
Romuald founded the monastery of Camaldoli in Tuscany; part of an Italian movement to revive the hermit life.

1046–8
The Emperor Henry III, from Franconia, cleared out three unworthy popes from Rome and began reforms in the papacy.

1049–54
Under the German Pope Leo IX the papacy recovered its lost influence.

1054
Breach between Rome and Constantinople, each side excommunicating the other; both were equally at fault. The dispute was mainly over southern Italy, where many Greeks lived, so that there were conflicting claims of rights. This was not the final breach, though it has often been seen as such.

1059–90
The Normans conquered southern Italy and captured Sicily from the Arabs.

1073–85
Pope Gregory VII (often called by his own name, Hildebrand) made powerful efforts to reform the Church and rid it of lay control. He forbade the investiture of bishops and abbots by lay princes, and tried to make priests celibate.

1077
Emperor Henry IV was obliged to do penance to the pope at the castle at Canossa in north Italy.

1084
Founding of the Carthusians at the Grande Chartreuse in the French Alps, part of a great movement of monastic expansion in those decades.

1093–1109
Anselm archbishop of Canterbury; a mind of such quality that he may be taken to mark the start of the flowering of thought in the high Middle Ages.

1095
Synod of Clermont in France: Pope Urban II summoned Europe to the first crusade to free Palestine from the Muslims.

1098
Founding of the Cistercians, who wished to keep the rule of St Benedict in a simpler form.

1099
The crusaders took Jerusalem.

1120
Founding of the order of Praemonstratensians at Prémontré. About the same time at Jerusalem were founded the Templars, a body of knights sworn to defend the holy places in Palestine, and the knightly Order of St John of Jerusalem (the Hospitallers).

1124
Start of the conversion of Pomerania and the south Baltic coast.

c. **1140**
Gratian, the canonist of the Bologna School of Law, published his *Decretum*, which founded the study of canon law in the new universities.

1153
Death of St Bernard, first head of the Cistercian house of Clairvaux.

1154–9
Pope Hadrian IV, the only Englishman to hold the office.

1156
The Carmelite order founded on Mount Carmel in Palestine.

1160
Death of Peter Lombard, Bishop of Paris. His four volumes of *Sentences* were the chief textbook of theology in the Middle Ages.

1170
Thomas Becket murdered at Canterbury.

1176
Peter Waldo, a merchant from Lyons, began to preach the life of poverty and simplicity; the origin of the Waldensians (Vaudois).

1198–1216
Pope Innocent III; the most powerful of popes politically, he deposed Emperor Otto IV, excommunicated King John of England and made Philip Augustus of France (nominally) take back the wife he had put away.

c. **1200**
Communities of teachers began to turn into universities – Bologna, Paris, Oxford, Cambridge.

1204
The fourth crusade captured Constantinople and set up a Latin empire (until 1261). The Greek Emperor Alexius V retired to Trebizond (modern Trabzon).

1209–29
Crusade against the Albigensian heretics of southern France.

1215–50
Reign of Frederick II, Holy Roman Emperor and King of Sicily; the most dangerous political enemy to the medieval popes.

1221
Death of the Spaniard Dominic, founder of the Dominicans.

1224–41
Mongol invasion of Russia and Eastern Europe; later the Mongols destroyed much of the Nestorian Church in Asia.

1226
Death of Francis of Assisi.

1226–70
Reign of St Louis IX, King of France.

1232
The Inquisition was made systematic, partly because of the Albigensians.

1243–54
Pope Innocent IV led a very secular fight against Emperor Frederick II.

c. 1250
By this time the Spaniards had won back Spain for Christianity except for the small kingdom of Granada in the south.

1256
Establishment of the Augustinian Eremites (Austin Friars).

1274
Death of Thomas Aquinas, whose *Summa* marked the climax of medieval divinity.

1291
Fall of Acre, last stronghold of the crusaders in Palestine and Syria.

1302
Pope Boniface VIII's bull *Unam sanctam* made the highest claims for the authority of the popes.

1309–77
The popes lived at Avignon.

1321
Death of Dante, poet of the *Divine Comedy*.

1357
Death of Gregory Palamas, defender of Hesychasm in the East.

1378–1415
Great Schism in the papacy: two lines of popes each recognized in certain countries.

1384
Death of John Wyclif; his followers, the Lollards, continued their preaching.

1409–49
The Conciliar Movement, series of councils to end the Great Schism and reform the churches.

1415
Council of Constance (1414–18) burnt John Hus, Wyclif's Czech disciple; beginnings of the Hussite churches and rebels in Bohemia.

1453
Turks captured Constantinople and turned St Sophia into a mosque.

1492
Spain won the kingdom of Granada and ended the Muslim foothold in the peninsula.

1492
Christopher Columbus landed in the West Indies.

1506
Start of the rebuilding of St Peter's in Rome.

1508–12
Michelangelo painted the ceiling of the Sistine chapel.

1509
Erasmus published *The Praise of Folly*.

1516
Erasmus's New Testament.

1517
Luther issued his ninety-five theses against indulgences.

1521
Luther excommunicated by the pope; at the Diet of Worms he was outlawed by the Emperor Charles V and a majority of the Diet.

1521–2
Luther hid at the Wartburg castle.

1523
Zwingli began to lead reform in Zürich.

1524–6
Peasants' Revolt in Germany.

1525–30
The Protestant Reformation spread steadily in central and south-western Germany and Switzerland; in 1525 Albert of Hohenzollern, Grand Master of the Teutonic Knights, turned the nominally ecclesiastical state into the Duchy of Prussia.

1525
Early group of Anabaptists in Zürich.

1526
Tyndale's English translation of the New Testament.

1529
Diet of Speyer in the Rhineland, at which some German states and cities protested against an effort to stop the reforming movement – hence the name 'Protestant'.

1530
Diet of Augsburg: the Protestants presented the Augsburg Confession, which became the classic Lutheran statement of faith.

1533–4
Anabaptists seized the city of Münster, but were overthrown by force.

1534
Henry VIII abolished the pope's authority in England.

1534
Ignatius Loyola founded the Jesuits in Paris.

1536–41
Michelangelo painted *The Last Judgement* in the Sistine chapel.

1537
Denmark and Norway adopted Lutheran Protestantism.

1541
Calvin was established in Geneva, remaining chief pastor there till his death in 1564.

1542–52
Francis Xavier led missions, first in India then on to Japan.

1545–7
First session of the Council of Trent, with the aim of reforming the Catholic Church; later sessions 1551–2, 1562–3.

1547–53
Reign of Edward VI in England, under whom England was made strongly Protestant – at least outwardly.

1550–2
Iceland adopted Lutheran Protestantism.

1552
Las Casas shocked those concerned with the American missions by his publications protesting against the oppression of the Indians.

1553–8
Mary Tudor's reign in England; attempt to restore the Catholic Church.

1553
The Spaniard Servetus burnt for heresy in Calvin's Geneva.

1555
Peace of Augsburg: the Catholic German empire accepted that in the Lutheran states and cities the Protestant faith of the Augsburg Confession was legal in Germany.

1555–6
Burning of bishops Latimer and Ridley and
of Archbishop Cranmer of Canterbury.

1559
The French Protestants (Huguenots) held
a national synod for the first time.

1559
Queen Elizabeth enabled a moderate Protestant
settlement of religion in England.

1560
Scotland became Protestant with John Knox,
a disciple of Calvin, as its leading minister.

1562
Theresa of Ávila began to reform the
Carmelites with her teaching of mystical prayer.

1562–94
French wars of religion.

1566
Protestant revolt in the Netherlands
which were ruled by Spain ; the resulting
war ended in 1579 with a largely Protestant
north (modern Holland) and a largely
Catholic south (which much later
became modern Belgium).

1567
John of the Cross joined Theresa.

1572
Massacre of St Bartholomew in Paris
and other French towns; the bloodiest part
of the attempt to end Huguenot power in
France.

1589
First Russian patriarch of Moscow.

1593
Sweden finally established a Lutheran church,
last of the Scandinavian countries to go
decisively Protestant.

1594–7
Richard Hooker published *Of the Laws
of Ecclesiastical Polity*, classical Anglican
statement.

1598
Edict of Nantes established toleration for
the Huguenots in Catholic France.

1601–10
The Jesuit Matteo Ricci worked in Beijing.

1608
The first 'reduction' (reservation for Jesuit-
led Indian community) in Paraguay.

1611
Authorized (King James) version
of the English Bible.

1614–43
Japanese attempt to destroy Christianity.

1618–48
Thirty Years' War in Germany, which in
its earlier years was partly an attempt by the
Catholic empire to reverse Protestant advances.

1620
The *Mayflower* carried the nucleus of a Puritan
congregation to America.

1642
Civil war in England, Scotland and Ireland,
leading to Commonwealth in 1649 and
Protectorate in 1653.

1647
George Fox began to organize congregations in
England, later known as Quakers or the Society
of Friends.

1648
Peace of Westphalia ended the Thirty Years'
War and made Calvinists (as well as Catholics
and Lutherans) legal in Germany.

1653–97
The Jesuit Antonio Vieira worked to improve
the lot of slaves in northern Brazil.

1660
End of Commonwealth and restoration
of monarchy in Britain.

1666
Attempt by Nikon, Patriarch of Moscow,
to reform the Church in Russia led to a big
and lasting schism, that of the 'Old Believers',
which still remains a division in Russian
Orthodox Christianity.

1675
Spener began the movement in German
Lutheranism known as Pietism.

1678
John Bunyan's *The Pilgrim's Progress*.

1682
The Quaker William Penn organized the state

of Pennsylvania on a basis of religious
toleration.

1685
King Louis XIV revoked the Edict of Nantes;
exile of many Huguenots from France to
Britain, Germany and America.

1686
James II driven from the throne of England,
Scotland and Ireland, partly because he was
a Roman Catholic.

1695–7
Pierre Bayle's *Dictionary* published
in Rotterdam.

1721
Tsar Peter the Great abolished the Moscow
patriarchate and put the Orthodox Church
in Russia under a synod. This system lasted,
with a brief interval at the revolution 1917–25,
until 1943.

1722–50
Bach in charge of music at St Thomas's church,
Leipzig.

1726
Missions in America lead to an evangelical
revival known as 'The Great Awakening'.

1738
John Wesley was converted and began
his travelling mission.

1742
Handel's *Messiah* first performed, in Dublin.

1751–65
First edition of the French *Encyclopaedia*, edited
by Denis Diderot, in seventeen volumes in
Paris; it has been called the monument of the
Enlightenment, and contained sharp criticism
of the clerical tradition.

1756
Voltaire's *La Pucelle*, a satire on Joan of Arc;
later works included *Candide,* on the problem
of evil, 1759; *Philosophical Dictionary*, 1764.

1762
Rousseau's *Emile*; really a book about
education, but including 'The Profession
of Faith by the Savoyard Vicar', a declaration
of religious radicalism.

1767
Closure of the Paraguay reductions.

1773
Under pressure from the powers, Pope Clement XIV dissolved the Jesuits, with a loss to missions and education.

1776
American Declaration of Independence.

1787
Constitution of the United States: separation of Church and state and equality of civil rights for the members of any religion.

1799
Schleiermacher, preacher in Berlin, published *Speeches on Religion*: religion was based not on argument but on the nature of the religious consciousness of humanity.

1789–94
French Revolution: the national assembly nationalized church property, banned monastic vows and tried to control the Church with the Constitution of the Clergy, which the pope and half the French clergy rejected. The 'Terror' of 1792–3 brought an attempt to de-Christianize France.

1801
Napoleon made a concordat with the pope, reviving the French Catholic Church, though it was still much restricted by the state.

1802
Lamarck at the Paris Museum proposed a theory of evolution, faulty but influential.

1804
Foundation of the British and Foreign Bible Society, which sought to translate the Bible into every language spoken by any significant number of people.

1807
Britain prohibited the slave trade (though not yet slavery itself) after campaign by William Wilberforce.

1810
The Spanish in America began to free themselves from the rule of Spain and set up the Latin American republics, thus causing grievous disputes between the Church and the states, often resulting in the dissolution of religious orders.

1814
Jesuits revived by Pope Pius VII after the first fall of Napoleon.

1817
Under the lead of the King the Lutheran and Calvinist Churches of Prussia united; this lead was followed in certain other German states, though not all. The most important success in Christian reunion since the Reformation.

1817
Robert Moffat began work in the South African mission and moved northwards; his work inspired Livingstone.

1826
Christian peoples in the Balkans began to free themselves from Turkish rule: Serbia and Romania succeeded in 1829, southern Greece in 1832, Bulgaria not until 1878; in return, Christians in Turkey began to be persecuted and expelled.

1829
Roman Catholic emancipation in Britain.

1833
The Oxford teacher J.H. Newman and the pastor and poet John Keble began the Oxford Movement to recall the Church of England to its Catholic heritage.

1833
Abolition of slavery in British possessions; William Wilberforce died.

1830–45
Organization of the Churches in Australia and New Zealand.

1840
David Livingstone began his missionary and exploring expeditions in Central and East Africa, which he continued with barely a break till his death in 1873.

1843
The Scottish Disruption, a split among Scottish Presbyterians over their relations with the Church establishment; mostly healed in 1929.

1845
Newman became a Roman Catholic, but the Oxford Movement continued among the Anglicans.

1846–78
Pope Pius IX – longest reign of any pope. He was much against the world of his time, condemning it most forcibly in the *Syllabus of Errors*, 1864.

1848
F.D. Maurice and Charles Kingsley founded the Christian Socialist Movement in London.

1848
Karl Marx and Friedrich Engels published the *Communist Manifesto*.

1858
Visions of Bernadette at Lourdes.

1859
Charles Darwin published *On the Origin of Species*; widespread controversy.

1863
Polish revolution against the Russians resulted in a grave persecution of the Catholic Polish Church by the Orthodox Russians.

1865
Samuel Crowther in Nigeria became the first black bishop, an Anglican.

1868
Archbishop Lavigerie of Algiers founded the White Fathers for the African missions.

1870
Rome seized by Italian nationalists, named as capital of united Italy; papal possessions annexed. First Vatican Council declared the pope infallible when speaking formally on faith and morals as a teacher of all Christians; the Old Catholic Church, originally those Catholics who could not accept the decree, founded in Germany, Switzerland and the Netherlands.

1872–9
Kulturkampf in Prussia; attempt by chancellor Bismarck to restrain the freedom of the Catholic Church.

1879
The French republican movement began to become increasingly anticlerical.

1891
Pope Leo XIII's encyclical *Rerum novarum* condemned socialism but opened the door to Catholic alliance with Socialists.

1894–6
Massacre of Armenian Christians in Turkey.

1894–1906
Dreyfus case in France; bitter disputes about antisemitism provoked the separation of Church and state in France in 1905.

1900
Boxer rebellion in China; Christians massacred.

1900–7
Modernist controversy; tension among Catholics over the right to study the Bible with historical criticism.

1910
Edinburgh Missionary Conference led to the modern reunion movement.

1915
Massacre of Armenian Christians in Turkey.

1916
French hermit Charles de Foucauld murdered in the Sahara.

1917
Bolshevik revolution in Russia, leading in 1918 to the nationalization of all Church property and then to a civil war in which many Orthodox bishops and priests were killed.

1921
Founding of the Church of Simon Kimbangu in the Congo, most flourishing of the many independent African churches.

1923
Expulsion of Muslims from Greece and Christians from much of Turkey; Asia Minor lost its strong Christian presence.

1927
Conference at Lausanne which later led to the foundation of the World Council of Churches.

1929
Lateran Treaty: Mussolini created the Vatican City, an independent state for the pope.

1929
Mother Teresa began work in Calcutta.

1933
Hitler took power in Germany; schism among the German churches on whether or not to cooperate. Hitler signed a concordat with Pope Pius XI but did not keep the undertakings.

1934
Synod of Barmen; German churchmen opposed to Hitler founded the Confessing Church.

1937
Hitler denounced by the pope in the encyclical *Mit brennender Sorge*.

1938
Kristallnacht: Nazi gangs destroyed Jewish shops and synagogues. Maltreatment of Jews became plain to Germany and the world.

1939–45
Second World War, which made possible the Holocaust, 1941–5.

1940
Taizé community founded by Roger Schutz in France, originally with the aim of helping Jews and other refugees.

1943
Stalin, needing backing from all Russians to resist Hitler, allowed the Russian Church to revive and again have a patriarch.

1947
Founding of the Church of South India, the most important venture in Christian unity since 1817.

1948
World Council of Churches founded at Amsterdam.

1948–9
Communists under Mao seized control of China; many Western missionaries expelled, though the Chinese churches were left alone at first.

1948
The new satellite communist governments in all Eastern Europe north of Greece began to obstruct and persecute the Church. Show trials of bishops – the nastiest was the trial of Cardinal Mindszenty of Hungary, 1948–9.

1949
Beginning of the evangelistic work of the American Baptist Billy Graham.

1958
Khrushchev began a new attack on the Orthodox Church, sustained but less murderous than Stalin's earlier attack.

1958–63
Pope John XXIII; he opened up the Roman Catholic Church, inflexible since the time of Pius IX. John was the first pope to be beloved by some Protestants.

1961
The Orthodox Churches joined the World Council of Churches at its New Delhi meeting.

1962–5
Second Vatican Council put the new openness into law; it allowed services in the vernacular rather than Latin, sought friendship with other denominations, and recognized good in non-Christian religions.

1965
The charismatic and Pentecostal movement, already strong in the United States, began to affect Latin America and also parts of Europe.

1966
Cultural Revolution in China; wild persecution of everything 'respectable' brought much suffering to Christian communities.

1967
Albania declared itself the first atheist state in the world.

1968
Murder of Martin Luther King, the Baptist pastor who stood for all that was best in the civil rights movement in America.

1968
Latin American bishops' conference at Medellín in Colombia showed a new openness about social reform.

1978
Election of the Polish Pope John Paul II, first non-Italian pope since 1523.

1980
Murder of Archbishop Romero of San Salvador, while celebrating mass.

1984
Radical Polish priest Jerzy Popieluszko, important in Polish Solidarity movement, murdered by secret police.

1986
Desmond Tutu made Archbishop of Cape Town.

1988
First woman bishop elected among the Anglicans (American Episcopalian, suffragan of see of Massachusetts).

1989–90
Fall of communist regimes in Eastern Europe and Russia; end of Church's state persecution.

1992
The Church of England accepted that women should become priests.

Further Reading

General History

J. McManners (editor), *The Oxford History of Christianity*, Oxford 1990
Select documents in H. Bettenson, ed., *Documents of the Christian Church*, 2nd edition, Oxford 1987

Reference
F.L. Cross and E.A. Livingstone (editors), *The Oxford Dictionary of the Christian Church*, 2nd revised edition, Oxford 1983

Christianity and art
Gertrud Schiller, *Iconography of Christian Art*, English translation, 2 volumes, London 1971

The Early Church

General
H. Chadwick, *The Early Church*, Harmondsworth 1967

Documents
English translations of the first church historian, Eusebius of Caesarea, are valuable, e.g. G.A. Williamson, Harmondsworth 1965

Persecution
W.H.C. Frend, *Martyrdom and Persecution in the Early Church*, Oxford 1965

The early Church and society
C.J. Cadoux, *The Early Church and the World*, Edinburgh 1925

Art in the early Church
J. Stevenson, *The Catacombs*, London 1978
A. Grabar, *Christian Iconography: a study of its origins*, London 1969

The Bible
H. von Campenhausen, *The Formation of the Christian Bible*, English translation, London 1972

Constantine
A.H.M. Jones, *Constantine and the Conversion of Europe*, new edition, Toronto 1979

The saints
P. Brown, *The Cult of the Saints*, London 1981

The origins of monks and nuns
D.J. Chitty, *The Desert a City*, Oxford 1966

Biographies
R.Williams, *Arius*, London 1987
P. Brown *Augustine of Hippo*, London 1967
H. Chadwick, *Augustine*, Oxford 1986
L. Bieler, *The Life and Legend of St Patrick*, Dublin 1949

The Conversion of the Pagan Tribes

The Franks
English translations of Gregory of Tours' *Historia Francorum*, e.g. by O.M. Dalton, Farnborough, 1967
J.M. Wallace-Hadrill, The Frankish Church, Oxford 1983
E.R. Chamberlin, *Charlemagne*, London 1986

The English
English translations of Bede's *Historia ecclesiastica gentis Anglorum*, e.g. by L. Sherley-Price, rev. ed., Harmondsworth 1968
H. Mayr-Harting, *The Coming of Christianity to Anglo-Saxon England*, London 1972
F.H. Dudden, *Gregory the Great*, 2 volumes, London 1905

The Germans
C.H. Talbot, *The Anglo-Saxon Missionaries in Germany*, London 1954 (translations of early lives, Boniface etc.)

The Spanish
R. Collins, *Early Medieval Spain*, London 1983

The Byzantine Church

P.N. Ure, *Justinian and his Age*, Harmondsworth 1951
J.M. Hussey, *The Orthodox Church in the Byzantine Empire*, Oxford 1986
T. Ware, *The Orthodox Church*, Harmondsworth 1963
P. Sherrard, *Athos: the holy mountain*, London 1982
J. Meyendorff, *A Study of Gregory Palamas*, English translation, London 1964
G.E.H. Palmer and others, edd., *The Philokalia*, English translation, London 1979, in progress

The Nestorians, Copts, Armenians, St Thomas Christians in India
A.S. Atiya, *A History of Eastern Christianity*, London 1968
L.W. Brown, *The Indian Christians of St Thomas*, rev. ed. Cambridge 1982

The coming of Islam and its effects
N. Daniel, *The Arabs and Medieval Europe*, 2nd edition, London 1979
J. Riley-Smith, *The Crusades*, London 1987
English translations of William of Tyre, *A History of Deeds Done Beyond the Sea*, translated by E.A. Babcock and A.C. Krey, 2 vols, New York, 1943

The High Western Middle Ages

C. Morris, *The Papal Monarchy: the Western Church 1050–1250*, Oxford 1989
R.W. Southern, *Western Society and the Church in the Middle Ages*, Harmondsworth 1970
B. Hamilton, *Religion in the Medieval West*, London 1986
R. and C. Brooke, *Popular Religion in the Middle Ages*, London 1984
C.H. Lawrence, *Medieval Monasticism*, 2nd edition, London 1989

Biographies
F. Barlow, *Thomas Becket*, London 1986
R.W. Southern, *St Anselm*, Cambridge 1990
Jane Sayers, *Innocent III*, London 1994
A.V. Murray, *Abelard and St Bernard*, Manchester 1967
A. Morgan, *Dante and the Medieval Other World*, Cambridge 1990
Several translations of early materials for the life of St Francis,
e.g. his own works by L.E. Sherley-Price, London 1959; Rosalind
Brooke's translation of the *Life of Brother Leo* and other early texts,
Oxford 1970.
A classic biography of Francis, beautiful and still worth reading:
P. Sabatier, *Life of St Francis of Assisi*, English translation, London 1894

The Reformation and Counter-Reformation

The Reformation
Owen Chadwick, *The Reformation*, Harmondsworth 1964
and later editions
S. Ozment, *Protestants: the birth of a revolution*, London 1993
E.G. Leonard, *A History of Protestantism*, 2 volumes, London 1967
R.W. Scribner, *The German Reformation*, London 1986
A.G. Dickens, *The English Reformation*, London 1964

Biographies
R. Bainton, *Erasmus of Christendom*, London 1969
R. Bainton, *Here I Stand: a life of Martin Luther*, London 1955
H. Oberman, *Luther: man between God and the Devil*, London 1985
G.R. Potter, *Zwingli*, Cambridge 1976
T.H.L. Parker, *Calvin*, London 1975

The radicals
C.P. Clasen, *Anabaptism: a social history*, Ithaca and London 1972

The Counter-Reformation
A.G. Dickens, *The Counter-Reformation*, 2nd edition, London 1989
A. Ravier, *Ignatius of Loyola and the Founding of the Society of Jesus*,
English translation, San Francisco 1987

The Spanish mystics
S. du Boulay, *Teresa of Ávila*, 1991
English translation of works of St John of the Cross: ed. E.A. Peers
E.A. Peers, *Spirit of Flame*, 2nd edition, London 1953

The expansion into America and the East after 1492
S.C. Neill, *A History of Christian Missions*, revised edition,
London 1986
C.R. Boxer, *The Christian Century in Japan 1549–1650*, Berkeley 1951
G. Schurhammer, *Francis Xavier*, English translation, 4 volumes,
London 1973–82
S.C. Neill, *A history of Christianity in India*, 2 vols, Cambridge 1984–5
P. Caraman, *The Lost Paradise: an account of the Jesuits in Paraguay*,
London 1975
R. Ricard, *The Spiritual Conquest of Mexico*, English translation,
Berkeley 1966

The Age of the Enlightenment

G.R. Cragg, *The Church in the Age of Reason*, Harmondsworth 1960
A.L. Drummond, *German Protestantism since Luther*, London 1951
N. Hope, *German and Scandinavian Protestantism 1700–1918*,
Oxford 1995
G. Rupp, *Religion in England 1688–1791*, Oxford 1986
R. Porter and M. Teich (editors), *The Enlightenment in National
Context*, Cambridge 1981
English translations of Voltaire's more famous writings, e.g. *Voltaire
on Religion*, ed. K.W. Appelgate, New York 1974; *Philosophical
Dictionary*, translated T. Besterman, Harmondsworth 1971

The Modern Age

J. McManners, *The French Revolution and the Church*, London 1960
J. McManners, *Church and State in France 1870–1914*, London 1972
K.S. Latourette, *Christianity in a Revolutionary Age*, 5 volumes,
London 1959–63
J.S. Conway, *The Nazi Persecution of the Churches*, London 1968
D.L. Edwards, *Christian England*, volume 3, London 1984
F. Lannon, *Privilege, Persecution and Prophecy: the Catholic Church
in Spain 1873–1975*, Oxford 1987
Jane Ellis, *The Russian Orthodox Church: a contemporary history*,
London 1986
S. Alexander, *Church and State in Yugoslavia since 1945*,
Cambridge 1979
S.E. Ahlstrom, *A Religious History of the American People*, New
Haven 1972
J.L. Mecham, *Church and State in Latin America*, revised edition,
Chapel Hill 1966

The Cristeros in Mexico
R.E. Quirk, *The Mexican Revolution and the Catholic Church,
1910–1929*, Bloomington 1973

Africa
Adrian Hastings, *Church and Mission in Modern Africa*, London 1967
Adrian Hastings, *The Church in Africa 1450–1950*, Oxford 1994

American fundamentalism
M.E. Marty and R.S. Appleby (editors), *Fundamentalisms and Society*,
Chicago and London 1993
M.E. Marty and R.S. Appleby (editors), *Fundamentalisms Observed*,
Chicago 1991
N.T. Ammermann, *Baptist Battles*, Rutgers 1990

Biographies
Eberhard Bethge, *Dietrich Bonhoeffer*, English translation,
London 1970
Cardinal Mindszenty, *Memoirs*, English translation, London 1974
P. Hebblethwaite, *Pope John XXIII*, London 1984
P. Hebblethwaite, *Pope Paul VI*, London 1993

PICTURE ACKNOWLEDGEMENTS